Bury Place

To Richard
Christmas 2010
Love Mum.

Frank Kermode

Bury Place Papers

Essays from the London Review of Books

....

LONDON REVIEW OF BOOKS

First published in Great Britain in 2009
by LRB Limited

ISBN 978-1-873092-04-0

Printed in Great Britain
LRB Limited
28 Little Russell Street, London WC1A2HN

CONTENTS

INTRODUCTION

Frank Kermode is too multifarious a writer to have anything as dogged as a theme for his critical work; too sane and stealthy to boast of anything as limiting as an obsession. But there are persistences, continuities, as he calls them in the title of one of his books. There is an interest in difficulty, for example, and especially the difficulty of understanding – either oneself or others. This interest is not discouraging, or downhearted. On the contrary. But it never turns difficulty into ease – a mildly surprising conclusion, given the grace and fluency of Kermode's style.

He is interested, of course, in the difficulty of understanding what is manifestly difficult: some texts, propositions, events, people. It often seems as if there is nothing to which he can't usefully bring his considerable learning and perhaps even more considerable curiosity. But his deeper and more continuous project involves a more direct (although double) question. Why do we find it so hard to understand apparently simple things, and why are our acts of understanding themselves often so hard to understand?

The notion of understanding occurs in key places in the first and the last but one of the essays in this very varied book, and could be said to run through all of them. In the first, 'Apocalypse Now and Then', Kermode comments on the fact that those who believe literally in signs of the end of the world often 'find it hard to understand why others reject them', while 'those who reject them find it hard to do so without expressions of disgust or accusations of fraud'. 'There seems to have been no intent to deceive,' he says. But of course there was (there almost always is) a failure to imagine the possibility of deception, and an even stronger failure to believe in the lack of a deceiving intent. Kermode's question is in part historical: how could this happen? But it is more largely interpretative: how are we to understand it when it does happen? It isn't a matter of building bridges (especially when the rivers and the people are gone) or of finding some absent middle ground; it is a matter of getting what people don't seem to get, and why they don't get it.

Similarly, in the later essay, looking at A.E. Housman's apparently odd commitment to the enduring study of 'a long, dull and difficult first-century astronomical-astrological poem by Manilius' rather than any of the livelier classical treasures, Kermode asks 'how we should understand this life-absorbing passion'. And immediately provides, as if by chance, a brilliant answer in the prolongation of the question itself: 'this life-absorbing passion for a craft that required not only a virtually unparalleled grasp of ancient languages and cultures but the possession of the exquisite divinatory intelligence required to make proper use of that knowledge'. Nice work if you can do it, as Cole Porter didn't quite say.

Kermode is not Housman and not a diviner. But he does devote much exquisite intelligence to matters of divination – even and especially of secular affairs. He would like to believe we could do without such obliquities. He is touched and amused by the fact that Housman appears to have thought that both laughing and crying were legitimate critical responses to poetry. He is drawn to the thought of a shared, unpuzzling world even if he sees that world as a now fragmented and perhaps never really tenable historical fantasy. Writing of Tony Tanner's intricate study of adultery in the novel ('there is hardly a page that lacks some original and enriching perception'), he worries about whether critical works like this 'will ever make much contribution to the common wisdom'. 'We may have here an avant-garde that will never be joined by the main army – happy enough behind the lines and content with its familiar rations.' Kermode is writing these words in 1980, and reflecting not only on Tanner but more generally on the 'new transgressive criticism' produced by Geoffrey Hartman, J. Hillis Miller, Edward Said and others, not to mention any of their French influences and inspirations. These were relatively early days in the Theory Wars, and Kermode was splitting his vote in a way that was both subtle and rare. He liked transgressions but rather wished that the avant-garde would wait and see if the main army showed any sign of catching up, or at least that the avant-garde would talk the main army's language now and then. But he knew what to expect from familiar intellectual rations, and we can hear the sceptical, more or less kindly quotation marks slipping into place around the words 'common wisdom', or at least around the word 'wisdom'. Kermode never wrote anything the main army couldn't understand; but nor did he write anything the main army could have managed on its own.

The discreet ambiguity in the title of Kermode's book *The Sense of an Ending* offers a neat emblem of this practice. We could have a *sense* of an ending when everything is just continuing; and we could make sense or fail to make sense of a given ending at any time. What we can't have is the unsensed thing, the ending *an sich,* the final occasion that permits and requires no understanding. This is part of what Wittgenstein meant when he said death is not an event in life. He didn't mean we don't die or that we can't experience the death of others as a grievous event. He meant that our own death is beyond our life, just off the edge of it. Our last moment is not death but dying.

All of the essays in this volume first appeared in the *LRB,* their arrangement is chronological and their dates run from 1979 to 2007. It's a sobering thought that these 29 pieces represent only a portion of what Kermode has written for this journal alone, and we haven't even started to think about the articles he published elsewhere, and his scholarly books, lectures and essays. Defending Paul de Man's rather slim academic publishing record – his first book, *Blindness and Insight*, appeared when he was 51 – Kermode says that in view of the density and strangeness of the work, and of its author's fame: 'it would take a very tough dean to say de Man had under-produced.' There are such deans, however, and I like to think of the same tough fellow entertaining a proposal to hire Frank Kermode under several different pseudonyms. He would be able to sack half a department and still look good.

So it is a sort of accident, assisted by taste and well-judged authorial irony, that the first essay in this book concerns visions of the apocalypse while the last considers old age. Not too far into its pages we encounter an essay on the consciousness of death in the West, as imagined and reconstructed by Philippe Ariès. Have we come upon a theme after all? Not quite. But we have found a region where our understanding is not only severely tested but put in its place. Death is like painting in this respect. It does 'the real talking', as Kermode says of the work of Howard Hodgkin, in its own tongue. We don't have to translate its language, we don't have to talk for or about death, and we don't have to write criticism of visual art or anything else. But we still need, in Kermode's fine words about paintings, 'to have our attention directed to them, our possible blindnesses cleaned, our sensitivity to their weathers refined'. And it may be impossible to keep quiet about death, if only because we need to make a show of being prepared for its weather. Expressing scepticism about Ariès's claim that death didn't really trouble the medieval imagination because it was so completely part of an ordered worldview, Kermode suggests that anyone who knows how to be happy knows how to worry about dying, or the death of others. 'Where there is an imagination of happiness,' Kermode writes, 'death is a scandal.' And 'a scandal is, literally, a stumbling block or trap; when there is no way round it, the only thing to do is to accommodate and explain it.' I have no idea whether Kermode is right about the middle ages, but we have to admit the sympathetic intuition which can find a scandal when there is not even supposed to be a surprise. Happiness in this view – no, the imagination of happiness – has invented the shock of death and driven us to explanation.

But we are not going to find Kermode offering himself as an expert on death – or indeed on anything else except certain aspects of Renaissance literature. 'This is not, as they say, my field', he writes in the preface to *Romantic Image*, his wonderful book on Yeats and Modernism. We might think that, over time, his field has become everything. This is a man who has written just as convincingly on Don DeLillo as on John Donne, on Kazuo Ishiguro as on Joachim of Flora. And he certainly does his homework, whatever his subject. But then this is one way of thinking of his special gifts as a critic. Nothing is a 'field' for him, there are no fences or trees in the way. The main army can camp anywhere; the avant-garde can camp anywhere else.

Kermode is not even going to pretend to be an expert on age, even though he had just turned 88 when the last piece in this volume – his review of Helen Small's *The Long Life* – appeared in the *LRB*. This is the highpoint of the book, not because it ends anything or even gives us the sense of an ending but because it is so full of the grace of Kermode's attention to the process of understanding. Small's remarkable study concerns 'old age in Western philosophy and literature', but of course most of her informants are just guessing. Kermode tells us, as Small does herself, that she is only 42; and more strikingly that Eliot and Larkin were, respectively, 54 and 51 when they wrote their seemingly definitive versions of human ending:

> Let me disclose the gifts reserved for age
> To set a crown upon your lifetime's effort.
> First, the cold friction of expiring sense
> Without enchantment . . .

And:

> What do they think has happened, the old fools,
> To make them like this? Do they somehow suppose
> It's more grown-up when your mouth hangs open and drools,
> And you keep on pissing yourself, and can't remember
> Who called this morning?

'Few of Small's witnesses are doing real old-age philosophy', Kermode says with a touch of mild malice. 'Those who have had actual experience of old age are likely to be dead or very tired or just reluctant to discuss the matter with clever young interlocutors'. 'Have had' is quite marvellous, and Kermode acknowledges without irony that 'much of the best thinking on this subject comes from philosophically sophisticated but honourably ignorant juniors'. There was Plato, for instance; and Eliot and Larkin, who unlike Helen Small, were not asking but projecting.

Kermode is writing from experience, of course, but not immediately about his experience, and what he now has to say about final prospects is not very different from what he said long ago about endings. 'The last years may not offer anything that could be called "completion".' Just so: that is why we have to invent terminal fictions that look as if they have a sense. These late years 'may contain "projects" with posthumous implications . . . or they may be spent in idleness or even wickedness, having few virtuous connections with the rest of the life in question'. 'Death may be, is likely to be, a little too early or a little too late.' 'Even wickedness' is a genuinely promising idea; and the idea of knowing the likelihood of death's being only a little too early or too late is wonderfully tantalising. Death is not an event in life, but it has real promise as an author of modernist short stories. If we know the date of these sentences they can't be timeless, but they are certainly ageless, written by a man whose prose will never drool or settle for mere cold friction. This is the virtue of the project of understanding, as distinct from just living or narrating.

Kermode is also interested in the question of age in another sense: the age we live in. He is a little too young to belong to the generation described in Noel Annan's *Our Age,* a 'large, attractive book', which he views sympathetically but with precise and characteristic reservations. The group in question comprises 'anyone who came of age and went to the university in the thirty years between 1919 ... and 1949' – a fairly restricted group, even if more than two universities were really in question. Kermode invites us to pause over the elaborate social coding of Annan's description of David Eccles as 'a Wykehamist with the manner (so Etonians said) of a Harrovian' – but also over the blunter evocation of Richard Hoggart as 'the grammar school extramural lecturer'. Our Age had its traditions, 'was a gentleman', as Kermode says, and pretty much ran the whole show, 'being powerful yet negligent'. Our Age also turned out to be rather keener on Margaret Thatcher than one might have thought. Yet in spite of many searching criticisms, open and implied, of this imperious English group, Kermode is quietly sensitive to what we might call ruling class pathos, the suggestion that these urbane and civilised people who 'had a pretty good time during the half-century or so when our world was in their charge' nevertheless ran the place into moral ruin just as surely as their vulgar and vulpine successors kept it there.

A slightly unlikely but highly qualified member of Our (or Their) Age was William Empson, who went up to Cambridge in 1925 and down again in disgrace in 1929. There are three essays on Empson in this book, and he and his teacher I.A. Richards are in one sense its heroes, variable and (in Empson's case) not always admirable advocates of what matters in literary study. Richards agreed with Eliot that maintaining 'a high degree of culture' was hard work but added: 'I do not see how this greatest of human efforts is to be made wholeheartedly unless the salvation we are seeking is for all.' Kermode comments, resisting and supporting the idea that Richards, for all his scientific interests, had a magical view of the work of words, that 'it is hard to conceive of a nobler magic' than the project of a salvation which is not just for us, 'and Richards never abjured it'.

Empson of course spent much of his later life attacking the very idea of salvation as long as it had a Christian tinge, but he had his interest in nobler magic too, and his idea of honour, eloquently drawn out by Kermode, is a matter of moral style rather than mere morality. Empson despised Pascal's famous wager (we might as well bet on the existence of God since we shall win if there is a God and lose nothing if there isn't) because he thought it made the one who accepted it 'the slave of any person, professing any doctrine, who has the impudence to tell him a sufficiently extravagant lie . . . Clearly, if you have reduced your morality to keeping the taboos imposed by an infinite malignity, you can have no sense either of honour or of the public good.' This is stirring stuff, and the public good is a surprising note. Kermode says: 'it does warm the heart to hear [Pascal's] line of argument dismissed as simply dishonourable.' The trouble with Empson is that he could dismiss other arguments for quite different, reckless or obsessive reasons. In Kermode's view, or views, he is 'a great critic', a man of 'passionate and polemical mind', author of more than one of 'the texts that taught a generation to read well and feel good about it', 'generous-minded, affectionate, a very likeable man'; but also a person who needs enemies not so that he can argue with them but so that he can abuse them. He was large-spirited, never petty, but he did like sweeping whole territories of discussion off the table.

Honour itself is not a patient word, and Empson also liked to talk of self-respect, as in the following brilliant and extremely useful passage from *Seven Types of Ambiguity*:

People, often, cannot have done both of two things, but they must have been in some way prepared to have done either; whichever they did, they will have still lingering in their minds the way they would have preserved their self-respect if they had acted differently; they are only to be understood by bearing both possibilities in mind.

Whenever I think of this sentence, which is often, I picture what is lingering in our minds as the stories we tell ourselves about what we do – the various stories we tell to meet our various needs – but I tend to drop the idea of self-respect, clearly central to Empson's sense of the matter. Isn't there something a little too self-regarding about self-respect, as there is about honour? I could, if I set my mind to it, preserve my self-respect while being completely wrong, even *by* being completely wrong, as Empson often did. But this is too shallow and easy a thought. Beyond the hint of excessive self-regard is the wonderful intimation of being faithful to others by first being faithful to oneself, and if I happen to think kindness or decency or courage or the avoidance of the unforgivable are what are likely to linger in most minds trying to tell themselves an acceptable story, we still could see all of these attributes as just roads to self-respect, paths to the place where neither honour nor the public good is betrayed. This is where Kermode situates both Empson and Richards, and of his own literary relations with the former he says that 'it seemed necessary to disagree with him and to take the consequences; but also to agree always that he was incomparable.' I think Kermode would also accept Empson's claim that 'it does not even satisfy the understanding to stop living in order to understand,' although he might like to delete the word 'even'. But then neither Kermode nor Empson believes that any form of satisfaction requires us to stop understanding in order to live.

When Kermode writes of the imagination of happiness, he is adapting a phrase from Henry James; and when he writes, in relation to the work of Ishiguro, of the imagination of disaster, he is quoting the phrase he previously adapted. Happiness, as we have seen, or the very thought of it, involves disaster, since it is so soon overtaken by the scandal of death. For Ishiguro, Kermode says, 'it seems there is a sort of calamity built into the texture of life' – as if the scandal of death had its special delegates or representatives for particular people. Kermode is, I think, a little harsh on the novelist's *Never Let Me Go*, but writes with extraordinary subtlety and immediacy about *The Unconsoled*. 'I have not,' he says at the end of six amazing paragraphs, 'succeeded in explaining that this is a wonderful book.' Well, no, he hasn't explained. But he has done something better. He has made us see and feel the wonder of the thing, and characteristically, what we see has to do with making sense.

I see this book as a sort of super-novel in which a failed novelist, urgently aware of his responsibilities yet lost, failing, is betrayed by the trivialities that interfere with his overwhelming need to remake the world, in this case by the treacherous means of writing a novel.

The echo of failed and failing points to something very important in Kermode's writing more generally. He can be as brilliant as Empson – think of the bravura passages on *Macbeth* in *The Sense of an Ending* – but he is never strident, because the thought of failure, or at least the imagination of what happens to happiness, is never far from his prose. It's not that everything ends in failure, only that the chance of failure stalks every human venture, and lively consciousness of this chance discourages triumphalism of all kinds, even negative.

Citing a famous proposition by Yeats ('The intellect of man is forced to choose/Perfection of the life, or of the work') Kermode says of Hemingway that 'he wanted perfection of the life as well as of the work but accepted the Romantic myth that you can't have both (the truth being that you can't have either).' Poor old Ernest: wrong twice. Kermode's voice here – and elsewhere – is a little like that of Auden's when he revises a poetic opinion in conversation. Of his lovely line 'We must love one another or die', Auden later gruffly said it wasn't true, because we die anyway. But Kermode isn't gruff, he's always subtle. I used to think some of his grander pronouncements – 'one may be sure of one thing, and that is disappointment' – were not only too grand but too gloomy. This particular remark is about the odds of success in interpretation, but Kermode goes on to generalise, or at least to speculate sadly: 'It has sometimes been thought, and in my opinion rightly, that the world is also like that; or that we are like that in respect of the world.' Even so, in context, and backed up by Empson's delicate sense of 'the waste even in a fortunate life, the isolation even of a life rich in intimacy', such a remark now seems to me beautifully shaded, a little mournful but far from hopeless. Disappointment is one thing we can be sure of. Not all the time, and it isn't the only thing we can be sure of; but it isn't going to go away. We need to read Kermode, even more so than we do Empson, for what he is not saying as well as for what is on the page.

I think of the character in Henry James who is said to possess 'an irony without bitterness and that came ... from ... having so much imagination'. Writing about the reports Winnicott's biographers make of their subject's supposed stinginess, Kermode imagines, with a splendid faintness of apology, a subtle variant on what is already a fairly subtle scene:

It would be shallow to assume, as a non-psychoanalyst writing about a non-psychoanalyst might, that it wasn't simply that he disliked paying bills, a reluctance shared by a great many ordinary people, but that he only wanted it to seem as if he did, which is more complicated and might lead to more gratifying interpretations.

If this is shallow, save us from the deep. James's character, or indeed James, couldn't have done better. This sentence allows both for the expertise and peculiarity of professionals, expresses some scepticism about their actual difference from anyone else, and divines a sinuous performance where it might seem as if there was only a symptom or a vice. Psychoanalysts (and 'ordinary people') read signs; literary critics read the staging of signs. Plenty of irony, no bitterness, and a great deal of quiet imagination.

This is where we should return to some of the other words I see as haunting Kermode's work, his critical heraldry, as it were: nobility, magic, honour, happiness, scandal. All of them can be found in some kinds of literature and in some kinds of that other (modest) literature which is writing about literature. But this preoccupation, a preoccupation with this particular set of emblems in this conjunction, can be found in the work of only one. The noble magic of that work does him honour; and we find happiness in the way he matches his wits with scandal.

MICHAEL WOOD

APOCALYPSE NOW AND THEN

....

The Second Coming: Popular Millenarianism 1780-1850 by J.F.C. Harrison

Thanks to the work of Norman Cohn, Christopher Hill, Eric Hobsbawm, Keith Thomas and others, we have, over the past few years, acquired a lot of information about millenarianism as a social and historical force. The belief that the end is nigh, or that a new series of times is about to begin, is very ancient, but it is also modern. It is, moreover, a belief upon which people are liable to act, often with disastrous consequences to themselves and others. Persistent, dangerous as well as very interesting, it is a faith that invites more seductively than most the attention of the historian, and Professor Harrison, noting some very peculiar manifestations of it in the period of the Napoleonic wars and the succeeding years, has found himself a very good subject.

He speaks of himself as writing 'popular' history and examining the 'structure of popular thought', but he is aware, perhaps a little uneasily, that apocalyptic patterns of thinking are by no means confined to the lower classes. Certainly the scepticism which they had always engendered prevailed in the educated classes at the time of his study and the association of popular millennialism with political radicalism, powerful though by no means necessary or universal, naturally strengthened the opposition of the Establishment. Yet all Christians had in some sense to accept the premises of the millennialists, however much they disliked their cant and their behaviour: they were to be found, indeed not to be missed, in the Bible. However subtle our reflections on the End, on the Last Days and what succeeds them, they have the same texts behind them as the beliefs of Norman Cohn's prophets, marching on a neighbouring city and mistaking it for Jerusalem, or the Peculiar People catalogued by Harrison, certain that the world will end on this day or that, or awaiting the birth of the Shiloh to the 65-year-old Joanna Southcott.

It may be that some variety of myth concerning the End is necessary to everybody, but there can be no doubt that the forms of it that have prevailed in our culture were established by the Bible – by

Daniel, Revelation, and the 'little apocalypse' of Mark and the other synoptics. Scholars still argue about the exact sense of the word 'apocalyptic' as it applies to the first Christians, but nobody doubts that the religion *is* apocalyptic, nor that it was born in a period of flourishing apocalyptism. Over two thousand years the basic ideas, numbers and allegorical figures have undergone an astonishing variety of interpretations and been put to a great many uses. The world-historical system of Joachim of Flora, almost eight centuries old, turns up all over the place in Blake, in D.H. Lawrence, in Hegel and Hitler, in the sects studied by Christopher Hill. Foxe's *Acts and Monuments*, which had its place in every Elizabethan church, provided a world history with England at its centre and the apocalyptic tropes and numbers as its scheme. Spenser based the first Book of his vast patriotic epic on the Book of Revelation; his Una is the Woman Clothed with the Sun, just like Joanna Southcott. Apocalypse can be an agent of imperialist propaganda as well as of radical politics.

By the time we get to Harrison's period, centuries of fundamentalism had passed, and it was among people to whom the Bible was almost the only book that the prospect of an imminent millennium called for action, whether political or not. It is with the sociology of these people that Harrison is concerned. He refuses to make much of the unusual degree to which patterns of apocalyptic thinking persist historically; methodologically cautious, perhaps overconfident that nobody will any longer take such ideas seriously, he looks at his millennialists in terms of their times. Since movements of the kind they launched need the inspiration of a prophet, much is said about charisma and Weberian types, but the prophets themselves are vividly described as individuals, and there is much of interest on the subjects of their ideological inheritance and their relations with contemporary intellectuals of less extreme sorts.

In times of severe political repression enthusiastic movements among the lower classes are likely to suffer along with more overtly political and subversive enterprises. Several dissident messiah-figures were charged with treason, but then found to be mad and sent to lunatic asylums, quite in the modern manner. There were personal contacts between the apocalyptic movements and such non-charismatic intellectuals as Godwin, whose anarchism is a wholly secular version of the antinomianism often associated with apocalyptic sects. Scraps of Boehme and Swedenborg got into the language and visions of the enthusiasts, but mostly they did their own thinking, or drew directly on the Bible. One interesting feature of their organisations is that men were not favoured over women, and females made as good prophets as men; this equality extends to their other arrangements, so that we might, at a pinch, see Mary Wollstonecraft as a secular version of Joanna Southcott.

Typically, a millennialist group would be made up of labourers, tradesmen, servants, and an infusion of the better-off and better-educated. Its beliefs, apart from those directly derived from the Bible, would be a mixture of popular beliefs in dreams, omens and the like, and a less localised magic (for instance, the belief that the visible world exactly signified the invisible). Also characteristic was a very naive attitude to figurative language, and a confidence in the magical properties of numbers.

It was from such an ideological bank that Richard Brothers borrowed the notion that he was destined to lead the Jews back to the Holy Land (sorting out the Jews is often a precondition of the millennium) and to rebuild the city and the Temple. He made very elaborate specifications for the first of these tasks, but invited Flaxman to design the Temple. The account here given of Brothers is very illuminating, and so is that of the better-known Southcott. Joanna made no claims except to direct inspiration. She knew she was an ignorant woman, but this was thought good, as she could provide a purer channel for the Word. She wrote a great deal, and two of her books were required to be possessed by all who were 'sealed' her followers. Given that she was the Woman Clothed with the Sun, they did not think her pregnancy odd; the Word easily prevails over common probability, and when she died some thought she might still rise and bear the child. Those who hold such beliefs find it hard to understand why others reject them, those who reject them find it hard to do so without expressions of disgust or accusations of fraud (see Rowlandson's caricature of Southcott being examined by the doctors). Yet there seems to have been no intent to deceive, and genuine dismay at the outcome, at least until, as always happens when prophecy fails, explanations were found which made the unexpected series of events concordant with the prophecies, which had only appeared to be disconfirmed. (See Leon Festinger's excellent book, *When Prophecy Fails*, a study of a modern sect similarly disappointed.)

The usual fate of these movements is failure and oblivion, even when there are Writings which survive the death of the prophet. The Southcottians lingered on, splitting into factions with new leaders, until the mid-century, and even, with much attendant absurdity, into the 20th. Brothers is characteristic of the leader who left no direct succession. When they succeed, as did the first Christianity and the Mormons, they have to become institutionalised. Harrison discusses the Mormons, and some other American phenomena, by way of seeing whether the comparison with British millennialism might prove illuminating. The Mormons survived the loss of their first prophet, and made an extraordinary march into the unmapped West before settling down into a calmer (though still very active) phase of their history. The Millerites made the mistake specifically avoided by the early Christians of naming the day of the Second Coming (22 October 1844); I do not know how these bibliolaters explained Mark 13: 32 'of that day or that hour knoweth no one, not even the angels in heaven, neither the Son, but the Father'. Harrison tells the diverting if painful tale of a Boston businessman who gave away all that he had, fearing to be encumbered with possessions on 22 October, but afterwards sued in the courts for its return, pleading that his mind had been deranged by the prophet Miller. The Shakers and others are likewise produced for comparative study. American millenarianism is a vast and wonderful subject. The Americans had more space, and seemed more inclined to form stable communes, they were equally interested in the Signs of the Times, but the Signs themselves seemed to be different.

In the England of the 1790s, you didn't have to be an enthusiast or visionary to conclude that the Last Days were imminent. They were to be a period of disaster, of the reign of anti-Christ, and a plague of false prophets. This has always been the apocalyptic condition most easily met, and it is, of course, the people who have most to gain and least to lose by a destruction of the existing order who get most excited by the Last Days and fear them least. Yet Harrison is careful not to accept in any simple form the notion that millennialism is always associated with social deprivation, or with radicalism. Some radicals were millenarians, some millenarians were radicals. Only the other day Bob Dylan had to explain that in becoming a reborn Christian he was not necessarily moving to the extreme right in politics, proof that enthusiasm is compatible with a good income and an interest in keeping things roughly as they are.

If the differentiae of millenarian sects, in the period that concerns Harrison, or in any period, are not political and not theological, how should they be described? It is certainly very important to assess their passion for allegory and numbers. It may be related to superstitions that had been shed by secular intellectuals, yet the expectation that the Beast and the Woman should be actual historical persons, and that the secret numbers of Daniel and Revelation should relate to world history, is as old as apocalypse itself. The sums were always possible, for the history of the world was short (in the 1790s it was only approaching its sixth millennium), and there were some numbers (666 is the most famous) which could be used as wild cards to make the answer to the question of the Second Coming work out right for the person doing the sum. As to hidden meanings, they were still sought everywhere by poets and priests; only in Germany had the literary criticism of the Bible reached the stage where it was possible for scholars to hold sophisticated views about Biblical fictions. What divided an enthusiast from a parson or a rational intellectual was more a fear of enthusiasm itself, of particular ways of expressing the sense of texts or dreams, than of the matter expressed. In this fear Swift is at one with Wesley. A prime differentia, in other words, is simple manners. Another related characteristic, as I've suggested, is a willingness to act on one's belief, which entails opposition from institutions set up to take care of it for one.

What does it all matter, now? Well, a moment's thought is enough to convince one that our world is full of charismatic fundamentalists, and not only in California, but also in Iran, in Africa, even within the Catholic Church itself. And there are other flexible fictions, workable if you have a very simple view of human history and a sufficiently gnomic set of texts and a leader to interpret them. Much practical wickedness may flow from the mistaking of figure for fact, and attempting to order the world into conformity with the figure. Belief in myths can be devastating, even if it is associated with great political causes; we hardly need Palestine and Ireland to remind us of that. Perhaps the value of knowing about such people as Brothers and their absurd delusions is simply that they exhibit, in a form that proved harmless, the motives which, endowed with political power, can bring tyranny and destruction on a scale undreamed of by calm intellectuals who know a myth from a fiction and a fiction from a fact.

25 October 1979

EDUCATING THE PLANET

....

It is a commonplace that among I.A. Richards's first achievements was a modern defence of poetry. In the years following the Great War, he saw the world as entering an unprecedented historical crisis. He believed that the collapse of the old 'Magical View' of the world had left us in a condition of bewilderment, of deep privation, of affective destitution. People (I think he supposed them to be a minority) who were not content to 'live by warmth, food, fighting, drink and sex alone' must 'require other satisfactions': but the sources of such satisfactions had been stopped by the advance of knowledge. As throughout his life, he saw in trouble and disorder an immediate invitation to action, though, as at first conceived, this action was of a subtle kind, hardly to be distinguished from contemplation. 'A sense of desolation, of uncertainty, of futility, of the groundlessness of aspirations, of the vanity of endeavour, and a thirst for a life-giving water which seems suddenly to have failed, are the signs in consciousness of this necessary reorganisation of our lives.' What distinguishes this sentence from similar exclamations of dismay, which would not be hard to find in the literature of the period, is that it ends with the affirmation of a need to act. The rest of it owes most to Eliot's *Waste Land*, as Richards acknowledged in a famous footnote. He valued the poem, not only as an exhibition of disorder and desolation, but as affording us means to contemplate them in a valuable way; it was modern, belonging to a world that had outlived the Magical View; but it offered what must take the place of that view if our psychological privations were to be ended.

In this poem, Eliot had achieved 'a complete severance between his poetry and all beliefs' and that is what modern poetry must do. Eliot mildly objected to this statement, but I doubt if Richards was much bothered. He confided in poems rather than poets, as we see from his version of Shelley's pronouncement: '*Poems* are the unacknowledged legislation of the world.' But in the second edition of *Science and Poetry* he took the opportunity of explaining himself, and extended what was already a famous footnote. *The Waste Land*, he claimed, 'realised what might otherwise have remained a speculative possibility . . . by finding a new order through the contemplation and exhibition of disorder'. The poem was a simultaneous image of both – a typical Richards formula, for he liked to hold antinomies in a single thought, to speak, for example, of the 'interinanimation' of separate words, and of what he came later to call 'complementarities'. But the immediate point is that this difficult modern poem was recommended as an example of the 'necessary reorganisation'.

Thus did Richards help to establish Eliot's poem as the *livre de chevet* of a generation of educated readers. He did more: for when he extended the note, Richards added to it some lines, now but not then famous, from Conrad's *Lord Jim*. 'The way is to the destructive element submit yourself . . . So if you ask me how to be? In the destructive element immerse . . . that was the way.' This is an instance of his uncanny aptness in quotation: the way to read *The Waste Land*, and the way to live in the new, more hostile world, is not to try to climb out, but to let the deep, deep sea keep you up. The second edition of *Science and Poetry* had not been out a year before Stephen Spender entitled his book on modern writers and belief (or unbelief) *The Destructive Element*, describing Richards's note as 'a focal point from which diverge rays towards the past and the future'. Certainly Conrad's words give some insight into Richards's future dealings with the destructive world.

When he wrote this longer footnote, he had been engaged on his modern defence of poetry for more than a decade. His ideas, widely circulated, did not go unopposed. Eliot himself, reviewing *Science and Poetry*, noted 'a certain discrepancy between the size of [the author's] problems and the size of his solutions'. 'Mr Richards,' he said, 'is apt to ask a supra-scientific question, and to give merely a scientific answer.' This is an objection often made, in one form or another, to Richards's procedures, and I believe it to be, in the end, false. The response of the young was less critical. Christopher Isherwood went as an undergraduate to Richards's lectures and hailed him as 'the prophet we had been waiting for . . . To us, he was infinitely more than a brilliantly new literary critic: he was our guide, our evangelist, who revealed to us, in a succession of astounding lightning flashes, the entire expanse of the Modern World.' For all its extravagance, that strikes me as a truer response. Richards was much more a prophet than a scientist.

The immediate, but by no means the only, consequence of the early prophecies had been to entrust to poets and their readers an unexpectedly central responsibility for dealing with the world crisis. A great borrower, Richards took from the neurologist Henry Head the notion of 'vigilance' – 'what happens in a given stimulus situation varies with the vigilance of the appropriate portion of the nervous system' – and explained the extraordinary availability of experience to the poet, and his power to organise that experience, as the consequences of his superior vigilance. The notion is, in literary terms, Romantic, and was stated in other language by Wordsworth and Coleridge. What Richards added to it was his conviction that only in such poetic vigilance could we find a means to construct a new world, difficult but inhabitable. And like Hölderlin he called upon the people (or the best of them) to assist the poet in this work. He is again in the native Romantic tradition when he insists that the poet is possessed of 'normality'. 'To be normal is to be a standard, but not, as things are and are likely to remain, an average.' The object of his new methods of teaching poetry was simply to make others as vigilant as poets, so that the gap between the average and the standard might be progressively closed. The whole plan was conceived as rational, and as supported by modern psychology and physiology.

That is why he could be accused of going in for science and so giving comfort to an enemy. And of course it was always part of his plan that a new poetry and a new criticism should benefit by the very expansion of knowledge that had helped to bring about the world crisis. Just as he had intended, when he decided to be a psychoanalyst, to take a medical degree, so he prepared himself for the task he actually undertook by immersing himself in psychology, physiology and philosophy. In doing so, he drew copiously on the resources of Cambridge at that time. That does not mean he agreed with everything he was told. With G.E. Moore, for example, he had what he might later have called a relationship of complementarity: 'I feel like an obverse of him. Where there's a hole in him there's a bulge in me.' 'Moore was vocally convinced that few indeed could possibly *mean* what they *said*. I was silently persuaded that they could not possibly *say* what they *meant*.' He held Wittgenstein in only moderate awe. Russell he dismissed in a brisk appendix to *The Meaning of Meaning*, though he had from time to time to repeat and revise his reasons for doing so.

However, mention of *The Meaning of Meaning* is a reminder that in his first and seminal book (for *The Meaning of Meaning* really is the foundation of nearly all Richards's later work) he had as collaborator C.K. Ogden, a walking encyclopaedia of philosophy and science. The union of prophet and polymath was not only extremely productive, but, as Richards often remarked, great fun. Never was a book of such gravity written in such high spirits. The opinions of the great go down like skittles. 'There's something insipid about agreeing with an author,' said Richards long afterwards, 'especially when you're young. You feel it's your business to be *other*.' He could give a precise and interesting date for the conception of the book: Armistice Day, 11 November 1918. That day he had watched drunken medical students sacking Ogden's shop in King's Parade; they met in the evening to see if they could identify any of the marauders. In the small hours they had a long conversation on the stairs under the flare of an aged bat-wing gas-jet. This was either outside Richards's rooms in Free School Lane or outside Ogden's attic above Mac Fisheries in Petty Cury: in two different accounts Richards specifies both places. By the time they parted they had roughed out *The Meaning of Meaning*. Ogden was at the time editing a weekly paper, *The Cambridge Magazine*. Its circulation rose to 25,000 and the only way he could solve the paper shortage was to buy books in bulk and pulp them – not, however, before he had looked through them.

Ogden believed in being reasonable if he could find a reasonable auditor ('Will you change your mind if I convince you?' he would ask). Richards found in him 'a central clarifying insistence, a flame of curiosity and impatience, a disdain for the acquiescences of sloth, a trust in mind' which spoke to the same qualities, differently but complementarily compounded, in himself. The collaboration seems to have been very intimate. 'It's a most extraordinary experience, finding you can agree with someone,' said Richards years afterwards. 'Decades later it wasn't the case that we could understand one another *at all*.' The book they called *The Beadig of Beadig* because of the heavy colds they suffered during its composition was, for all its laborious and combative argumentation, an entertainment. Ogden, in fact, seems to have regarded it as a way of relaxing from his work on the translation of Wittgenstein's *Tractatus* and Vaihinger's *Philosophy of 'As If'*. But it was an indispensable prelude to the subsequent careers of both authors; and it belonged firmly to the Cambridge of the immediate post-war years.

And indeed at this time Cambridge was virtually the whole world. Some day, I hope, we shall be told more about the intellectual horizons of the early Richards – not only about the precise nature of his collaboration with Ogden, and his beneficent mutual misunderstanding with Moore, but also about his dealings with the psychologists and with Cornford. The four remarkable books of the Twenties were all very Cambridge books. Nevertheless they were read everywhere, and changed attitudes to poetry and criticism throughout the English-speaking world.

It is a curious fact that they were also misunderstood everywhere. W.H.N. Hotopf, author of the most serious book yet written on Richards, notes with astonishment that of all the eminent philosophers and critics who have written on Richards there are very few who 'do not betray some fairly important misunderstanding' of his position.[1] What happened in the world at large, I think, was that some notion of the *Principles* got through, but with much loss of detail and some general distortion. The reasons are doubtless many: careless reading, impatience with the psychology and linguistics, a tendency also on the part of the writer to say too many things in too many ways, and to say them, sometimes, obscurely. But to demand minute consistency and a slow clear progress of argument is to ask the wrong gift of Richards, and to misunderstand his prophetic role. What mattered was the prior conviction of the value of poetry and the importance of language, and of the teachability of right reading. The utilitarian-psychologistic theories were instruments that lay to hand.

It was his fate, then, to be both influential and misunderstood, in Cambridge as elsewhere. Though he was a don for most of his life, Richards was not, I think, a very academic man, and the partial institutionalisation of his method in the English Tripos could not have satisfied him. His unease is demonstrated in the continual recurrence of his worry about correctness in interpretation. As is well-known, he was committed to new and heretical views about meaning in poetry, dis-

[1] *Language, Thought and Comprehension: A Case Study of the Writings of I.A. Richards* (Routledge, 1965).

counting the simple intentionalist position and placing a high value on ambiguity. Where the conventional pedant found in poetry instances of 'incorrectness' or lack of clarity, Richards saw 'interinanimation', 'a movement among meanings'. All discourse, he maintained, is 'over-determined', and ambiguity is 'the indispensable means of most of our important utterances.' Professor Kittredge, for example, believed that good writing was writing that left the reader with no need to go in for 'inference and guesswork': Professor Richards asked what interpretation could be if it *wasn't* inference and guesswork.

But he was very clear that this didn't mean you could say anything you liked about a poem. It is possible to be wrong. Hence the list, in *Practical Criticism*, of the ten 'chief difficulties' (more properly, causes of error) in criticism; hence the denunciation, in the Clark Lectures he gave almost half a century later, of what he vehemently labelled 'omnipossibilism'. And in between he had often returned to the topic. 'Whatever accounts are offered to the reader must leave him – in a very deep sense – free to choose . . . This is not . . . any general licence to readers to differ as they please . . . For this deep freedom in reading is made possible only by the widest surface conformities.' I think he was troubled, in later years, by demands for a freedom that defied such a consensus. While he and Ogden were at work on *The Meaning of Meaning*, they looked at Saussure's *Cours de Linguistique Générale*, which had appeared only a few years before, but dismissed it in a page or two. *La langue*, they argued, was a useless abstraction; the project for a semiology, though 'a very notable attempt in the right direction', makes a fatal division between signs and what signs stand for: thus it 'was from the beginning cut off from any contact with scientific methods of verification'. At about the same time, the Russian Formalists were active: but they were soon suppressed, and perhaps news of them did not reach Cambridge.

In the Sixties, however, both Saussure and the Formalists made a long-delayed and rather spectacular reappearance on the scene, and the consequences have been many, and often omnipossibilistic. Richards gave a characteristically warm though not unqualified welcome to Jakobson's experiments in poetic analysis, but the new libertarian semiologists of France and America cannot have pleased him. He believed steadfastly that there were such things as wrong readings. And of course he also believed that one could progressively acquire competence in reading, that error could be corrected. The question arises: who shall distinguish right from wrong? And his answer, inevitably, was: those who have acquired competence, the teachers. Thus the belief in the possibility of corrigible error leads directly to a belief in the need for institutions of criticism.

Yet it seems clear that he did not greatly care for such institutions. Of the English School he has few good words to say. 'It's hard on the poets to make everybody study them like this . . . As far as I can see, making it into an academic subject has not increased the amount of *enjoyment* taken in the poems.' The senior members of the critical institution, participants in the consensual establishment of right reading, must perforce be scholars. And although he had a great respect for scholarship, Richards was dismayed at its side-effects. It prevents us 'from supplying our greatest need – teachers able to help humanity to remain humane'.

In the early Thirties, times were changing, and so was Richards, but this need did not change, and the defence of poetry continued. One of the doctrines of *Principles* is that the effect of good readings, of equilibrated impulses, achieved poise, is cumulative: we are talking not about discrete, self-sufficient Paterian moments, but about provision for the future, in the form of what he later called 'feedforward'. Certainly his own experience confirmed the doctrine: directions changed, horizons widened, Richards would 'cross the tracks' into educational enterprises improper to Cambridge. But in a sense he did not change, only built on his past. *Coleridge on Imagination*, published in 1934 when his wider enterprises were already well started, shows no diminution in his hopes for a central and humane criticism of poetry. It is in the 'searchings for meanings of a certain sort', he says, that the being of a poem consists; and that search is the best response to the vast alterations in consciousness that beset us, our only way of recovering 'a less relaxed, a less adventitious order for the mind'. It is the point of *Science and Poetry*, reinforced by an understanding of Coleridge as the herald of the revolution in consciousness. To attack science, he says, is a futile error, a 'myth reflecting our unease'. The point is to match and master the new human world, as science does the physical world. And the task still falls to the poet. When all knowledge is either myth or without meaning, he becomes responsible for the very principle of human order. The writing and reading of the necessary new poetry is arduous, but it must be done.

It is here, near the end of his first defence of poetry, that Richards comes closest to Shelley. 'Poetry acts in another and diviner manner,' says Shelley. 'It awakens and enlarges the mind itself by rendering it the receptacle of a thousand unapprehended combinations of thought.' And Richards: 'Because the Universe as it is known to us is a fabric whose forms, as we can alone know them, have arisen in and through reflection; and because that reflection, whether made by the intellect in science or by "the whole soul of man" in poetry, has developed through language . . . the study of the modes of language becomes . . . the most fundamental and extensive of all inquiries. It is no preliminary or preparation for other profounder studies . . . The very formation of the objects which these studies propose to examine takes place through the processes . . . by which the words they use acquire their meanings.'

These words look back to work already done, and forward to a different future. But we may hear in them a note of exaltation that will sound strange to anyone who thinks about the teaching of poetry in modern universities. Perhaps we have lost confidence in the poets, as Richards himself partly did. Certainly most of us are not convinced that he was right when he said, in *Coleridge*, that 'critics in the future must have a theoretical equipment of a kind which has not been felt to be necessary in the past.' In the Thirties, there was an automatic reflex of opposition to the New Criticism, of which he was the chief patron; and any other *nouvelle critique* must expect a largely contemptuous and unexamined rejection now. Richards saw it happening. Like the Old Testament prophets he liked to quote in his epigraphs – on the whole a disappointed body of men – he found us duller of apprehension and more apt to backslide than he had hoped. Interpretation was teachable: but the institution, with its narrowly conceived and conservative view of scholarship, came between the teacher and the taught.

That was doubtless one reason for 'crossing the tracks'. The approaching war was another. That poetry could arduously satisfy human needs no longer met by religion and ignored by science was a position tenable only, perhaps, by an élite capable of strenuously and courageously sitting still. It was already under threat, not only from the retreat to primitivism Richards deplored in Yeats and Lawrence, but also from history itself – from Spain most immediately. 'Today the struggle.' Julian Bell, whom Richards knew, died there, but not before he had diagnosed the disturbed visions of civilised discontent he found in Freud and Richards as 'mild troubles'. Poetry seemed unlikely to save us after all.

But even before Spain made a cruder form of action seem urgent, Richards had been considering the problem of right reading on a larger scale, as a problem of universal communication. Of course he always supported Basic English as a general solution, but his Chinese book, *Mencius on the Mind*, which appeared in 1932, first revealed his new direction. It is an anti-institutional book, for Richards thought it more important to be bold than to be academically cautious. *Mencius* uses Chinese, a language 'not strictly governed by an explicit logic', to explore the principles of 'Multiple Definition' and extend our consciousness of what we do with language. He wrote it at Harvard, while lecturing on Joyce and Dostoevsky, but the manuscript was stolen, and abandoned by the thief on a Chinese rooftop. Back in Cambridge, England, he wrote it again. Then the first version was recovered from the roof. One version was affected by Richards's determination to avoid 'the intellectual currencies of the Harvard scene'; the other by his equal determination not to get caught up in the 'local logical game' at Cambridge. Which one we got I don't know: perhaps a blend of both.

All this seems characteristic of the independence and the plunging boldness of his approach. He liked best to start a book and then, writing with great speed, find out what the book wanted to be – an admirable method, I think. He was aware of the risks: what justified them was the possibility (repeatedly but not obtrusively mentioned in the prefaces to many books) that the enterprise might be of benefit to humanity. He looks to Mencius, not for information about the truth, but for what, in his view, all philosophy ought to provide: 'the opportunity of considering modes of meaning carried to their revealing limits'. And he asks us to read his books in the same way, as steps on the road to 'a single comprehensive view of comprehending'. That his linguistic equipment might be fallible didn't matter. 'The detail of my commentary may be a tissue of misconceptions and yet the trouble I share with my readers will be justified' by the importance of the problems. I have spoken of his 'uncanny aptness' in quotation. His epigraphs are also witty. The one to *Mencius* is from *Troilus and Criseyde*, where Pandarus is explaining to Troilus that even if his own record as a lover is bad he can still be useful as an example: 'Thus ofte wyse men ben war by folis,' he says. 'By his contrarie is every thing declared.'

And we shall never, I think, have a true sense of the man unless we understand this gay calculated audacity. He rushes forward, as if some gap had opened on the future. He wrote *Interpretation in Teaching*, a difficult book of over four hundred pages, in six weeks, and in the leisure time of those same six weeks turned out the none too simple *Philosophy of Rhetoric*. To bring that off you cannot afford to make a cautious survey of the path before you dash down it. All you can hope for is that you are well enough programmed, or 'taped', as he used to say – that you have adequate 'feed forward'. And you must be very inventive. From *The Meaning of Meaning* on, Richards prodigally invented new terms; some, like the 'Canon of Actuality' and the 'Utraquist error' of *Meaning*, died young; others, like the 'stock response' of *Practical Criticism* and the tenor-vehicle distinction of *The Philosophy of Rhetoric*, have stuck. All were expendable; what mattered was the forward movement. One thinks of the lines, addressed to Mrs Richards, which recall the descent of a glacier, the scrambling across innumerable half-hidden crevasses before being overtaken by darkness on the abrupt edge:

> At the stiff-frozen dawn
> When time had ceased to flow,
> – The glacier ledge our unmade bed –
> I hear you through your yawn:
> 'Leaping crevasses in the dark,
> That's how to live!' you said.
> No room in that to hedge:
> A razor's edge of a remark.

And so he did not hedge, but wrote precipitately, and precipitately he crossed the tracks. If one looked outside the university, where highly educated people made such a hash of one's protocols, and equally highly educated people regarded 'English' as a joke or a soft option, one saw vaster problems of interpretation, life-and-death problems calling for immediate action and new methods. In the Richards of the Twenties there is a certain not fully conscious élitism – a few would find their salvation in poetry, most of them probably in Cambridge. But the world as a whole needed order, and order could be taught. The world was largely analphabetic; it lacked the means to communicate between different cultures; it lacked the knowledge to resist systematic corruption by fraudulent manipulators of language. Basic English was meant to take care of some of these problems, to help order the world. *Basic English and its Uses*, published in 1943, begins: 'This is a reconstruction book. It looks to the future and assumes that the reader enjoys a moderate faith in man.' Very characteristic; and so is the assumption that the corruption of communications is the source of all modern disasters, including war. Working with language, one fought fire with fire; and one used all forms of modern communication in order to combat their harmful effects. In 1976, he was still saying that 'TV or satellite-distributed sentence-situation-depiction games are going to be the way to educate the planet.'

Educating the planet was the larger enterprise he took on after he stopped educating Cambridge. In retrospect, he saw *Interpretation in Teaching*, published in 1938, as 'the grand hinge' of his career. However salvific poetry might be for some, the world at large urgently needed instruction in the reading of prose. In came the new prose protocols, and in commenting upon them Richards hoped to found a new discipline. As knowledge, information monitored by feed-forward, had grown towards superior organisation in his own mind, so he hoped that there might be, in this matter of imparting knowledge, a useful and ordered accumulation. He saw *Interpretation in Teaching* as 'the beginning of . . . a vast collective *clinical* study of the aberrations of average intelligence', and wondered why *Practical Criticism*, a work of much more limited ambition, should have prospered while this one, 'though offering a deeper examination of concerns nearer everyman's essential capacities, was comparatively little studied'. But of course he did not regret the effort. 'I had . . . to do something about the general condition of incompetence I had uncovered. I felt (and still feel) it to be too threatening to the human prospect to be left uncured.' So he wrote in the second edition of *Interpretation*, 35 years after the first. *Interpretation* had looked back to Coleridge, having as its aim the increase of 'organic interinanimation of meanings, the biologic growth of the mind in the individual and in a social inheritance maintaining the human advance': but it looked forward, also, to years of ingenious and indefatigable labour in those causes.

In short, the diagnosis of grosser diseases than those of the academic intellect now absorbed most of his attention. Reviewing Eliot's *Notes towards the Definition of Culture* in 1948, he agreed with the author that 'a high degree of culture (or Education) in an equalitarian society can only be attained if the great majority of men can be raised to a level, and kept at a level, which has never been remotely approached in the past.' But the truth of this did not, for him, entail the closing down of unnecessary schools and universities. 'High things are hard,' he wrote. 'And I do not see how this greatest of human efforts is to be made wholeheartedly unless the salvation we are seeking is for all.'

Salvation for all! Richards believed that because it was necessary to change everybody, everybody could, given the right, continuous application of intellectual energy on the part of the clerisy, be changed. From the time of *The Meaning of Meaning* on, he had been sure that atavistic assumptions about language and meaning made ordinary men vulnerable to people who manipulated them for base ends: he particularly feared the application, in times of peace, of methods of manipulation devised for war.

Later, as I've mentioned, he tried to use television and radio against themselves, against their venal use. He did not succeed, and he came to think, like many apocalyptic spirits before him, that the times must get worse before the world will be ready to make so great an effort. 'Much can be done if things get *bad* enough,' he said in 1968. 'Things are going to get bad rather soon, and so I'm hopeful.' The theory and the method were ready and waiting. Unlike some prophets, Richards believed in theory. Having bad theories makes people misinterpret things: good theories are at least prophylactic. 'The duties of good critical theory . . . are analogous to those of a good police in a society as nearly anarchic as possible.' He was speaking then of a theory that would protect poets, but good theory would protect ordinary citizens as well. For the poet is normal; there is no difference in kind, only in the measure of sensibility or vigilance, between him and the ordinary man whom the language-manipulators cheat and stupefy. That is part of the theory, and it is also part of the prophecy: the gap between the citizen and the poet must and will be closed.

Richards has been called a mystic, and there is at least a little justice in the description. Behind all his work there is a vision (a poet's vision, but a vision available to every man) of interinanimation, of opposites reconciled, of peace, as when Isaiah spoke of wolf and lamb feeding together. And there is also that confidence in a participation beyond the ordinary range of sense, the transmission of poetic experience, a sort of fruitful silence beyond the movement of meaning. His tireless forward thrusting, as if to press through a gap into the future, sometimes seems to have that silence as its ultimate goal.

> If ever in the windings of the dance,
> *To-be-said* and *saying* in perfection fit,
> Another silence listens . . .

And if he was a mystic, he was not the only one we know of who exhibited from day to day an intense practicality. If you want to affirm a principle of order you must work in chaos, and understand the ills besetting 'the poor loveless, ever-anxious crowd'. Basil Willey called Richards 'the Coleridge of our time', and one can imagine the fervour with which Richards read those lines:

> Ah! from the soul itself must issue forth
> A light, a glory, a fair luminous cloud
> Enveloping the Earth –
> And from the soul itself must there be sent
> A sweet and potent voice, of its own birth,
> Of all sweet sounds the life and element!

For interinanimation, and the complementarity of opposites, and the apprehension of the world as a single organism, are creative acts of the human mind, of human language 'carried to its revealing limit'.

It has indeed been argued that Richards, the enemy of Word Magic, was himself a word-magician. Like Russell and Whorf and Wittgenstein, in their different ways, he thought that the purgation of error from language could lead us into a magical peace, a silence beyond all this fiddle. 'This conception,' says Dr Hotopf, 'is magical because they attribute such great power to language, and write as though their mere insight had already given them that power.' To hold that since language mirrors the structure of reality, we can make the structure of reality *our* structure is sympathetic magic. So says Dr Hotopf. It may be so: but Richards is a rational magician. As a prophet, he sees the prospect of order; and the image of that order, that interinanimated whole, is language. Within it we may move in our own minds, to a human peace. When *to-be-said* and *saying* are one, so are being and becoming.

Language is our programme for that journey into silence. And not ours alone, not just the programme of those already educated: 'the salvation we are seeking is for all.' It is hard to conceive of a nobler magic; and Richards never abjured it.

20 March 1980

NOVELS ABOUT ADULTERY

....

Love and Marriage by Laurence Lerner
Adultery in the Novel: Contract and Transgression by Tony Tanner

It calls for no great acumen to spot a connection between adultery and theft. According to Dr Johnson, 'the essence of the crime' lay in the 'confusion of progeny', for by imposing bastards on her husband the adulterous wife diminished the inheritance of his legitimate issue. Since *his* infidelities were without this material consequence, they counted for much less – a tumble with a chambermaid was 'mere wantonness of appetite'. Boswell says that this opinion showed Johnson's usual solid judgment and knowledge of human nature: but he was moved to ask whether it wasn't a little hard that 'one deviation from chastity should so absolutely ruin a young woman.' Not at all, said Johnson. 'It is the great principle which she is taught. When she has given up that principle, she has given up every notion of female honour and virtue.' Like Eve before her, she has by one wicked act disordered the entire fabric of social happiness and stability, of which property is only another aspect.

Female honour is so narrowly conceived because of its simple, intimate relation to male inheritance. Male honour, much more complicated, has nevertheless the responsibility of protecting that same inheritance: it must react to any challenge offered to name, station, or the honour of the female who has been given that name and that station. Duelling codes are an extension of legal and theological bans already imposed by society, presumably because these bans seem insufficient. But when marriage changes and considerations other than property grow important, the law grows gentler and ideas of honour, after reaching a climax of punctilio, tend to decompose. Duelling dies out and adultery grows more interesting; it produces more varied narratives; in fact, it becomes a central theme in a new form, the novel.

That's too glib, of course. The novel may have benefited from the dissociation of the notion of adultery from that of property, but there are other associations less easily dissolved. What about jealousy, an atavism no doubt, but still painful, and also having to do with the family, but not the family as a financial corporation? We are all early acquainted with this ugly passion. Yet, curiously, it is not a prominent feature of the novel. I've been trying to compile a list of novels which show a lively interest in it, and can think of very few: Gissing was a bit obsessive about it. Tolstoy describes a rather special case in *The Kreutzer Sonata* and Graham Greene another in *The End of the Affair*. There is *Herzog*, and there must be more. But it seems almost as rare as duelling, which, still important in Richardson, crops up anachronistically in Flaubert, and even more so in Wyndham Lewis. Wronged spouses in novels mostly seem to be miserable rather than furious or sullied – the Prince de Clèves, for instance, and Karenin, Ford's heroes and Tony Last. The drama seems better suited than the novel to the treatment of the pathology of jealousy, perhaps because it has a primitive association with pollution; after Shakespeare, it's hard to know what more could be said on this subject.

Laurence Lerner, in his book *Love and Marriage*, develops Weber's point that marriage is threatened by too high claims for sexuality, finding in the literary tradition an inarticulate wisdom, an awareness that no social arrangement can bear the intensity of demand represented by Tristan and Othello, Lancelot and Phèdre. Jealousy is an erotic excess; the novel in its nature as the genre corresponding to a more domesticated sexuality condemns this excess, as *Madame Bovary* is in itself a condemnation of Emma's reading. And certainly Tony Tanner's book on adultery hardly as much as mentions jealousy. In a second volume, he proposes to discuss *Anna Karenina*, *The Scarlet Letter*, *The Good Soldier* and *Lady Chatterley's Lover*, among other books; they will hardly afford him opportunities to say much more.

So the novel, like bourgeois marriage, its central theme, has its emotional limits. Within them, it will enact the themes of property and family, the great contracts and their transgression. This is the apparently simple programme of Tanner's book: but it does not stay simple for long. For he finds the analogy between the history of the novel and the history of its subject to be very complex. The novel is a 'transgressive mode': it broke the contracts offered by earlier genres and offered new ones. Locke argued that relations of contract were substitutes for family dependence; Tanner applies his words to fiction, for the shift in marriage arrangements is paralleled by a shift in the novel to 'individual obligation' and a perpetual change in the terms of the contract, the constant incursion of new and transgressive forms. In marriage as such there is no narrative; especially in bourgeois marriage, so long as it is stable, there is simply nothing to do and nothing to say. Adultery alters all that by introducing a pseudo-contract between incompetent parties. The novel mimes this change, grows ever more problematic, flouts and violates the contracts, tells the story that could not have existed before. Its method, like its material, involves the intrusion of false contracts into the stability of true ones.

Tanner makes this opening point with much energy and fertility of illustration, but we have still to learn the scope of his ambition and his power. For this is an extraordinary book, which may well be seen as marking an epoch in the criticism (that is, the reading) of fiction. It has many faults, mostly related to his own transgressive effort. It is monstrously long – the section on *Madame Bovary* alone runs to some seventy thousand words – and one often has the impression that the glosses and *aperçus* are coming out under such high pressure that the writer cannot spare the time for the more menial task of organising them, or even splitting them up into paragraphs. He often seems to be breathlessly reminding himself of where he has got to 'at this stage', and announcing what it is he proposes to do next, or after he has said just a few more things about what he has just been saying. The text is sprinkled with polyglot misprints – I counted over fifty without trying hard – as if there were more important matters to think about than getting individual words right; and they look odd in a book that attends so intimately to puns, slips, metatheses and homophones.

Yet somehow these lapses seem natural to the enterprise. Interesting as the general argument is, readers are, I think, bound to attach more importance to the brilliant assault on three great novels – *La Nouvelle Héloïse, Elective Affinities (Die Wahlverwandtschaften)* and *Madame Bovary* – which Tanner reads as it were to destruction, tearing at them with every instrument he can lay hands on, and pausing only to pursue, in dozens of digressions and excursions, notions about other books which come up in the course of the main action. Roughly speaking, any thinker can become an instrument in Tanner's hands as long as he isn't primarily a literary critic – Locke, Vico, Freud, Lévi-Strauss, Lacan, De Rougemont, Bataille, Foucault. The poaching is done with any light and any net that comes to hand, and I cannot think these streams ever yielded so much to a single transgressor.

At this stage (as Tanner would say) I should offer some account of what kind of achievement this is, but before I do so I want to make some remarks about its significance. It studies marital contract and transgression as these are represented and mimed in novels; and in doing so it reminds us of another contract, and transgresses it. I mean the old contract between critic and reader (here suggested by the title, the blurb, and all the amenities of scholarly publication), which was founded on the assumption that although the writer was likely to be better-informed on the particular subject, he and the reader were essentially the same kind of person, similarly educated and likely to be brought to agreement, or left in informed disagreement, by a familiar, sanctioned mode of discourse: 'This is so, is it not?' It is an assumption of likemindedness, of literate community, of the possibility of consensus. Outside that community stood the largely indifferent army of the less competent – of those who might, in an understandable sense, be regarded as unable to read in any adequate way *Madame Bovary*, *The Golden Bowl*, or whatever. But the community of the competent was still of a certain magnitude: works of literary criticism were and are published in the ordinary way, and not as xeroxed manuscripts or microfiches.

And here is the transgression. Tanner signals it by his refusal to consider what has formerly been said, by other literary critics, about these books. He moves out of the consensus with its familiar ways of arguing, and offers a manner of reading which will seem bizarre even to some readers whose manners of reading already seem bizarre enough to 'general readers'. It is not 'academic', being at odds with the normal criticism of the academies; indeed, it represents a violation of the institutional consensus and suggests the break-up of that consensus. There are even stronger signs of the break-up in the United States, though it is possible to see the American transgressor as a sect with a programme (suggested in *Deconstruction and Criticism*, the new collection of essays from Yale), whereas Tanner has no firm theoretical base. He can observe the contract if it suits him (for example, he will ask whether the subtleties he is considering are 'deliberate', consciously arranged by an author – a question unlikely to be asked by most of the Americans). Like Birkin in *Women in Love*, he feels there is no such thing as pure accident: he reads every word of the text, not skipping great tracts of it as an ordinary reading unwittingly does, because it is in the unread places that one finds the intimate consonance, the surprising secret, the significant transgression. (Indeed, one may see in such criticism the ultimate conquest of modern interpretative method by Freud.) Thus Tanner violates the old contract, does virtually as he pleases, digresses, speculates, pursues some fugitive sense across the frontier into silliness, or what the consensus would call silliness.

Obviously the book is not an easy read, but there is hardly a page that lacks some original and enriching perception. Let me mention some of his observations on Goethe's novel. Mann called it the most daring novel about adultery, though in fact nobody in it actually commits adultery (the same is true of Rousseau's book, in which the rejection of adultery as disastrously subversive is almost hysterical). What happens instead is a quasi-adulterous act between married partners, each substituting (in fantasy) house-guest for spouse. On the relations between these four people Tanner exerts all his ingenuity. He studies anthropologically the relations between host and guest. He asks why three of the characters involved have closely related names (Charlotte, Otto, Ottilie), and why the child born of the central and rather louche sexual act should resemble not its parents but the lovers for whom they were surrogates, and why it should be named Otto rather than Edward, after its father. The running-together of names is a denial of the separations proper to marriage. It is echoed in other breakdowns of separation, as when Charlotte allows a blot to run together the words of a letter; or when a plan is formed to alter the features of the landscape by deliberate flooding; or when we learn of a count and a baroness who have a liaison but live separately. The fixities of marriage, and the fluid forces that may wash over them or erase them, are represented in other ways – for instance, by the topography of the house, which has a woman's wing with locked door, but has also secret spiral staircases: 'for every door expressing a taboo of no-passage, there is some other architectural feature suggesting possibilities of other modes of entry ... every consciously arranged separation suggesting new combinations

by another route . . . The house is thus like a code in which the inhabit-
ants can formulate different messages according to where they position
themselves, the syntax of their arranging . . . '

The 'central act of non-adulterous adultery' is for Tanner a critical
moment in the history of the European novel because in it adultery
and licit sex completely overlap: the monstrous intrudes into the normal, the contractual; law turns into its opposite; the child 'begotten in
double adultery' separates the parents it ought to bind together. And
the central figure of the book is separation/relationship. The title suggests it, for *Verwandtschaften* are family relationships, and not elective;
to call them so is to establish the thematic paradox on the title page.
It is a paradox reflected in every marriage, which by means of a contract turns a voluntary non-blood relationship into a binding blood
relationship. All this is reinforced by the chemical figures, represented
in the narrative by the experiments of a visiting English virtuoso lord,
and in the language by repeated allusion to affinities.

I have given the merest hint of the complexity of Tanner's observations. He persuades Goethe's novel to represent, in great depth, most
of his theories about the nature and necessity of transgression in bourgeois marriage and in the novel. *Madame Bovary*, a much more highly
wrought work, is, I suppose, his real test piece. He undertakes to 'open
up the text in a way that will lay bare some of its most important lines
of force, its most energetic intentions', beginning with a marvellously
minute study of Charles's cap and his first day at school. The cap is a
random assemblage of sexual and uterine puns, the school desk the
first in a series of ambiguous containers that includes the box used in
the operation on Hippolyte's foot and the carriage in which Emma
rides with Léon. The significance of the new boy's need to yell out
his name ('*Charbovari!*') takes pages to unravel; he is stampeded, like
Emma later, into a neglect of the necessary gaps between words (or
persons, such as husband and lover). Most of the characters have pun-
ning names: Binet is 'save-all' and 'duplicate', and his lathe produces
an endless line of identical napkin-rings, emblems of the bourgeois
marriage Emma must escape; the labels of Homais are also emblematic, establishing with arbitrary precision the boundaries between one
thing and another. All this is reinforced by Tanner's endless ingenuity
in the detection of pun and metathesis, as well as his ability to take a

much longer view, to see the novel as a whole in relation to other novels and to the other forms of discourse proper to its historical moment and ours.

It remains a question whether this remarkable book, or others of its kind, will ever make much contribution to the common wisdom – whether the rest of us will in future learn to read more of a novel than we are inclined or encouraged to do by prevailing contracts, and whether we shall come to understand the powerful analogy between the history of the form and the history of marriage. I suggested at the outset that there is an aspect of adultery (roughly, the aspect of pollution) which the novel registers only inadequately. Yet it is true, I think, that there is an analogy. The history of marriage and that of the novel could both be told in terms of the progressive waning of authority: the disappearance of the omnipotent father and the omnipotent author, the invasion of contract by transgression. If the contractual fixities were never threatened by change there would be nothing to say of a marriage, and a meagre future for fiction. But just as many marriages still resist adultery, and many readers resist novels that too manifestly ignore the old contracts, so will there be resistance to this new transgressive criticism. We may have here an avant-garde that will never be joined by the main army – happy enough behind the lines and content with its familiar rations.

15 May 1980

BUMPER BOOK OF DEATH

....

The Hour of our Death by Philippe Ariès translated by Helen Weaver

This book is a history of the collective consciousness of the 'Latin West' (with this country and New England included by association or out of courtesy) during the last thousand years; its focus is death, or changing attitudes towards death, but it is part of the argument that such attitudes must be related to our feelings about many other matters.

Ariès is a researcher of genius, and I shall be saying later that his gifts are sometimes the cause of certain faults or excesses. As in Burton's *Anatomy of Melancholy*, of which this work is a modern avatar, there is an armature of theory which is almost lost under the vast quantity of illustrative material. Much of this is unfamiliar, for Ariès has looked in unusual places – wills, journals, epitaphs and the like – in an attempt to avoid the more formal literary and iconographical kinds of evidence, though he uses that evidence whenever he needs to. What he wants to do is to get behind the standard theological, liturgical and rhetorical formulas, and touch some common imaginative deep structure from which we generate our changing attitudes to death.

The thesis maintains that there have been, in the millennium under consideration, five distinct historical phases. The first, and longest, was the phase of what he calls the Tame Death: at this time death was not feared but thought of merely as repose. The manner of suffering it, its effect on survivors, their ways of representing it, of disposing of the corpse and remembering the departed, all reflected this calm acceptance. The Tame Death was as devoid of terror as it was of medical attendance; when possible, it was public and ceremonious. The worst fate that could befall one was sudden and unexpected death: it is a measure of the changes that have occurred between the early and the late years of the period that nowadays it is on the whole thought a benefit to die without knowing it – for example, in sleep.

The second phase is that of the Death of the Self. The individual begins to conceive of his death as personal, and as preceding an intimate accounting with God. Elaborate wills, giving among other things detailed instructions for the disposal of the body, for masses, tombs and epitaphs, accompanied a new anxiety about Judgment and the after-life generally. Anonymous burial, the normal lot of all but the rich and powerful, gave way to the desire of more ordinary persons to have some memorial. Death was well on the way to becoming 'untamed', and in the third phase the melancholy appropriate to the death of the self gave way to the more fantastic responses of the Baroque; death even grew erotic. There followed, in the Romantic period, the age of the Beautiful Death. The loved one might now be identified with nature, and a cult of the dead, indeed of death itself, might co-exist, as in *Wuthering Heights*, with exotic Gothic terrors. Last comes our own Invisible Death.

Such, in brief, is the historical scheme. Ariès admits that it can't really accommodate all the facts he has collected, or all the ideas they have given him, and he urges us to look out for the *obiter dicta*, the less schematic speculations, that he comes up with in the course of the work. These are undoubtedly interesting, and make the work even more like Burton's: but most readers, I think, will come away, not with a handful of ideas, but with a mass of strange, often gruesome information.

For instance, there is the changing history of graveyards. At the beginning of Ariès's thousand years it was the custom to bury bodies inside, or just outside, the church, so that they might have the protection of the saints. There were ecclesiastical and practical objections to this practice, but they were overborne. Later it was probably the fashion for personal monuments that led to intolerable overcrowding in urban graveyards, which had formerly been rather temporary places of deposit, the bones being removed later to an ossuary. In the 19th century people began to complain that the urban cemeteries were unhygienic. The great Paris graveyard, Les Innocents, was closed, and corpses were dispatched to the environs by the trainload. Ariès asks why the city sites, fundamentally unchanged for centuries and presumably always rather grisly, came so suddenly to seem intolerable. Had there been a change in the sense of what a city ought to be? Or was this a new form of an old fear, a new mechanism of rejection? We can never answer such questions satisfactorily, because the evidence provided is so extensive and complicated. It won't support a simple thesis. At times it has appeared that the living are anxious to keep themselves well apart from the dead, and the revulsion against vast urban burial grounds might well be an instance of this: yet at much the same time the desire to commune with one's dead seems to have grown stronger, and Ariès cites some instances to show that in roughly the same period there was a revival of interest in mummification. One late 18th-century gentleman had his wife made into a mummy, and kept her in the house after he remarried – a state of affairs imaginable, in our time, only by Thurber. Somebody else wanted to patent a method of vitrifying corpses and making of them glass beads to be worn by the bereaved.

We read here of medieval emperors who, at death, were instantly boiled to remove the flesh, which occupied one tomb; bowels, heart and, noblest of all, bones were each consigned to separate tombs. We see a photograph of the great ossuary at Palermo, stuffed with the bones and skulls of monks. We read of a hundred different ways of thinking about dead bodies and getting rid of them. Customs that must have seemed natural and universal turn out to be merely cultural and local. All that is certain is that the body has to be disposed of somehow; whether it is to be tended or even remembered, let alone prayed for, whether it is to be loved or feared, depicted as beautiful or disgusting, seems to be optional. We continue to make such choices. Here in Britain we prefer to burn the dead, in the United States the preferred procedures are at once more profitable and less briskly like garbage disposal.

Among thousands of almost equally startling bits of information, Ariès offers us the news that in Britain today widowers are ostracised, and that in the first year after the death of the wife their mortality rate is ten times that of men of the same age not so bereaved. I mention this fact because I do not quite know what to do with it, and there are a great many more of the same kind. One sees why Ariès needed his big scheme to accommodate them. He also needs, and has, strong views as to what are good and bad ways of thinking about death. Both the scheme and the *parti pris* tend to distort the evidence.

The argument is for deep historical change. Of course such change does occur, but Ariès wants its course to be chartable in terms of abrupt turning-points, violent contrasts. He is always anxious to dispute received opinion. A notable instance of this anxiety is his pronouncement that human beings never knew the fear of death until the 17th century. 'Of course, they were afraid to die; they felt sad about it, and they said so calmly.' This formula distinguishes the fear of dying from the fear of death, which is probably fair: but it also switches from being afraid to feeling sad, which probably isn't. But Ariès badly wants to establish that there was a major change in feeling at a particular historical moment.

Behind this need there is a very strong feeling that in the centuries since we gave up the tame death we have gone terribly wrong on the subject. Death is regarded as a scandal. It 'should have disappeared along with disease, but it persists; it is not even any longer in retreat'. Ariès believes that we need to humanise, or rehumanise, death, to change its image. At present that image strikes him as more cruel than ever before: a man or woman in a hospital bed, stuck all over with tubes, lacking the nobility of even the most grotesque St Sebastian.

Yet it is hard to believe that death has only recently become a scandal. Even in the centuries when it was tame, when it was accepted without fuss, when the passing was orderly and the mourning quick and simple – there must have been something scandalous about it. Rachel mourned her children and would not be consoled: it seems improbable that she had no successors before the present century. Where there is an imagination of happiness, death is a scandal. That is one implication of the Genesis myth, and it was of particular interest to Milton, admittedly a post-tame-death poet. His poem is always astonished by the brutality and finality of death's intrusions into bliss; even before it has ever happened to anybody it is thought of as a dreadful penalty:

> the pain
> Of death denounced, whatever thing death be.

The most appalling indication of the enormity of the loss suffered by Adam and Eve is Eve's proposal to meet death halfway by suicide:

> Why stand we longer shivering under fears
> That show no end but death, and have the power
> Of many ways to die the shortest choosing,
> Destruction with destruction to destroy?

Since their deaths would presumably have prevented all the deaths that have happened since, Eve's seems a reasonable argument, but of course it is also wicked, and Adam knows better than to annoy his Judge, the inventor of death, with such 'acts of contumacy'.

A scandal is, literally, a stumbling block or trap; when there is no way round it, the only thing to do is to accommodate and explain it. That is why the human imagination has a plasticity in regard to death no less admirable than what it displays in its dealings with sex. The arts of dying, like the arts of disposing of the dead, remembering them, assisting them, are therefore extraordinarily various, and fashions change in time: but whether they change with the decisiveness postulated in this book is very doubtful. When you listen to the arguments in *Measure for Measure*, you may be impressed by the Duke's grand formulation of the *Contemptus mundi*: there are ways of dealing with the fear of death, and the Duke specifies some of them, but Claudio is closer to the real thing and speaks like a man with a dread of it in his guts. *Measure for Measure* admittedly scrapes into the 17th century, but it is hard to believe that nobody ever felt like Claudio before that date.

Ariès, however, might value the play as a document of transition. He alludes to *Hamlet* only in passing, though it is also full of interest for his argument. The reader of this book will abandon any notion that the graveyard scene is merely an instance of the literary macabre: the burial grounds of the period would have been littered with bones and skulls, and the gravedigger would have known who had lain where, and even what were the corpse's prospects of slow or rapid decomposition. Hamlet's reaction to the skull of Yorick is especially apposite. Ariès notes a change from the *memento mori*, the generalised injunction to remember that you must die, to the *memento illius*, the reminder of a particular person. Hamlet treats the jester's skull as both of these. You could also say that rapid remarriage – using the funeral baked meats cold at the wedding reception – was good medieval thanatology, acceptable to Gertrude, but not to Hamlet – another mark of transition. Anyway, that is the sort of thing Ariès is always looking for.

He wants to discover a 'hidden language' – a deep structure which has sharply different period manifestations. 'The desires and fantasies that had risen from the depths of the human psyche were expressed in a system of symbols provided by the Christian lexicons. But [each] age spontaneously chose certain symbols in preference to others, be-

cause they better expressed the underlying tendencies of collective behaviour.' In favour of this view it can be said that whole tracts of the
language of death might remain unused for centuries. For example, St
Matthew's pronouncements on judgment, Heaven and Hell, though
perfectly familiar to the literate, seem to have had little influence on
attitudes to death until the late Middle Ages. The Last Judgment was
not until then a matter of much concern; even at Chartres it is not represented as terrible. Its depiction on baptismal fonts suggests merely
that to have been baptised ensures one a place among the sheep rather
than the goats: the matter was already settled. But soon it grew in importance, and flourished in the popular imagination and in painting.
Another instance is Purgatory, familiar to the theologians and Dante,
but having no popular imaginative acceptance until the 16th century;
prayers for the souls in Purgatory, like the Mass for the Dead, are a
relatively late innovation. The notion that one needs the help of in-
tercessors at the time of judgment also appears quite late, and the Ave
Maria, which requests such intercession at the hour of our death, came
in in the 16th century.

This is all persuasive. Yet even at the time when the moment of
death assumed such critical importance, there were voices strongly
insisting that the final account would take notice of a whole life, and
not just its end. The simultaneous existence of conflicting opinions is
something of a nuisance to Ariès. It might suggest that although there
are recognisable differences in prevailing attitudes to death at various
periods, most of the possible responses can co-exist, so that the irrup-
tion of apparently new or neglected forms of expression need not be
read as marking an epoch in the subject. But that is too simple, too
dull, for Ariès: anything that seems obvious, or is widely believed, must
be challenged. Is there a relationship between the high mortality rate of
the plagues and the development of the macabre in funerary art? No,
for that might imply the too early onset of the fear of death. So macabre 'images of death and decomposition do not signify fear of death
. . . They are the sign of a passionate love for this world and a painful
awareness of the failure to which each human life is condemned.' Max
Weber remarked that only capitalist man wants to go rich to his grave.
'In fact, the truth is exactly the opposite': it is pre-capitalist man who
wants to '"go to his grave loaded with gold and riches" and to hold on

to his fortune *in aeternum*.' He accepted the idea of dying but could not bring himself to 'leave houses and orchards and gardens'. Yet another common error is the belief that the family is now on the wane: in fact, it dominates our society as never before.

There is probably something in all these paradoxical contentions, but they are too unqualified to convince. Researchers of genius love to find intricate and occult patterns in their material, and they love to show that everybody else has been not slightly but entirely wrong.

Characteristically, he has little praise for his rival inquirers into the depths, the psychoanalysts. Freud and Abraham were, he thinks, right to deplore the modern refusal to mourn, but wrong in their analysis of it. They assumed that complex dealings with the love and hate felt by the survivor for the deceased were universal, that the death of the other always induces the same sort of psychic situation. But Ariès has been labouring to show the great diversity of the human response to death, and to prove that it is subject to periodisation: so he concludes that the analysts were unwittingly dependent upon a local and cultural model of mourning, which they mistook for a universal condition: their ideal mourner is a 19th-century invention based on the 18th-century invention of the Beautiful Death. Before that there was grief, but not guilt, no persistent prostration.

I suppose the analysts would dismiss these arguments as mere symptoms of denial, saying, for example, that mourning recapitulates inescapable infantile losses and conflicts common to all mankind; death is always construed as an act of violence, however the culture works to conceal and deny the fact. For them, Ariès's denial of denial is simply another form of the same denial. He himself shows how various are the forms denial can take – for example, in his study of the practice of concealing or revealing the face of the dead, of changing fashions in tomb sculpture. But these are cultural, not psychic changes. The analysts have a deeper deep structure. Ariès rejoices in diversity; analysts, despite all the variations of doctrine, are what used to be called uniformitarian.

His love of change can be seen in the emphasis he places upon the fear of premature burial, as the starting-point, virtually, of modern attitudes to death. For centuries, nobody seemed to bother about it, but then an epidemic fear developed. Finally it disappeared again, so that although it instituted a major change it was in itself no more than a period fashion. This seems very doubtful. I myself have known a man with a pathological terror of being buried alive: he extracted all manner of undertakings from his friends, who were to carry out a series of tests and instal alarms in the coffin. I daresay the consulting rooms are still haunted by such unfortunates, and Ariès himself cites instances from earlier periods. The fear of premature burial – and the fear of the prematurely buried – may be closer to universal than he allows. Epidemic manifestations may have temporary and local explanations, but that the dead and living states should be clearly distinguished, that any intermediate state is felt to be intolerable to all concerned, may be matter for the analyst rather than the historian.

Ariès's attitude to psychoanalysts is nothing like so hostile as his attitude to doctors. He looks back with admiration at times when death occurred without medical attendance, at home; the dying knew they were dying, and how to behave, and the neighbours dropped in to say goodbye. Nowadays the doctor is in charge, prolonging our lives into the worst terminal indignities, then dismissing our bodies as evidence of no further relevance, or of medical failure. A strong dislike of modern modes of dying may be one of the forces that animate this very excited and eloquent book.

Indeed, I have given a rather poor impression of its scope, variety and interest. It is likely to be read less as an example of a fashionable way of doing history than as a sort of bumper book of death. It is very large, but then so is its subject, and part of the pleasure for everybody will be that, large as it is, it doesn't include everything. The main pleasure, of course, is that it protects us from its subject by making it a subject, a mere matter of cultural history.

1 October 1981

HEMINGWAY HUNT

....

Along with Youth: Hemingway, the Early Years by Peter Griffin
The Young Hemingway by Michael Reynolds
Hemingway: A Biography by Jeffrey Meyers

A few months ago I went one Sunday evening to a Broadway theatre, not to see a play but to enjoy what was meant to be a thrilling contest between Norman Mailer and Gore Vidal. The place was packed; except for those sponsored by some publisher, the audience had bought very expensive tickets, and they displayed a keenness more appropriate to a prizefight. Indeed a prizefight was what they expected, Mailer and Vidal having been rough with each other in the past. In the event nothing much happened – a few not very good jokes and a good view of two heavy gentlemen whose rough-housing days lie very properly in the past. Still, it was interesting to reflect that this large and fashionable crowd had turned out on a Sunday night to watch the two men doing something they would both have regarded as work of the left hand. Writers are supposed to do best the essentially private work of writing, and they would hardly wish to be exposed to public view when engaged in it, nor would anybody but a singular pervert want to watch. All they could do in the circumstances was to collaborate as fully as possible with their public images, which are in any case of much greater interest to most people than their books.

American writers have long had appalling difficulties with the media – passionately concerned as the media are with everything about famous writers except their writing. Formerly it was possible to be both in and out of the game, as Whitman put it – to have a private as well as a public self. Mark Twain went to great lengths to impose himself on the crowd, and he was a more successful performer than Messrs Vidal and Mailer, but he was also able to hold a self in reserve. For Hemingway it was all much more difficult. His private life was extraordinary to begin with, and he enlarged its extraordinariness for the benefit of all. The image of it was projected onto the mist of the media like a Brocken spectre, a ghost upon which the original proceeded to

model himself. What happened when this act of possession was per-
fected is still best understood from Lillian Ross's notorious *New Yorker* profile; a portrait less of a man than of a demoniac, his talk partly
in a sham Indian dialect and partly filtered through the sports pages.
The trade of the novelist, he wants to argue, is very taxing: 'They can't
yank a novelist like they can a pitcher. Novelist has to go the full nine.'
Or: 'Nobody's going to get me in any ring with Mr Tolstoy unless I'm
crazy or I keep getting better.' He will go the distance with most other
writers. The artists from whom he is willing to learn and whom he presumably doesn't wish to fight are not writers. 'I can make a landscape
like Mr Paul Cézanne. I learned how to make a landscape from Mr
Paul Cézanne by walking through the Luxembourg Museum a thousand times with an empty gut, and I am pretty sure that if Mr Paul
was around, he would like the way I make them.' Mr Hemingway will
never say anything quite the way it was, and there is no reason to suppose he ever walked through the Luxembourg Museum with an empty
gut, since his wife in those Paris days had an adequate income. All he's
saying is that he learned something from Cézanne, which could well
be true. He also says he learned how to do counterpoint from Mr J.S.
Bach, which is slightly less persuasive.

Critics have been trying for a half a century to distinguish the writer from the talking ghost, and some – Edmund Wilson, for instance
– found it easier to do the trick than Hemingway himself. When he was
young, he worked very hard at never saying anything the way anybody
else would say it, and his success was remarkable. Later he often managed to do it again, when the ghost didn't seize the pen and make him
sound like one of his own imitators. Part of the trouble was that he was
no better than anybody else at finding good ways of talking about his
writing: like everybody else, he had to speak of it as almost anything
but writing – baseball, boxing, game-fishing, lion-hunting, bullfighting or war. In a way, he was as ungenerous to himself as he was to most
other writers, including some he certainly did learn from, like Ford
Madox Ford, Gertrude Stein and Sherwood Anderson. Yet very good
writers, including Ford and Pound and Joyce, recognised Hemingway's
gifts, the serious gifts about which he never bragged. And it might be
said that the author of *In Our Time* could go quite a few rounds with
the author of *Dubliners*, or even that the author of 'The Short Happy

Life of Francis Macomber' could have mixed it for a while with Mr Tolstoy.

Two of these biographies are concerned only with the youthful Hemingway as the sort of person who could become the sort of person he later became; they stop at pretty well the same point, when Hemingway is about to take off for Europe with his bride Hadley Richardson. He is 22 and she close to thirty. He has done a good deal of journalism and written some stories, none published. I suppose one justifies the writing of quite long books about a writer before he truly became a writer by arguing that nothing about so great a figure can be wholly irrelevant, but it seems to me that both Mr Reynolds and Mr Griffin have pushed this argument a bit far. When you've read these books you will be exempted from ever attending to another word about Hemingway's home town Oak Park, a posh suburb of Chicago; and although it may seem a little ungracious to say so, for she was an interesting woman, you may feel some regret that a thousand letters from Hadley to Ernest have survived.

Although Reynolds and Griffin (who has two further volumes in store) here cover much the same ground, they have different emphases. Reynolds says little about the early journalistic career in Kansas City and Toronto because others have covered it adequately, but he is not short of material, having had access to the John Fitzgerald Kennedy Library (where Hadley's letters, alas without Ernest's thousandfold replies, are stored) and many other major collections; indeed all the biographers appear to have been received with unusual generosity by the Hemingway family and the custodians of all this precious material.

Reynolds is particularly interested in Oak Park in the days of Ernest's youth. An uncle of the writer's, regretting the lack of squirrels, which he regarded as essential to an upper-class suburb, introduced them from Arkansas. The squirrels turned out not to be sufficiently genteel, but by the time that was clear the Great War had started, so nobody blamed Uncle George. 'Today there are no Hemingways left in Oak Park, but there are plenty of squirrels.' So, in summary, runs the ominously leisurely opening paragraph, and it is followed by much more significant detail about crime-free Oak Park, the nobs' refuge from wicked metropolitan Chicago. The first automobile arrived at the same time as Ernest, and by the time he was 14 decadence had set in, as the local newspaper, *Oak Leaves*, reports: 'The music of the bagnio finds its way to every piano, and our young people habitually sing songs, words and music produced by degenerates,' and demi-mondaine Paris fashions aggravate 'tendencies which civilisation demands be held in sure control'. Before long, the young were doing 'brothel dances' like the Fox Trot and the Tango, and suburban commuter trains were bringing into Oak Park burglars, muggers, gamblers and other villains from Chicago.

Meanwhile young Ernest was collecting knives and fishing a lot. By the time America entered the war in 1917 many of his contemporaries were almost old enough to volunteer. Ernest had a weak eye and wouldn't have been accepted anyway, but he went to Kansas City and worked on a local newspaper. He learned a lot, among other things that the Kansas City whores thought semen a specific against tuberculosis, that city politicians were corrupt, that military uniforms attract girls, and that much might be done with brief sentences. Then he joined the Red Cross as a non-combatant, went to Italy, got wounded, and came back, before he was twenty, wearing a uniform to which he was not entitled and working up fantasticated stories about his military experience. In fact, he had over two hundred shrapnel wounds and a genuine limp: but that wasn't enough, and he claimed that after sustaining these wounds he carried another wounded man a hundred and fifty yards to safety, or alternatively that he was buried by the explosion three days before he rose again. Though for very good reasons he wore a uniform to suggest that he had, Hemingway did not serve in the Italian Army. It was about this time, we are told, that William Faulkner wore a Royal Canadian Air Force officer's uniform with wings, and cultivated a limp, to none of which he was entitled.

All this may sound very silly, but war is a great breeder of lies and the young Hemingway was behaving like a lot of other people. Still, the progressive adornment and transformation of the story of his wounding is very like the treatment he gave other episodes in his life, whether in his everyday boasting or in his writing. The need to be extraordinary, to excel not only in war but also in competitive sports and displays of physical strength, may, as Reynolds suggests, have something to do with the influence of Theodore Roosevelt, who was always urging youth, in a time when there seemed to be no more wars in prospect, to do the next best thing and fight one another or kill animals. If this is so, and it seems probable, the influence of Teddy is not yet dead: reinforced by the example of Hemingway himself, the American version of pastoral is still very evident, and middle-aged town-dwellers take off at weekends for their log cabins, wearing their L.L. Bean lumberjack gear, to pit their wits against the birds, as one of them expressed himself to me.

Hemingway seems not to have been very good at most of these manly activities, and Griffin in particular likes to point out, fondly enough, that his bad eyesight prevented him from being a good shot, that he was careless with fire-arms, that he lost at tennis, that his reflexes at boxing were slow. But he threw his body into every sort of violent activity with gruesome gusto. Meyers has a frightful appendix listing Hemingway's accidents and illnesses, over thirty of the former and some of them almost fatal. The cost was great. In *For Whom the Bell Tolls*, which he wrote when he was about forty, he represents the 52-year-old El Sordo as an old man wondering why the prospect of death is unattractive even at his great age. At the time Hemingway still had his most remarkable antics to come, during the Second World War, but by the time he reached El Sordo's age his battered, diseased and drink-soaked body really was old, and ten years later there can have seemed no real alternative to disposing of it. Like some of his kindred and associates, he had a tendency towards suicide. His father, a brother and a lover killed themselves, one wife was the daughter of a suicide, and at least two wives threatened suicide. Add to this the inexorable demands of the public image and there was no other way to go.

His mother gets some of the blame, for she liked the idea of him as a man, not as a writer. She insisted on treating him as a hero – 'my boy is *every inch a man* . . . It's great to be the mother of a hero' – but she was ashamed of his books and thought them dirty. He came to detest her and apparently not without cause, but she contributed to his personal myth and probably to his choice of women. It appears that he had very few love affairs, for, as Faulkner remarked, he thought he had to marry them all. The nurse Agnes von Kurowsky is the model for Catherine in *A Farewell to Arms*, but he seems not to have slept with her, nor with Adriana Ivancich, the dreamgirl of *Across the River and into the Trees*. Griffin is the best source for information about Agnes;

for Adriana, of course, one needs Meyers.

Although Reynolds leaves quite a lot out, he still has too much to say and goes in for fine writing:

The cars went on up the road out of sight, around the point at the edge of town. Ernest sat down on the porch with his luggage. He was happy. He had not been unhappy all winter or spring. This was different though. There had been things to prove to himself. Now they were done. . . He had done the job.

Here *style indirect libre* is indistinguishable from parody. What with one thing and another he doesn't even get Hadley into the book till page 143, and much of the second half comes from her fluent pen.

Griffin, with two more volumes in hand, is equally leisured. He will let you know what Jack Hemingway had to drink when they met at the Boston Airport Hilton, Jack having come east for what is rather oddly called the internment of his mother's ashes. If it is remarked that Hemingway's father said grace, Griffin will spell out the grace. He will tell you what brand of cigarettes Hemingway smoked in the Italian hospital. But there are compensations: rooting through all those archives, he comes up with a letter written by Ernest at the age of six, in which he describes how he whacked a porcupine with an axe. Later when he was caught redhanded by a game warden with an illegally killed heron, he fibbed. He fibbed again, more astonishingly, when he told his horrified parents that he was engaged to the film star Mae Marsh, and again when he said he was set on becoming a wartime pilot, knowing all the while that no combatant service would have him. But one feels that Griffin is really telling us all this to make his hero more rather than less remarkable. Probably his greatest disservice to Hemingway is his reprinting of some really terrible early stories. It is a lot easier to understand their prompt rejection by editors than the miracle by which this author came to write *In Our Time* before he was 26.

Griffin has access to the 'Memory Books' of Ernest's mother, a treasure trove of information about the infant Hemingway, and of course there is Hadley. 'For walking in the country, Hadley had bought herself a scotch plaid cape. It was not lined but very pretty' etc, etc. Not all the minute detail is quite credible. Italian soldiers are unlikely to have called Hemingway *giovanni Americano*, and when Johnny Miller missed his stroke while rowing he was not catching crabs.

How Griffin is going to get Hemingway's extraordinarily eventful last forty years into only two more volumes if he goes on at this rate is a question only time will answer. Jeffrey Meyers, in his full biography, has to despatch the period dealt with by Reynolds and Griffin in 62 pages, one-tenth of the whole. He, too, has had access to all those collections; he is less expansive but manages to add a few points on the early life – for example, on the Kansas City period and Mae Marsh. He can even adorn the tale of the hero's wound: Hemingway claimed he was shot twice through the scrotum and had to rest his testicles on a pillow. Hemingway was in hospital with a lot of men who had wounded genitals. Apparently he thought of Jake in *The Sun Also Rises* as having had his penis shot off while his testicles remained intact, though in the book the hurt remains more obscure. Obviously a lot of fantasising on such subjects intervened between Hemingway's wound and Jake's. He also claimed to have felt his soul, or at any rate something, being pulled out of his body like a silk handkerchief from a pocket, and this was remembered for the bullfighter's death in *In Our Time*; and, as Meyers rather oddly remarks, it 'recurs in a sensory passage' in *A Farewell to Arms*. Without minimising Hemingway's trauma, Meyers nevertheless points out that Proust spent more time in the army than Papa.

All the same, Hemingway, in one capacity or another, saw a great deal of war. He covered the Greco-Turkish conflict of 1922, the Spanish Civil War, and the Second World War. It was the biggest game of all, the one to which all the others aspired, as all sexual relations aspired to marriage; and it was the saddest also, again like marriage. One prepared for the next marriage by having a serious liaison, and for the next war by killing animals and studying the grace of bullfighters under pressure.

Meyers is not a lively writer, but he is certainly informative and, compared with some, succinct. His account of the Paris years is a useful supplement to *A Moveable Feast*, qualifying the nasty portraits therein of Ford and Wyndham Lewis and explaining how it was that Hemingway acquired quite a reputation as a writer without actually publishing anything. Here, too, began his career as a bully. If it's true that perfect strangers occasionally went up to him and hit him it can only be because they wanted to please him. He liked to beat up weaker and older men. I had heard of without really believing in the fight he had with the poet Wallace Stevens at a drunken party in Key West. It does seem to have happened, when the novelist was about forty and the poet about sixty and as usual overweight. Hemingway despised Stevens for asking him to hush the matter up, as likely to damage his reputation as an insurance lawyer. It's all the more touching to recall that some years later, when Stevens, having turned down the job himself, was asked to suggest a name for a new Chair of Poetry at Harvard, he proposed Hemingway. This wasn't as daft a suggestion as it may sound, for Stevens felt at the time that reality was being particularly oppressive, and saw the main duty of the poet as finding a style to resist it. Perhaps he was right. In any case, it would have been an interesting appointment.

Meyers provides much information about the four marriages. Gertrude Stein said of her ex-friend that anybody who marries three girls from St Louis hasn't learned much, but the truly remarkable thing is that any of the wives lasted as long as they did with a husband who made himself extremely dependent yet demanded absolute freedom. Hemingway must have seen himself as rather like the writers about whom Henry James liked to expand, men who recognised marriage as fatal to art but who couldn't always manage without it. There is just a touch of updated *Yellow Book* about Hemingway's marital history. He even turned against men friends when he thought the relationship was getting too intimate. But women were the major problem. He felt guilty about Hadley, and tried to make it up to her in *A Moveable Feast*; he turned Catholic for Pauline, but that only led to rows about birth control; he came to detest Martha. The record of wives and mistresses is largely a record of failure. It seems Hemingway believed that by expending semen you were giving up juices necessary to good writing, a view that puts wives in a difficult position. He wanted perfection of the life as well as of the work but accepted the Romantic myth that you can't have both (the truth being that you can't have either). His work is more interesting than his life, but they were connected, and people are right to think that on the whole the work got worse as the life became more absurd or tragic.

Living life to the full and never being a coward like his father took its toll in all those accidents and fights. The legend spoilt things for him. When he went back to Pamplona for the bullfights he found the place ruined by tourists, sent there by his books. He himself was the main tourist attraction of Key West. He spent his time with drinking and fishing cronies, flatterers of the man, not readers of the books. He could still be very good, as in the African stories, but he needed another war to recharge his batteries, and the Spanish conflict provided it. He lived life to the full, enjoyed his fame, made many new friends – including Martha Gellhorn, whose legs 'begin at her shoulders' – and got out of it a book that is certainly very good in parts.

When the next war came along he developed a megalomania of which the most extraordinary aspect is the fact that he got away with so much because he was such a great man. He personally hunted German submarines off Cuba and ran his own intelligence operation. He even got special petrol allowances for the sub hunts, and went on with his valueless counter-espionage despite the disapproval of the FBI. In 1944, at preposterous risk and entirely without military necessity, he was the first to get to Paris. This was the greatest of all the rough games. He probably killed some Germans. He felt the best he had ever felt; he was insanely brave yet always boasting about his courage. He carried arms to which he was not entitled, was admired for his tactical know-how by some experts, and behaved rather like an irresponsible version of General Patton. When his behaviour got him investigated, he was advised by two staff officers of Patton to commit perjury, which he did. He got off; Meyers remarks that he 'was licensed to do as he pleased and famous enough to get away with anything'. His wife Martha now thought him mad as well as an intolerable liar. Staying at the Paris Ritz with Mary Welsh, later to be his fourth wife, he placed a photograph of her husband in the toilet bowl and shot it with a machine pistol. There was a flood, dealt with by the tolerant management. Most professionals would describe his military conduct as absurd and dangerous to his own side. However, Fidel Castro says he and his friends took *For Whom the Bell Tolls* into the mountains and learned guerrilla tactics from it.

Catching up with one's own lies can be a costly business, and at not much over fifty Hemingway was physically broken, a self-styled 'defeated man', an alcoholic with an astonishing number of diseases. He had bad eye trouble, high blood pressure, liver and kidney diseases, a fatal form of diabetes; he was severely depressed and also impotent. He had a paranoid fear of the FBI, insisting that he was being followed. (He was.) Yet he managed to write a good book, *A Moveable Feast*, before he began treatment at the Mayo Clinic. He suffered ECT treatment many times and lost his memory. He killed himself with a sportsman's efficiency at 62.

This is the death of the author old-style, not post-structuralist but Americanised *poète maudit*; the latter is headline news but very few care about the former. Probably the moment when Hemingway's life made most sense to him was when he was seriously wounded and in love with a woman who dropped him; *A Farewell to Arms* was not the only product of that happy conjunction. Swaggering strength and an altogether abnormal capacity to absorb punishment co-existed with an overdeveloped susceptibility to insult, injury, and illness real or imagined. It is true not only that paranoiacs have enemies but that hypochondriacs have illnesses. Hemingway's daily recording of his blood pressure was abnormal but so was his blood pressure.

Also the truth about liars may be very extraordinary, and the mere facts about what happened to Hemingway would be fictions in most lives. His fantasies always had a bottom of fact, which is what gives some force to the Old Man and Colonel Cantwell in the late novels. 'A writer's job is to tell the truth,' he said. 'His standard of fidelity to the truth should be so high that his invention, out of his experience, should produce a truer account than anything factual can be.' There is a big difference between fantasticating one's experiences to impress fellow drunks in a bar, when they get more absurd as the drink goes down, and turning facts and attendant fantasies into truth in a book. Hemingway was a liar with a passion for the truth and an understanding that it could be had only by devising a technique of great economy and purity. It was hard to keep on doing it.

He admired technique above all, whether it had to do with guns or bulls or game-fishing or war or prose. He sometimes exaggerated his knowledge of all such matters. A Spanish bullfighter, a hostile witness to be sure, remarks that Hemingway knew nothing about bullfighting, but admitted that he knew more than any other American though less than any Spaniard. However, even Spaniards know very little about it: only the matadors do, and not many of them. On this account Hemingway should not have claimed an ability to make fine critical discriminations about the art of bullfighting. But he did know quite a lot about prose, too much perhaps, so that his own technique became excessively mannered, too much on show, too much the servant of the public image, the Brocken spectre. Of these three biographers Meyers has the best sense of the relation between the workshop and the shop window, and of the nature of the demon that possessed the man.

17 April 1986

ON A CHINESE MOUNTAIN

....

The Royal Beasts by William Empson
Essays on Shakespeare by William Empson

The Royal Beasts contains works of Empson's previously unpublished or published long ago and very obscurely. There is a short play, an unfinished novel, a ballet scenario and a batch of poems, all early. It is the third posthumous volume and much the most important, though a fourth – a collection of essays on 17th-century poetry and drama – is promised for 1987. Since it will presumably contain Empson's essays on Donne, which have a peculiar centrality in his work, this final volume will be needed for any considered estimate of a writer much honoured by fellow critics (at any rate in England) even when they found him most exasperating. However, it will hardly match *The Royal Beasts* in interest.

The volume has a valuable seventy-page introduction and some useful notes by John Haffenden, who arranges the material as far as possible in chronological order. The play or melodrama, *Three Stories*, was written when the poet was 20, and performed, with him in the cast, by the Cambridge ADC. Long supposed to have been lost as Empson pursued his career in the East, it somehow turned up, and is certainly worth having. The poems mostly belong to the late Twenties. Some appeared in Cambridge magazines but were excluded from the first collection of 1935. A dozen are now printed for the first time ever. The novel was written in China in the immediately pre-war years; the ballet belongs to 1942, when Empson was working for the BBC and writing propaganda for Chinese consumption.

Between Cambridge and the BBC he had published *Seven Types of Ambiguity* (1930), *Poems* and *Some Versions of Pastoral* (both of 1935), and a second volume of verse, *The Gathering Storm* (1940). He also wrote many reviews and – as we now learn – a book on the faces of the Buddha, obviously the product of intense research and imaginative energy, but totally lost. He had been a professor in Japan from 1931 to 1934, and in 1937 joined the faculty of Peking National University

in Hunan, where the northern universities had retreated before the
Japanese advance. These were the years when he taught English literature without the aid of books, at the same time getting on with his
writing. *The Royal Beasts* has a whole library behind it, but he must
have carried it in his head. He was the only non-Chinese around, and
obviously enjoyed the whole dangerous and uncomfortable enterprise.
He returned to England when the European war began, but went back
to China afterwards, coming home finally in 1952. By that time he was
already a legendary figure, partly because of the precocious *Seven Types*
but also for the poems, which enjoyed a revival of attention around
1950.*The Structure of Complex Words* had come out in 1951, *The Collected Poems* in 1955. Now a professor at Sheffield (he had wanted to
work in Yorkshire), he published *Milton's God* in 1961.

During his years at Sheffield, and afterwards, Empson entered with
spirit into the life of the literature professor and took part with idiosyncratic vehemence in the professional controversies of the day. But
although he didn't mind being a prof, there was an element of suspicion or mistrust in his dealings with other profs. He wished they could
all be different and often suspected them of holding detestable and
smug views on Intention or God. In his critical writings one sees again
and again that he is trying to deal justly with these contemporaries, but
sooner or later exasperation at their dullness takes over. I think he was
very conscious of the breadth and variety of his own experience and so
thought us all narrow and tame, venturing our pathetic little audaci-
ties from positions of bourgeois security. 'It is not human to feel safely
placed' is a line that expresses a deep conviction.

Not being fully human, the professors frequently missed the simple meaning of the great literature they were supposed to know about.
What they admired in him was his extraordinary subtlety, his sometimes shocking novelties: but although he was properly proud of such
powers, I think he came to set even more store by his access to quite
simple truths about literature and life that were being overlooked.
There is a famous page about Gray's 'Elegy' at the beginning of *Some
Versions of Pastoral* which shows how the cleverness and the simplicity
worked together. Commenting on the stanza beginning 'Full many a
gem of purest ray serene . . . ' he points out that it means 18th-century
England had no *carrière ouverte aux talents*.

This is stated as pathetic, but the reader is put into a mood in which one would not try to alter it . . . By comparing the social arrangement to Nature, he makes it seem inevitable, which it was not, and gives it a dignity which was undeserved. Furthermore, a gem does not mind being in a cave and a flower prefers not to be picked; we feel that the man is like the flower, as short-lived, natural and valuable, and this tricks us into feeling that he is better off without opportunities. The sexual suggestion of *blush* brings in the Christian idea that virginity is good in itself, so that any renunciation is good . . .

And so it goes on, one of the texts that taught a generation to read well and feel good about it. Here we feel we are really seeing through Gray; his poem has a 'massive calm' but it doesn't take a Communist to see that it is a political cheat; 'the "bourgeois" themselves do not like literature to have too much "bourgeois ideology".' Splendid: but it is the sentence beginning the next paragraph that gives the Empsonian surprise: 'And yet what is said is one of the permanent truths; it is only in degree that any improvement of society could prevent wastage of human powers; the waste even in a fortunate life, the isolation even of a life rich in intimacy, cannot but be felt deeply, and is the central feeling of tragedy.' One hears rather little about permanent truths in modern criticism; to Empson it was obvious that they existed and that it was dishonourable (another word he didn't mind using) to 'wince away' from them.

Watching everybody wincing away made him more and more peppery and also, on occasion, less reasonable. He was the cavalier and the wincers mean-minded puritans. The authors he venerated he went on listening to very carefully, but there was a sort of boisterous uncharitableness in his treatment of their expositors. He was not an easy man to argue with; he liked to say he was only the *animal méchant*, and it is true that he had to put up with some fairly ferocious attacks in his time: but there was a touch of Prince Rupert also, a feeling that *à outrance* was the only way to fight. Of course a man can't go on charging all the time, and what one remembers mostly is a morose geniality of manner, an amiability isolated and wary. But above all one thinks of him with affection and deep respect, the one genius that the modern explosion in the critical population has produced. So it seems, at any rate, to my generation. Recently Christopher Norris has been meditating, with his usual tact, the resemblances and differences between the Empson of *The Structure of Complex Words* and the Paul de Man of *Allegories of Reading* – a sign, perhaps, that the most neglected (and most theoretical) of Empson's books will have something to say even to the young, who may suppose that really serious rhetorical analysis only got going in the late Sixties.

However, *The Royal Beasts* is not criticism, though it shows the intellectual force of the critical books of the Thirties, and sometimes reminds us of them. It is striking, for instance, that the play *Three Stories* should, at such an early date, show Empson experimenting with elaborate double plots. The main plot is about a young man who serves as secretary to an old novelist, and as lover to the old man's young wife. There is some good rather 'brittle' dialogue, some bright talk about sexual morality; and the old man gets shot for patronising the young one. In between the two halves of that plot there occurs an apparently unrelated scene about a man named Smith, who is the captive of Dracula. Some of this scene is written in that free-associative style Empson used in his first published poem, 'Poem about a Ball in the 19th Century', and in another here printed, called 'Address to a Tennis Player'; the notes to the poems express some doubt about the virtues of this manner, and they seem justified, but he kept the first poem in the *Collected* and perhaps rightly, for some of his best works ('It is this deep blankness is the real thing strange . . . ') have put the half-awake, entranced style to better use.

The formal experiment in *Three Stories* isn't just the Dracula sandwich: as the title says, there are three stories. The other is a framing romance, a mythical induction and epilogue in heroic couplets: in this story the wife is in chains, the young man comes with a sword to slay the dragon; he does so and they live happily afterwards, as they don't in the verismo version. It's admittedly a curious affair, properly admired in the Cambridge of its day. Haffenden quotes the *Granta* review, which smartly praises the author for achieving 'an almost complete mastery of his Oedipus complex' and using it 'for very intelligent purposes . . . If we interpreted it rightly, it amounted to something like this: that the ethical problems of life differ from the scientific problems only if one conceives them romantically, and even then, the apparent romanticism achieved, they become scientific again.' Much later, Empson told Martin Dodsworth that the structural idea had been 'to take a story and interpose a scene of apparently total irrelevance in the middle': we can now confirm the accuracy of that recollection as well as offering belated congratulations to the *Granta* reviewer.

In the chatter about sex the name of A.M. Ludovici is mentioned, a writer now remembered, if at all, for having infuriated T.E. Hulme by writing a little book on Nietzsche ('Mr Ludovici, writing on Nietzsche, might be compared to a child of four in a theatre watching a tragedy based on adultery . . . The most appropriate means of dealing with him would be a little personal violence') and patronising Epstein. Ludovici was also a feminist. Haffenden provides an interesting note from a diary Empson kept in 1926 which says that despite 'the grave national crisis' (the General Strike) what he wants to talk about is Ludovici and his creed of Heterosexual Healthiness. Against this doctrine the young poet argues that natural man really wants only a honeymoon; he will impregnate a woman and then 'swing back to the homosexual . . . A purely heterosexual man is dangerously uncivilised.' We shall see the relevance of this observation to *The Royal Beasts*. The note goes on to remark that Freud had shown how 'to make sure of the family . . . we took sex aside and turned it Oedipose.' You can see that Empson at 20 had a lot going for him, and there is abundant testimony to the fame he enjoyed in what he called, after they kicked him out, 'that strange cackling little town'.

This collection includes more of the poems that contributed to his early reputation. He remarked in a letter to Ian Parsons, who was to publish his first books, that 'there is a rather portentous air about compact verses without notes, like a seduction without conversation,' and of course he wrote notes fairly freely, though claiming to believe that what made them necessary was weakness in the poems. We could certainly use some notes to these unpublished poems. There is a pretty piece he wrote at 13 and a rueful one about being sent down. 'Letter VI' is instantly attractive, an epithalamion:

> Never to be thrust on your unwilling notice
> Still less before the public, annotated.

Yet here it is, though unannotated. There is as usual a lot of astronomical troping. 'Insomnia' feels like a good poem; it is one of those where for a while you congratulate yourself on hanging on to the sense, but then fall off, or look for notes. There is one theme which often appears with variations: a move into unintelligibly vast space, or downwards in a cave, or in a labyrinth:

> Simply we do not know what are the turnings
> Expound our poising of obscure desires,
> What Minotaur in irritable matched burnings
> Yearns and shall gore her intricate my fires.

Haffenden has some useful remarks on the poems, not unlike those of the *Granta* reviewer on the play: they try to solve the contradictions between the world of science and the feeling of being human; in the circumstances of the late Twenties it seemed the way to do this was to 'build . . . with slow labour and due regard for fame, a private cosmos', as Empson put it. He always believed the main reason for writing poems was to be rid of psychological tension, though there was a social obligation to be intelligible: so it isn't surprising that the poems are so tormented, and look down long vistas of possibility, moving from one metaphor to another in an attempt to express a meaning that cannot be literal. Yet Empson always insisted that there was nothing in the poem for you if you couldn't follow the argument; and if his 'audience within himself' couldn't, the poem failed in its therapeutic function, which was to save the poet's sanity. All this is very clearly stated in Empson's interview with Christopher Ricks in *The Review* (June 1963). Presumably the audience, within and without, needs to get some notion of how it felt to have to write the poem, and then to write it. This is a clue to much that goes on in the criticism; it explains Empson's lengthy campaign against W.K. Wimsatt, the aesthetician of the New Criticism, and it also explains why American critics, who tend to class Empson as a New Critic, are sometimes unable to believe that he wasn't 'anti-intentionalist'. In fact, he is the most convinced of intentionalists, and although he does a certain amount of unfair sneering at his opponents, his most ravishing, as well as his most wrongheaded, interpretations are always meant to be about what happened in a poet's head. Later on I shall give some instances I myself think important or weird.

The strangest of these works is the ballet scenario, 'The Elephant and the Birds', with Empson's comments on it and some interesting ancillary material supplied by Haffenden. Empson worked on it in 1942, when he was at the BBC, and seems to have gone on thinking about it for some time after that. The ballet combines two quite different stories, the Greek myth of Philomel and Procne, and an Indian legend about the Buddha's incarnation as an elephant. As Haffenden says, the idea was to ask a double-plot riddle: what does the tale of rape and cannibalism in Thrace have in common with the Buddha's self-sacrifice in his animal incarnation?

Empson knew a lot about Buddhism, which he saw as representing a stage of religious development from which Christianity, with its equation of love with torture, was a regression. Moreover he had argued, in his lost book *Asymmetry in Buddha Faces*, that by giving each of the Buddha's profiles a separate expression the sculptors produced a sort of icon of unity in dissimilarity, and of the way in which 'one arrives at two ideas or ways of dealing with things which both work and are needed, but which entirely contradict one another,' as he remarked in a review of 1928. He was also interested in the Gandhara sculpture and the argument as to whether or in what degree the eastward penetration of Alexander gave a Greek form to images of the Buddha. The ballet has something to do with holding East and West in a single thought.

Empson worked it out in great detail, not only the conduct of the narratives but the stage settings and music. He seems to have got Leslie Hurry to show interest, and sent a copy to John Hayward for comment. Hayward was used to this kind of request: he advised Eliot on 'Little Gidding' and a few years later Auden on the libretto of *The Rake's Progress*; and for somebody who professed no expert knowledge of ballet he acquitted himself rather well. It occurred to him that elephants were not very balletic; or, as he put it, there might be 'some considerable difficulty in finding adequate symbolism for the Elephants' weight, majesty and dignity'. And he made a number of practical suggestions: though dumpy in real life, the nightingale need not appear so on stage; swallows should be accompanied by violins, etc. Empson's reply is in his familiar tone of cheerful insult: 'My dearest Hayward, I was much shocked by your kind letter . . . Your views on my little ballet show I think the appalling corruption into which the European ideas about ballet have fallen . . . ' He had seen Japanese dancing in the Noh plays, and the Cambodian *asparas* at Angkor, and much preferred them to occidental galumphing.

One may ask why he should have spent so much energy on this recondite project when he knew that in the unlikely event of the ballet ever being danced it could only be danced absurdly. However, he did think the European ballet – he mentions *Swan Lake* and *The Firebird* – had the power of restoring mystery to already known legends; and he wanted somehow to bring that kind of thing into contact with Eastern legend and Eastern dance, as in the double profiles of the Buddha. At this distance of time it may seem that it was pretty fantastic to hope for the realisation of such a project in the dreary middle of the war: yet the old Sadler's Wells Ballet was not unadventurous and it might just have come off, however disappointingly. In any case, it enlarges one's idea of the man to have a sight of this rather weird enterprise.

We learn even more, I think, from 'The Royal Beasts'. It is a philosophical fable of great ingenuity and much charm, though it is easy to see why it was never finished. Empson wrote what there is of it on a Chinese mountain, without the aid of books, and although he presumably did some reading for it before leaving England (Zuckerman on apes, at least), it is remarkable how, under such conditions, he disposed of so much considered information.

Swift invented reasonable horses to show what a rational animal would be like. Empson invents an animal distinct from man and the higher apes, which nevertheless has strong affinities with man: for instance, it uses language. It is fur-covered, has a long tail and lemur-like eyes. But probably the most important difference is that the Wurroos have a breeding season. The questions that come up when a representative Wurroo (called Wuzzoo) is brought together with a British colonial administrator are many and profound. Formerly the Wurroos had kept to themselves, beating and expelling intruders: but a prospector finds gold in their territory. Wuzzoo brings some; his people don't want-it, but they do want protection from the evils that could follow its discovery. Not wishing to be treated like the native human populations, they ask to be regarded as beasts belonging to the King, feeling sure that he treats his animals better than his human subjects. So the immediate question, are they men or not? acquires some political urgency.

This is where their breeding season becomes important. Haffenden quotes a long unposted letter to Zuckerman in which Empson says that his Wurroos 'have become rational without using Freudian machinery'. A month of orgiastic copulation, with special rules, special music, obscene drawings, and so on, and then back to sexless fur-picking, which goes on for the rest of the year. Wuzzoo volunteers the information that he once had the same woman for three seasons, but says this was thought odd. One sees here a resemblance to the ideal arrangements suggested in the younger Empson's notes on Ludovici, but the main point is that the family is an arrangement unknown to the Wurroos, who therefore aren't Oedipal, and need a civilisation that can be established without the creative energies born of sexual repression.

George Bickersteth, Empson's colonial administrator, is an intelligent human and sexually quite ordinary; he gives up a native mistress and brings out a wife from a rectory. She is quite attracted to Wuzzoo, whom she teaches English, and he has to explain what is possible between them and what not. This helps to show that the Wurroos are both very similar and very different from humans; and there are other related boundary problems, such as the visitor's sleeping place (indoors, or outside with the dogs?), and, in the megapolitical realm, jurisdiction over territories with vague frontiers controlled by obscure treaties. Empson is surprisingly calm on the colonial question, if one thinks of the sort of thing the Left Book Club was saying about it at the time: his interest is more abstract, he is trying to think about Man.

Wuzzoo is friendly but knows he is not a man and, as he mildly tells Bickersteth, he thinks very badly of men. But the administrator has to warn him of the possibly severe consequences of not being human, such as being hunted for one's fur. Empson mentions more than once the decision of the Church in the matter of the natives of Tierra del Fuego: it proclaimed them human. And here he sets up a big court scene in which counsel argues the case of the Wurroos. This starts brilliantly with a plea for their non-humanity, very legal and scientific: humans cannot copulate with Wurroos, as experiment had shown, and any further attempts along that line would be liable to the charge of bestiality. Moreover blood transfusions between men and Wurroos fail. Counsel further argues that the case is unprecedented, since previous history records no instance of a species to be inserted in the space between animal and man. (This is untrue, as *homo selvaticus* filled this space, though it is true that, like Caliban, he could copulate with humans and wanted very much to do so; nor did he have a breeding season.) The legal arguments in favour of the humanity of the Wurroos seem much weaker, and it is with the philosophical and practical issues arising from their rational non-humanity that Empson is concerned. Were they capable of redemption? Should missionaries be sent? The Archbishop of Canterbury makes a good speech. The Buddhists make a strong claim that in their religion the Blessed One is open to the entire animal kingdom. Wuzzoo himself thinks Christianity fine for men, and also likely to be more creative, because more repressive, than Buddhism. But the main theological problem raised is one that had a permanent interest for Empson. The Archbishop remarks that if we got to Mars and found it inhabited, we should certainly want to convert the natives. Empson is thinking, not for the first time, about the plurality of worlds, and the need for multiple redemptions. Was Christ to be crucified all over the universe? If it became necessary, would he be recrucified here? Granted this sacrificial versatility, could he even appear under many guises, so that one might think of a particular person (Donne's Elizabeth Drury, for example) as Christ?

Although Empson has a lot of fun inventing a system of music appropriate to a 'sexless' species, and imagining the Wuzzoo attitude to babies ('Do your women *like* having to look after these things? Of course they are only raving lunatics for a year or so, but then they only get on to nagging and whining. Is that why women have to be kept under, because otherwise they wouldn't let you breed the things at all?'), and although the whole performance is notably high-spirited, this matter of plural worlds and redemptions was a serious one. Empson pondered it often: so, as it happens, did C.S. Lewis around the same time, but the emphasis was different. Perhaps Empson's interest in the theological implications of Bruno's plurality of worlds (which he sees as very complex) really stems from his almost obsessive interest in Donne, whom he regarded as the poet of the New Philosophy as it was circulating around 1600, the year of Bruno's execution, and for a while after that. In fact, I think, the religious issue, and the poetry of Donne, were deeply involved with each other in Empson's head, and the effects of the involvement are odd and important. 'In the Twenties, when my eyes were opening, it was usual for critics to consider that Donne in his earlier poetry held broad and enlightened views on church and state, that he was influenced by the recent great scientific discoveries, and that he used the theme of freedom in love partly as a vehicle for these ideas . . . I was imitating this Donne, the poet as so conceived, in my own verse at the time with love and wonder, and I have never in later years come across any good reason for the universal change of opinion about him at the start of the Thirties.'

The inhabited planet stood for a place where lovers could be free, independent, in a world of their own. Identifying so profoundly with Donne (so that he was sure he knew what had been going on in the young poet's mind), Empson had a deep quarrel with others who could not share this view, a quarrel which developed alongside his quarrel with the supreme torturer who required Satisfaction from his Son in all the worlds that otherwise stood for human and poetic freedom.

Though it may take a bourgeois professor to say so, Empson was wrong about Donne and the New Philosophy. Donne knew about Copernicus and made jokes about Kepler and Tycho Brahe and Galileo, but he habitually thought about the world in pre-Copernican terms, and treated the New Philosophy as further evidence that all human knowledge was extremely fallible, a point sufficiently proved by the failure of the old philosophy and of all human philosophies; only in heaven will you see things 'despoyl'd of fallacies'. But Empson knew a lot about the New Philosophy, so in an odd way he assumed that Donne must regularly have put it into his poetry, or his poetry would not be as like Empson's as the latter thought. Others thought so, too, including Dr Leavis. And yet it is not true. The mere difficulty of following the arguments of Donne's poems (which in any case did not stem from his frequent use of new scientific ideas) has steadily diminished since the Grierson edition of 1912 did so much to purge the text and make the allusions available: but nothing can really make Empson's poems easier because they use metaphor quite differently.

For example: Donne's 'Nocturnal upon St Lucy's Day' is certainly a difficult poem, but if you know, or get up, the elements of alchemy and a bit of quite antique cosmology you can hold on to the argument; that isn't, of course, all you need to do, but it is a prerequisite to the rest. The following lines, which come at the beginning of a poem called 'New World Bistres', seem to me quite different:

> The darkest is near dawn, we are almost butter.
> The churning is fixed now; we have 'gone to sleep'
> In body, and become a living pat;
> It is then that the arm churning it aches most
> And dares least pause against the ceaseless turning.
> I am sure he will soon stumble upon the gift,
> Maypole his membranes, Ciro be his eyes,
> A secret order, assumptive distillation;
> Fitting together it will be won and seem nothing,
> Mild artifact, false pearl, corpse margarine.

Here one can get most of the jokes and allusions, even the general run of the thing: but not, so far as I can see, the unbroken thread of argument. Even the title is baffling, and becomes even more so if you look up 'bistre' in the *OED*, as the poet is likely to have done. To put it coarsely, he was imitating a Donne of his own imagining.

However, he was quite unwilling to budge on such points, and once showed me a copy of the *Kenyon Review* containing the long essay 'Donne the Space Man' with copious annotations and additions strengthening his position, and so striking at those who by doubting it dishonoured Donne. At the time of Donne's quatercentenary in 1972 he and I found ourselves trying to collaborate on a stage piece for the Mermaid Theatre. I can no longer remember how Bernard Miles came up with this very bad idea, or why we both agreed to try it. I had known Empson a bit since his return from China, we had lunch and sometimes met as neighbours in Hampstead, but there was an element of unease in the relationship, which I think he accounted for by including me in a black list of Neo-Christians, a charge difficult to deny, since one's protests could be thought to be evasions or distorted admissions. There was trouble from the start, since Empson wanted it made perfectly clear that in 'The Good Morrow' the man and woman had been making love on the planet Venus, a reading he characterised as belonging to an older and more reliable school of thought about Donne: by wincing away from this view I was meanly trying to make the poet less interesting. We had the devil of a time trying to get something together that would work, and then he had to go to Canada before the show came on, adjuring me not to meddle with his share of the script. Two or three days before the first performance the actor playing Donne –

Alan Dobie – walked off; he had done a lot of work but was perhaps sickened by certain contradictions in the script. The piece was hardly a success, and I am glad to think the Empson scholars are unlikely to trace *that* manuscript. The point is that the preservation of his lifelong view of Donne was really self-preservation; he reacted like a wicked animal if anybody seemed to disparage his scientist-poet.

The measure of this virtuous *méchanceté* can be got from the ferocity with which he attacked Helen Gardner's edition and, almost at the end of his life, John Carey's critical biography. According to his review, Carey's book says 'no one need bother any more about Donne,' and the tone is fiercely contemptuous; the main argument is about the Elegy 'To his Mistress Going to Bed', and especially the line 'Here is no penance, much less innocence,' or 'There is no penance due to innocence.' The second of these is the reading of the first edition, held up on moral grounds till 1669; the former is the reading of some good manuscripts. The choice of reading does make a difference to the sense of the whole poem. Empson is certain that the 'due to' reading is the right one, and he gives reasons for this, though the main reason is that he wants a young poet to be saying, with the utmost cleverness of course, that this sexual encounter is innocent in itself. Carey's version of what was going on in the poem (and many are possible) required him to adopt the other reading, and Empson thought that reading exceedingly base. What is extraordinary is the combative rancour of Empson's comments. Helen Gardner joined in to say, quite reasonably, that the 1669 version means: 'why wear this last white garment? It symbolises penitence or virginity, and neither is appropriate.' Empson's reply is that her reading is textually 'impossible'. When another correspondent points out that in the course of his review he misread some of Carey's commemorative verse, Empson allows that the reading now proposed is right, but that the wrong one was there all the same, and the passage would have been heard 'as an adroit piece of double talk'. This is as defensive as he ever gets. When he castigates Carey's version of the poem as sadistic ('panting, bug-eyed Carey') he uses words like 'malignant' and 'ignorant'; I myself think Carey has got the poem wrong, but his version is no more fanciful than Empson's, in which the girl is an upper-class person who has left her husband drunk at some city banquet and hurried round to the poet's rooms. Claiming to know too much weakens the claim to knowing the important thing.

Empson's quarrel with the God of the Christians is also associated with his views on the young Donne, but got its fullest airing in *Milton's God*. There is, in that remarkable work, an excursus on Pascal which above almost anything else in this writer gives one an impression of the genuine moral power of his criticism. He is assaulting the professors who can't see that Satan, in his initial address to the troops, speaks out of a conviction that his cause is just. He finds their attitude 'confidently low-minded', and it reminds him of Pascal's Wager:

He argued, while more or less inventing the mathematics of Probability, that, since the penalties for disbelief in Christianity are infinitely horrible and enduring, therefore, if there is any probability however tiny (but finite) that the assertions of the religion are true, a reasonable man will endure any degree of pain and shame on earth (since this is known beforehand to be finite) on the mere chance that the assertions are true. The answer is political, not mathematical; this argument makes Pascal the slave of any person, professing any doctrine, who has the impudence to tell him a sufficiently extravagant lie. A man ought therefore to be prepared to reject such a calculation . . .

'If you win, you win everything,' says Pascal; 'if you lose, you lose nothing.' Empson has many more subtle points to make, but it does warm the heart to hear this line of argument dismissed as simply dishonourable. He associates it with that 'unpleasant moral collapse' which he thought had during his own lifetime struck 'our present literary mentors' – neo-Christians with 'no sense either of personal honour or of the public good'.

You can see how a man who was willing to rough up Pascal, not to mention God, as dishonourable and rather low-class would not worry about calling 'our literary mentors' disgusting, malignant, horrible, and so forth. Critics have to prove that they aren't the literary version of Evelyn Waugh's Hooper trespassing on Brideshead. The examination of their credentials came to occupy more of Empson's time than writing about poetry as such, and although the result can be entertaining and even heartwarming there must surely be a sense of loss.

That's why the Shakespeare collection is not likely to be thought one of his major works. His fondness for a good row, and for working out difficult puzzles, give the book much interest, and the whole thing is manifestly a product of his great veneration for Shakespeare, so it is a pity there is so little about the poetry. He had come to think that much criticism was too fancy, took far too little notice of basic story and plot, character, theatrical conditions; he was in reaction against the anti-Bradleyanism of his Cambridge days, the time of L.C. Knights's *How many children had Lady Macbeth?*, as well as against the more high-falutin criticism that poured out in his later years, the product of academic market pressures or perhaps a corrupt neo-Christianity. People had stopped understanding what poets actually do; Empson would dogmatically explain this, dwelling on what seemed to others minor issues like the supposed marriage of Marvell to Mary Palmer or the way some manuscripts were filched.

   The Shakespeare essays, written over 27 years (the latest, a review of Harold Brooks's edition of *A Midsummer Night's Dream*, appeared in this paper in October 1979), share these characteristics. The racy manner almost prevents one questioning the confidence with which we are told Shakespeare or the Archbishop of Canterbury would or must have done this or that; or that in 'The Rape of Lucrece' Shakespeare says nothing about the subsequent fall of the Roman monarchy because, as anybody who knows what it is to live under political censorship would be aware, he couldn't. Here, in the essay on the poems, I thought he was so busy making this sort of point against the Hooper-critics that he failed to register the Troy tapestry episode as a rich bit of double-plotting, finding it hard to excuse except as 'a substitute for dangerous thoughts about royalty'.

   And those 'would's' and 'must's' change easily into 'did's': 'I think that a visitor was left to wait in a room where a cabinet had been left unlocked . . . he saw at once that they would sell . . . Thumbing through the notebook, he . . . ' On 'The Phoenix and the Turtle' he is so involved in the mysterious story of how the compilation in which it figures was got together that he writes, on the poem itself, what must be the weakest of all his criticism. No wonder he wonders how Shakespeare went straight on from this to his great tragic period.

   The fifty-page essay on Falstaff and the seventy-page essay on *Hamlet* are as much as anything a running commentary on John Dover Wilson, who is treated with as much respect as Empson ever offers, but gets a lot of ribbing as well. Their difference concerning Falstaff is, crudely, that Dover Wilson thought he must choose one of the two options that seemed to be on offer, whereas Empson, claiming the support of the first audience, saw that you had to take both: the audience would certainly be all for political order, good kingship and so on, and against Riot, but they would also be for Falstaff – 'the first major joke by the English against their class system; he is a picture of how badly you can behave, and still get away with it, if you are a gentleman.' This seems acceptable, but it is argued at length and in that tone of ferocious facetiousness which can sometimes be tedious. Sometimes he seems to want all the good tunes. First he turns down Dover Wilson's parallel between the deaths of Socrates and Falstaff, saying it could not have been intended; but on second thoughts he takes the parallel into his own argument and credits Wilson with an 'eerie flash of imagination'. However, there is no doubt that anybody who feels like writing about Falstaff should work through this piece.

Of *Hamlet* Empson, who certainly had a smack of Hamlet, rightly remarks that it 'opened a new territory to the human mind'. Again he tries to receive it as the first audience might. Shakespeare was required to rewrite an old play for an audience which remembered it only as a joke, and would now ask questions they hadn't in their simpler days. The solution was to make the question of delay very conspicuous instead of pretending it didn't exist. 'The only way to shut this hole is to make it big. I shall make Hamlet walk up to the audience and tell them, again and again, "I don't know why I'm delaying any more than you do; the motivation of this play is just as blank to me as it is to you; but I can't help it."' This of course helps to explain the new self-conscious theatricality of the play. Empson goes into all the famous problems with great patience and vigour: the sheer length of the piece, the relation between the three texts, *Der Bestrafte Brudermord*, the complicity of the Queen, the odd placing of the soliloquies, especially 'How all occasions' (which he says was only played when an encore seemed called for), and so on – a sort of *What happens in Hamlet* in miniature. Among the good things he says about Hamlet himself is this: 'Hamlet never loses class, however mad. He also keeps a curious appeal for the lower classes in the audience as a satirist on the upper class': perhaps one of the ways in which one can say that he himself has a smack of Hamlet. It also seems characteristic that when he says he thinks the madness in Elizabethan drama, of which there is a lot, probably derives from Hamlet, he apologises for producing irritating guesswork, though this conjecture has a much more solid basis than many that aren't called guesswork at all.

The commentary on Dover Wilson continues in a briefer essay on *Macbeth*, but in a 65-page essay on the Globe he turns his critical gaze on others. He pins his faith on J.C. Adams, whose book on the Globe is over forty years old, though updated in 1961. He wants to amend Adams, and does some close work on theatrical structures, scorning much scholarship that came later and running a special campaign against Glynne Wickham. There is some rousing stuff about the staging of the opening battle in *Coriolanus*, but to say anything very useful about this essay you would have to be more up to date about the whole big controversy than I am. The essay on *The Dream*, and another on the last plays, are more eccentric than interesting. The last has a go at Derek Traversi and a milder one at me: I mention this in case some keen reader accuses me of wincing away from the charge of being at least Christian and possibly even an advocate of slavery.

The Shakespeare book is likely to be thought of as second-rate Empson and read more for its manners – the bulldog-like hanging on, the Hamlet-like flyting – than for its content. He was a great deal more than a tough controversialist, but he was certainly that, and he always found it hard to change his mind. In *Seven Types* he remarked that it was only in *Don Juan* that Byron escaped from his infantile incest-fixation on his half-sister, 'which was till then all he had got to say'. Later he added a note to say he now understood that Byron did not meet Augusta till he was grown up (till he was 24, in fact). It seems very like him to have owned up but not to have altered the text. It is very much the attitude he would take toward God. He never loses class. And take him for all in all, we shall not look upon his like again.

20 November 1986

HOW DO YOU SPELL SHAKESPEARE?

....

William Shakespeare. The Complete Works: Original-Spelling Edition
edited by Stanley Wells and Gary Taylor
William Shakespeare: The Complete Works
edited by Stanley Wells and Gary Taylor

When Oxford decided to do Shakespeare they clearly made up their minds that the scale of the operation must be very grand, and a team of scholars has been working hard for eight years to get it done quickly, done right, and done with the greatest possible display and novelty. One has to admire not only the industry of Professor Wells and his associates, but their flair for publicity, as evidenced by the enormous solemn fuss about the poem 'Shall I die?', now accorded an honoured place in their canon, and also by the proclaimed scope and originality of their enterprise, which, though not essentially different from other such enterprises, is different in many eye-catching ways, and must have set the Press some unique problems.

The work is not yet fully finished. What we have at present is two vast volumes, the Complete Works in modernised and again in original spelling, and a fair number of the single-play volumes edited by a lot of able people who are presumably in agreement about the general editorial line and who can provide the detailed introductions and notes missing from the big collections. Of these more portable and more useful books I can't say much; they will be judged by comparison with the New Arden editions, some of which are now showing signs of age (some of them always did), and possibly with the New Penguin. There is a Cambridge set now well under way; the Oxford *Hamlet* is the third considerable edition of that play in five years, following hard upon Harold Jenkins's magisterial Arden and Philip Edwards's serious Cambridge version.[1]

It may well be asked by non-Shakespearians and non-publishers whether all this editorial activity is needed, and by whom, and the Oxford team anticipates the question by asserting the boldness as well as the unparalleled scope of its enterprise. It is worth asking how much there is in this claim.

The Original-Spelling volume greatly increases the size of the undertaking and is probably the greatest novelty. In some respects it is a very odd compilation. Back in 1960 John Russell Brown wrote an article, celebrated in the trade, in which he argued against the value of old-spelling Shakespeare, saying among other things that the amount of 'silent alteration' an editor would have to introduce would make such a text almost useless for close study; that it would be naive to suppose the spelling reproduced was that of the author; and that to believe the old spelling imparted 'an Elizabethan flavour' to the words was a pseudo-historical nonsense, for the strangeness of the spelling isn't something the Elizabethan reader could have been expected to notice. Brown's article caused a stir because, as he remarked, it ran counter to assumptions rarely questioned. W.W. Greg had been firm about it in the Prolegomena to his authoritative book, *The Editorial Problem in Shakespeare* (2nd ed., 1951), where he argued that modernisation seriously misrepresents Elizabethan English when it changes 'murther' to 'murder', 'mushrump' to 'mushroom', 'vild' to 'vile', 'wrack' to 'wreck', and so forth. Less controversially, he indicated that modernisation can in some cases destroy rhymes, and hinder the business of emendation (but surely nobody would be ass enough to try that without recourse to the original). Greg's case really depends upon a conviction that the needs of critics and of ordinary readers are different, which is true, and another conviction, that there is always a chance that the original

¹ Edwards's *Shakespeare: A Writer's Progress* is far from being the usual routine survey, for Edwards is a distinguished veteran Shakespearian, who for many years has displayed much critical independence: his book is brief but useful. Another introductory volume is *The Cambridge Companion to Shakespeare Studies*, edited by Stanley Wells. This is Mark 3 of the Cambridge *Companions*, and contains chapters by well-known hands on the Life, the Thought of the Age, the Language, the Playhouse, comedy, tragedy, history, text, stage history, and history of criticism. A distinct improvement on Mark 2. Meanwhile studies of Shakespeare's *nachleben*, like all other Shakespeare studies, continue without remission. Notable is Jonathan Bate's *Shakespeare and the English Romantic Imagination*, a study of something we thought we knew about but largely didn't. Richard Foulkes's *Shakespeare and the Victorian Stage* is a lively and sometimes surprising collection of essays about stage design, historical verisimilitude, Irving, Victorian interpretation, German and Italian Shakespeare, and the productions of provincial companies more impressive and influential than we might nowadays expect.

spelling has some trace of the author's hand and should therefore be preserved. Of course he knew better than anybody how slim this chance was.

Brown saw that Greg's general case, though somewhat dogmatically stated, was less strong than it appeared. Why not work from photographs instead of type facsimiles or old-spelling editions? His opponents minimised the treachery of type facsimiles and stressed the fallibility of photographs: but that was before Hinman's Norton Facsimile of the First Folio (1968) – a remarkable achievement. By using only the best leaves of a great many copies of the Folio, Hinman produced photographs of an 'ideal' version, so that his facsimile is in practice a better copy than any genuine exemplar, and anybody who wants to see what Jaggard's compositors actually printed, without modern editorial interferences except for line numbers, should look there.

In 1965 Fredson Bowers, who more or less inherited Greg's authority, took a look at the problem in the light of the enormous recent expansion of bibliographical techniques, in part at least brought on by himself. Though he did not deny that an original-spelling text was desirable, he maintained sadly but strongly that it couldn't yet be achieved: there was still so much to be done in the way of studying printing-house practices, compositors' vagaries and so forth, along the lines of Hinman's extraordinary investigation of the printing of the First Folio, published in 1963. A great deal of recondite research has gone on since then, but work of this kind, as the present Oxford editors admit, usually opens up rather than closes the prospect of more work, and one would have expected Bowers's prediction, that an old-spelling edition of Shakespeare was a matter for the 21st century, to have held at least into the Eighties.

It is also a reasonable inference that such an edition would take a lot of people a long time: yet this has apparently not proved to be the case. An old-spelling Oxford edition was mooted long ago by R.B. McKerrow, but he produced only the *Prolegomena* (1939) before he died, and Alice Walker, who took over the project, did not issue a single play. With this discouraging history behind him, Professor Wells seems not to have been thinking of old spelling when he mounted the present assault on the Shakespearian summit. 'The newly proposed Oxford editions,' he wrote in 1979, will be in modern spelling. This procedure, traditional in editions of Shakespeare, removes unnecessary barriers to understanding, making it possible for the reader to concentrate on the text itself, undistracted by obsolete and archaic accidentals of presentation. Thus, his reading experience is closer to that of Shakespeare's contemporaries, who also read the plays in what was, for them, a modern form. We plan both a new single-volume edition of Shakespeare's works for the Oxford Standard Authors (OSA) series, and a detailed scholarly edition, devoting a volume to each play, for the Oxford English Texts (OET).

Wells went on to give by far the best account of the problems of modernising (*Modernising Shakespeare's Spelling*, 1979), but said nothing whatever about an old-spelling edition, and it is reasonable to infer that eight years ago the very idea of one must have seemed terrifying to the Press if not to the general editor, who was in any case ready with all manner of good reasons for doing without such a thing. So it is at least a little surprising that the decision was reversed, and that the work, once undertaken, occupied not the decades of editorial drudgery envisaged by McKerrow and Bowers, but five or six years at most of doubtless frenzied activity, years during which work continued on the modernised version, on the single-play volumes, and on the *Textual Companion*, still missing but promised for later this year.

Apparently the editors decided that the objections to old spelling were less cogent than they had thought. Does the present volume show their second thoughts to have been right? To answer with confidence one would need to have worked with the edition for a long time, and I have only sampled it. The most obvious difficulty is 'silent alteration', and so I thought I might look at a few passages celebrated for their difficulty, and see how the 'original spelling' of this Oxford edition compared with the original spelling.

1. There is a well-known crux in *Antony and Cleopatra*, I. iv. 47, where the original (Folio) text speaks of an 'Arme-gaunt Steede'. In Oxford OS we read 'Arme-iaunct'. The modernised text has 'arm-jaunced'. Presumably these readings will be defended and explained in the volume we have not yet got, but the point is clear: an emendation of 'Arme-gaunt' has been read back into Elizabethan spelling, and the word 'Arme-iaunct' is a pretty modern guess at what the author, or a compositor, or a proof-reader, wrote or rewrote. It is, in fact, a fake antique.

2. There is another crux in the same play, solved by the despised 18th-century editor Warburton in one of the most brilliant and certain of all Shakespearian emendations. Antony is complaining that all is lost by Cleopatra's treachery. His followers have deserted him:

> All come to this? The hearts
> That pannelled me at heeles, to whom I gaue
> Their wishes, do dis-Candie, melt their sweets
> On blossoming *Caesar*: And this Pine is barkt,
> That ouer-top'd them all.

Warburton read 'spanieled' in the second line. Antony has picked up the idea of 'discandying' (melting) from Cleopatra a little earlier.

> Ah (Deere) if I be so,
> From my cold heart let Heaven engender haile,
> And poyson it in the sourse, and the first stone
> Drop in my necke: as it determines so
> Dissolue my life, the next Caesarian smile [smite]
> Till by degrees the memory of my wombe,
> Together with my brave Egyptians all,
> By the discandering of this pelleted storme,
> Lye grauelesse . . .

The idea is of the hailstones melting ('discandering' = 'discandying') and so killing her, her son and her other children, and then all the Egyptians. But the word for melting stays with Antony and he remembers its other association with candy, a sweet resembling ice: so he launches into a strange conceit, supposing the 'hearts' of those who followed him, dog-like, to have let his gifts (their 'wishes') melt in their mouths (the candy discandies), and then go and drop the sticky remnant fawningly before Caesar, represented as a tree in blossom, while Antony is a tall barked pine. In this extraordinary sequence the verb 'pannelled' must refer to the fawning action of a dog, which is why Warburton, conscious no doubt that Shakespeare had elsewhere linked fawning and slavering dogs with candy, emended to 'spanieled'. In the Oxford modern-spelling edition this emendation is accepted. In the original-spelling version we get 'spannell'd', 'spanel' or 'spanner' being an old form of 'spaniel' presumed, no doubt, to have been familiar to the compositor, though not current in Shakespeare's time so far as the *OED* is aware.

The point is that the Oxford editors, having accepted the emendation and printed 'spaniel'd' in the modern version, have to invent a likely-looking older form as what the compositor misread as 'pannelled'. This is a guess, and a 'silent alteration' – and it is not easy to see that a modern reader is better off with it than he would be with Hinman's photographs and a modern edition to tell him or her how the original 'pannelled' has been altered to 'spaniel'd'.

3. The most famous crux of all is in *Henry V*, when it is said of the dying Falstaff that 'his Nose was as sharpe as a Pen, and a Table of greene fields'. Theobald's emendation is widely though by no means universally accepted, and occurs in the Oxford modern version as 'a babbled', in the 'original' as 'a babeld' – again an attempt to reproduce the manuscript reading a compositor might have misread as 'a Table'. I don't know that every expert would think this a probable misreading, but it is in any case pure conjecture, and argues back from Theobald's bright guess – which took little account of the peculiarities of secretary hand – to a version which looks more plausible and scientific. No doubt the whole matter will be argued out in the missing *Textual Companion*, which, as we see from the bits and pieces of it sent out in advance, devotes so much grave argument to the text of 'Shall I die?' that it is sure to be very expansive on rather larger issues.

4. At the beginning of the third act of *The Tempest* Ferdinand remarks that 'these sweet thoughts, doe euen refresh my labours,/Most busie lest, when I doe it.' Much ink has been expended on this difficulty, which Oxford-modern resolves by printing 'busil'est' – an emendation duly defended in Stephen Orgel's excellent single-play Oxford version ('my thoughts of Miranda are most active when I am busiest at my work'). The Oxford-original gives 'busielest' as what the compositor or possibly the scribe misread or wrongly divided in an attempt to make sense where there seemed to be none. There is of course no guarantee, and some would say 'lest' means 'least', while others might give up and say there is here, as elsewhere, an indeterminable corruption: that, as anybody who has ever read proof knows perfectly well, minds wander, and it is sometimes impossible to explain how things came to be as they are. But the original-spelling editor is obliged to produce a rational fake.

5. The Oxford editors have decided that the differences between the Quarto and Folio versions of *King Lear* are so considerable that they must treat them as two separate plays: they therefore print them as two separate versions, *The History of King Lear* (Quarto) and *The Tragedy of King Lear* (Folio). This is one of their bolder innovations, but at present I am interested in what happens when the two versions differ only slightly and not, on the face of it, as the result of revision. Here is what Kent says about Oswald in the Quarto:

> . . . such smiling roges
> As these, like Rats oft bite those cords in twaine,
> Which are to intrencht, to vnloose . . .

In the Folio this is:

> such smiling rogues as these,
> Like Rats oft bite the holly cords a twaine,
> Which are to intrince, t'vnloose . . .

Since they give both versions, the editors naturally have both 'intrencht' and 'intrince' in the original-spelling text; in the modernised version they have 'entrenched' (Quarto) and 'intrinse' (Folio). But it is quite difficult to believe that these are independent versions, or that one is an improvement made in revision. The holy cords must always have been 'too intrinse' and never 'too entrenched', since the rats are biting at knots that cannot be untied, not at knots that have dug themselves into something. The Quarto must be wrong, perhaps because the compositor or proofreader changed an unfamiliar to a familiar word; and the editors, pursuing their idea of two independent texts, have given canonical status to a sophistication. 'Silent alteration' would here have made a small point against the independence theory, or at any rate complicated it. Once again we shall have to see how the *Textual Companion* argues the matter, or consult the single-volume edition, not yet published. It will also, no doubt, offer explanations for pastiche stage directions. It certainly shouldn't be supposed that this old-spelling edition remains very close to the original, and in the absence of annotation in the volume itself the reader who hasn't got the *Companion* will always be uncertain, even when the spelling of everything looks reassuringly Elizabethan, as to what is editorial and what is not.

These complete editions are alike in their sparing provision of ancillary material, and the passages I've been discussing are of course random samples, for hundreds of such cases exist. The modern-spelling
version, like many of its rivals in the market, is content to provide bare
texts, rather handsomely printed though in double columns, plus a
general introduction, a list of contemporary allusions to Shakespeare,
and 17 illustrations, many though not all of them perfectly familiar.
The general introduction includes a short Life of Shakespeare, a section on the drama and theatre of his time, a brief survey of the early
printing of the plays, and a final section called 'The Modern Editor's
Task', which usefully indicates the remarkable variety of problems set
by the different sorts of copy used when the plays were printed, but
also raises the question as to when variation between two Jacobean
versions becomes so great that it is best to think of them as distinct and
independent.

This is the point at which the Oxford editors have been boldest.
In *Hamlet* there is a Quarto of authority, probably set for the most part
from Shakespeare's own papers, which contains 230 lines not in the
Folio version of 1623, and does not contain 80 more that are in the
Folio. Since the latter was set mostly from a theatrical manuscript, the
editors regard it as a revision of the Quarto which Shakespeare presumably authorised. Not feeling that they could print the longer early
version as well as the slightly abbreviated Folio one, they have used
the latter. Formerly editors following F have included the Q parts, but
here they are printed as an appendix to the play, on the ground that if
you put them in you have a composite that was never performed. The
editors seem proud of this decision, though it means that their text no
longer includes some famous verse from the opening scene and the
Closet scene, a lot of Osric, and the whole of the final soliloquy, 'How
all occasions do inform against me . . . '

We may well applaud this move as brave and logical, and it is true
that modern editors tend to err on the side of timidity: yet there is
something to be said against it. The habit of editors is understandably
to climb back as far as possible towards the version they think had
the final approval of the poet; they know very well that the best they
can hope for is a rough approximation, but, given a choice between an
early version and a version used in Shakespeare's lifetime and possibly

under his direction, they will, if forced to choose, choose the latter, even if the reason for the cuts is uncertain (since the Folio version is extremely long without additions from Q, the reason is unlikely to have been simply performance time; a net cut of 150 lines would save only ten or twelve minutes, and by the same arithmetic the remaining 3900 lines would occupy around four and a half hours; to get it done on a winter afternoon at the Globe you would need to cut another two hours of it, roughly half the play).

However, the real objection to leaving out the bits of the first scene and the Fortinbras soliloquy is simply that they belong to *our Hamlet*. The problem is one that comes up in Biblical studies: it is recognised for instance that two independent and mutually contradictory versions have been combined in the opening passages of Genesis, but the canonical Genesis is the one we have, not the disentangled fragments. They are, we may say, too intrinse to unloose; they are entrenched in tradition and have for millennia been one book and not more. The Oxford editors profess amazement at the timidity of their predecessors, all save one, who was brave enough to put the intrusive Q material into square brackets. G. R. Hibbard, editor of the Oxford single-volume *Hamlet*, argues strongly that the Folio was printed from a fair copy made by the author himself; naturally he would make changes, some slight, as he worked his way through, and 'the cuts and the additions seem to be parts of a definite policy designed to make the play more accessible to theatregoers in general by giving it a more direct and unimpeded action, pruning away some of its verbal elaborations, and smoothing out its more abrupt transitions.' But he admits that many of the changes seem not to further this cause, and it is obvious that the most striking of F's additions, the comments about the boy actors, didn't exactly promote direct and unimpeded action. Hibbard also relegates the Q parts of the opening scene, and the great soliloquy, to an appendix. We are being told to get used to a new *Hamlet*.

The whole question of the text of *Hamlet* is horribly complex, and the editors must have been tempted to print Q as well as F, but they decided that it would be 'extravagant' to do so, and, forced to choose, chose the more 'theatrical' version. However, they made an exception for *King Lear*, because in that case the differences between the two versions affect the story-line, especially in the last two acts. A tendency to think of this play as extant in two versions has been growing of late. The arguments are extremely technical, as several books have recently shown, but the immediate question is whether readers of such plain texts as these will benefit much from the editors' decision. They may not be very interested in the conduct of the military operations which lead up to the deaths of Cordelia and the King – as Albany says of the death of Edmund, 'That's but a trifle here' (both texts). It is a perpetual irritation to scholars that so many people still think of these plays as they first came on them in such editions as the old Globe, and it is their pardonable professional deformity to exaggerate the differences superior information can impose. This doesn't mean that editors should simply mark up the texts of other editors, only that the scope for sensible change is less than it pleases them to believe. Bowers was right to warn his colleagues that the incredible refinement of bibliographical technique in our time might not succeed in making many substantial emendations to Shakespeare's text, and it is worth remembering that Hinman's work on the printing of the Folio, which made available vast quantities of new information about the way it was put together, the habits of various compositors, etc, didn't, so far as I know, establish or make certain a single new reading.

The principal effort of the main Oxford editors has gone into the text. Each play, in both original and modern spelling, is given a page of bland appreciative comment ('In *Titus Andronicus*, as in his early history plays, Shakespeare is at his most successful in the expression of grief and the portrayal of vigorously energetic evil'; in *Romeo and Juliet* 'Shakespeare's mastery over a wide range of verbal styles combines with his psychological perceptiveness to create a richer gallery of memorable characters than in any of his earlier plays,' etc). It is claimed that the chronological order of composition has been freshly established, but the evidence isn't available here, and will, when it appears, chiefly concern the order of the earlier plays. Some may think it a nuisance to have the second and third parts of *Henry VI* before the first part, with *Titus* in between: it was sensible of Heminge and Condell to give them in the usual order. *Pericles*, a special case because it survives only in a quarto which is dependent on memorial reconstruction, and does not appear in the First Folio, is the kind of challenge the editors most enjoy. They offer a 'reconstructed' text in the modern-spelling volume and a diplomatic reprint in the original-spelling, which excuses them from the job of inventing Elizabethan-compositor's spellings.

The ancillary material in the original-spelling version is identical with that in the modern version, except for an impressive essay on 'The Spelling and Punctuation of Shakespeare's Time' by Vivian Salmon. It is mostly what it says it is, but it is also a defence of the original-spelling version, suggesting that the funny appearance of the old spelling is less offputting than Professor Wells supposed in 1979. As far as can be told, Shakespeare was himself a fanciful speller ('scilens' for 'silence') and despite some efforts to control them the compositors made almost as free; certainly they added letters to fill lines, substituted letters they had for letters they had temporarily run out of, and so on. Sometimes they can be identified by their orthographical habits. Nor were they the only re-spellers; occasionally they worked from copy prepared by a scribe, notably the well-known Ralph Crane, who also had his own way with a text; and there were proof correctors, who perhaps added their penny-worth. But Ms Salmon is still alert to the evidence for genuine Shake-spearian spellings, and hopes that when fully armed with the *Textual Companion* as well as 'a critical old-spelling edition' we shall join in the game of identifying 'patterns of Shakespearian orthography'. Well, perhaps. At least if we make ourselves aware of spelling conventions we can judge for ourselves 'the meanings and the forms which Shake-speare and his fellow actors found appropriate to a printed text, un-affected by the cumulative modernisations of generations of editors'. 'The general reader' is included in this invitation, though it is not ex-plained why he would be worse-off with Hinman's photographs.

My overall impression is that despite the undoubted learning and skill of the editors the edition suffers in two main ways. First, it is al-together too anxious to surprise us. There may be an argument for calling Falstaff 'Oldcastle' in *1 Henry IV*, and there is certainly an argu-ment against doing so, but it is characteristic of this edition that the former argument prevails.[2] There is a case for calling 2 and 3 *Henry VI The First Part of the Contention* and *Richard Duke of York*: it isn't a very good case, since by the time *1 Henry VI* was written and so entitled it

[2] David Bevington, the editor of the single-volume *I Henry IV* (Oxford, 324 pp., £19.50 and £3.95, 19 March, 0 19 812915 7), stubbornly calls the character 'Falstaff'.

is evident that the second and third parts had acquired the titles by which they have been known ever since, but these editors have committed themselves to the odder choice of title and of order.

There will doubtless be a vast amount of detailed comment and criticism when the whole operation is completed. At the moment it seems that the single-play volumes and the modern-spelling collection, despite the absence of apparatus and the continual self-advertisement, can hold their own against most opposition. The *raison d être* of the old-spelling collection is doubtful: for defences of its silent alterations and for readings at present lacking any explanatory support we shall have to wait for the *Textual Companion*. At £50 it is going to be an expensive supplement, but if you want to know exactly what is going on in the Collected Editions you will have to have it. One can't help thinking there were some flaws in the strategic thinking of those who planned this large publishing enterprise.

21 May 1987

A LITTLE OF THIS HONEY

....

Oscar Wilde by Richard Ellmann

Richard Ellmann's Life of Joyce, generally regarded as the best literary biography of our time, was the work of his middle years. The last third of his own life was largely given to this biography of Wilde, which was in some ways a very different sort of undertaking. There were surviving acquaintances of Joyce, but nobody who knew Wilde is available for questioning; the material, though copious, must be sought in libraries. But Ellmann was an exceptionally gifted researcher, never bragging about his finds, just folding them quietly into his narrative, as he does in this book.

For such a labour one would need not merely an admiration for the subject but a temperamental affinity, such as Ellmann obviously had with Joyce. He loved the clutter of Joyce's mind – that 'mind of a grocer's assistant' – and he also knew how to value the passion for occult patterns underlying the mess. In Wilde he chose another Irish subject: but the fantasy is different, the blarney more scented, and the achievement, in the opinion of many, of a less incontestably high order. Wilde's life, spent in a more or less continuous blaze of publicity, was far more absurd, far more spectacular, and finally far more luridly tragic, than Joyce's. His perfect biographer might be rendered incapable of writing the book by the very qualities that made him a suitable choice.

Hesketh Pearson, who wrote the best biography before this one, was advised by Shaw not to attempt it. For, as he saw it, everything that could be said had already been said – by Frank Harris and others, including Shaw himself; and although Wilde was 'incomparably great as a raconteur . . . and a personality . . . those points cannot be reproduced.' There is obviously some truth in this; we can hardly imagine what it must have been like to know Wilde and to hear him talk, for all the evidence suggests that there has never been anybody like him. There is nothing Ellmann or anybody else can do except report such talk as has survived – mostly epigrams and paradoxes, now for the most part too well known, too machine-made, and too often imitated, to induce hysteria. How, then, can a biographer justify going ahead? Ellmann's solution, broadly speaking, is twofold: to add to the stock of information about Wilde, and to treat him as both a great writer and a misunderstood moral genius.

The second of these is the more controversial project. This biography is at its magnificent best in its last third, for Wilde wrote very little after his disgrace, and could only with difficulty be proposed as at that stage a model of conduct, so the literary and ethical issues aren't so controversial. The section Ellmann entitles 'Disgrace' covers only the last six of Wilde's 46 years, but it occupies a quarter of the book. It could scarcely have been better done. The narrative is familiar in outline, but here the detail is everything. Even in our time, inundated as we are with accounts of even worse suffering and even worse desolation in even worse prisons, this account of Wilde at hard labour, sick, starving, cold and solitary, fills one with pity and disgust. The governor of one of his gaols is reported as saying that no middle-class person of sedentary habit (and middle age) could expect to live more than another two years after serving a sentence of two years at hard labour, and after reading this book one can believe it. Wilde, though fat, was tall and strong, and he lived on for four years: but in some respects it was only half-life.

In describing that famous fall – the three trials and their sequel – Ellmann has more to add than his own reflections. For example, it was known that the Marquess of Queensberry, the 'infamous brute' whom it was Wilde's worst bit of luck to cross, also had it in for Lord Rosebery, who at the time of the Wilde libel action was Prime Minister. Queensberry had followed Rosebery to Homburg, stalking him with a dogwhip (presumably, says Pearson, because he didn't happen to have a horse with him), and grievous bodily harm was prevented only by the personal intervention of the Prince of Wales. Queensberry's resentment was reasonably supposed to have arisen from the suicide of his son Lord Drumlanrig, private secretary to Rosebery, but its precise cause was the Marquess's suspicion that his son had been Rosebery's lover. The suicide may have been occasioned by fear of blackmail, or possibly by a desire to save Rosebery from a politically ruinous scandal. His tenure as prime minister was brief and insecure, and though it did occur to him to come to Wilde's assistance at the time of the libel action, he refrained for fear of losing the imminent general election. Later, when the jury disagreed at Wilde's first trial, there was a chance that the matter might end there, but 'the abominable rumours against Rosebery' were held to necessitate a second trial. Ellmann typically puts this little horror – or bad-luck story – together from a contemporary item in the *New York Times*, a manuscript journal in the library of the University of Texas, and a published letter of T.M. Healey's.

Among other things, it shows that Wilde was not as fortunate as he may have imagined to have very grand acquaintances, the first claim on whose attention is likely to be the need to look after themselves, and the second to look after their own very grand acquaintances.

He had also to learn some hard lessons about his less noble friends. Always ready to cast himself in some mythological role, he had in his time been Narcissus, St Sebastian, Marsyas (the musician who was flayed alive for challenging Apollo); he was in the end to see himself as Timon. He fits the part pretty well. Having in happier times been prodigally generous, he was reduced in his last years to begging. When he stopped Nellie Melba in a Paris street and asked her for money, she gave him what she had in her purse. But Henry James's friend Morton Fullerton made a more typical response – he must have written this letter with Shakespeare's play open on his desk:

I am distressed to have left your touching appeal unanswered for so long. But I have been on congé in the *patrie* of Stendhal, and had cognisance of your *gène* only yesterday. You do me too much honour in asking me to come to the rescue of an artist such as you. And if I could have known of the situation 3 weeks ago when I had money in my pocket I should not have hesitated for a moment, especially as I had just received your play [*Earnest*] and was in the state of mind of one who says of a thing without thinking: 'it is worth its weight in gold.' But at present, after an expensive journey, I am unable, with the best goodwill in the world, to seize the event and to accept the *rôle* in this particular comedy – I use the word in its Hellenic and Gallic sense, *bien entendu*, in the sole sense in which it exists for the admirers of *Lady Windermere's Fan* and of *The Importance of Being Earnest* . . .

Presumably there was no point in appealing to James himself, since he called Wilde an 'unclean beast' and refused to sign a clemency petition. There were closer friends who shunned him: Beardsley, for instance, who owed him so much; John Gray, an early lover, for whose *Silverpoints*, prettiest of Nineties poetry-books, Wilde had paid;

Lilly Langtry, to whom he had, at one time, brought a daily lily, and who claimed to have sent him money without having actually done so. Beerbohm did not spurn him but kept his distance. Of his old friends Robbie Ross, who had introduced Wilde to homosexuality at the age of 32, stood by him to the end, and he was supported by Reginald Turner and Frank Harris. They were joined by Jean Dupoirier, proprietor of the Paris hotel in which Wilde died, and perhaps of all his friends the most disinterested and serviceable.

It is easy to say that Wilde brought his distress on himself. The penury of his last years was in part due to his inability to live other than extravagantly, and in even greater part to his resuming relations with Lord Alfred Douglas – not only because the allowance from his wife was expressly conditional on his not doing so, but because, as he knew very well, Douglas was sure to bring him further disasters. It was the clearest possible proof of Wilde's self-destructiveness that knowing all he did about the treachery of this lover he should again put himself in his hands.

If one emotion prevails over all others in Ellmann's book it is loathing and contempt for Bosie, Wilde's great love and worst enemy – a callous bully, cruel in his rages and coldly exploitative, pretty and vain, autocratic and whining, jealous and promiscuous. Ellmann has no difficulty in bringing out the young man's close resemblance to the father he loathed, and against whom he unscrupulously used Wilde.

Ellmann conceived the whole life as tragedy, finding even in the triumphant part of it many premonitions of disaster. He attaches great importance to the fact that Wilde contracted syphilis while at Oxford, and has no doubt that the disease contributed to his early death: indeed he remarks that this 'conviction is central to my conception of Wilde's character and my interpretation of many things in his later life'. Wilde presumably thought himself cured, but it could no doubt be argued that he still feared the disease, and that the fear affected the writing of *Dorian Gray*, for instance.

Here as elsewhere Ellmann likes to underline the evidence that Wilde had forebodings of some future disaster, which induced him to live fully and dangerously in the present. And he certainly did take risks even before he became a practising homosexual. In an Oxford where you could be charged with the offence of 'keeping and reciting immoral poetry' it was risky to make a cult of St Sebastian, and Matthew Arnold's university was hardly the place to announce that the right way to live was to do as you like, and get what you want. Even in the larger world of London there were limits, and he achieved celebrity by continually flirting with them. When, in 1881, Gilbert satirised him in *Patience*, he was still only 26, and had published little except his first book of poems. He owed his fame to his daring in dress, talk and conduct. Such fame is inseparable from envy, and the friends made in the course of such a life could easily turn into bitter enemies, as Whistler did. No wonder Wilde had forebodings, especially when he became more or less openly and indiscreetly homosexual.

There is a sonnet in which Wilde quotes the plea of Jonathan: 'I did but taste a little honey with the end of the rod that was in mine hand, and lo! I must die.' In the Bible story Jonathan has broken Saul's prohibition against eating, the announcement of which he'd missed. He doesn't die, because the people rally and save him. Wilde's poem is ostensibly about spoiling one's life by preferring pleasure to arduous study, but Ellmann thinks he is surreptitiously hoping that like Jonathan he can have his taste of honey and still be saved. It seems more likely that the poet was remembering Jonathan's earlier remark: 'how my eyes have been enlightened because I tasted a little of this honey.'

Taken together, the texts fit nicely the image of the *poète maudit*, death being the price of his gift, and sex the agent of death. This is how Wilde might wish to see himself; he can hardly, even in his most extravagant daydream, have expected to be saved by the people. The point is that he was in this instance matching himself with a fashionable stereotype rather than anticipating doom and possible redemption.

Even if Wilde himself hadn't had premonitions, there would still have been, in the ordinary way of things, events in his life to which a biographer can give the quality of tragic portents. Ellmann describes Wilde's visit to a prison in Nebraska, his consultation with a palmist called Cheiros, and several other incidents, in those terms. Once he found on a tomb the epitaph *une heure viendra qui tout paiera* – incidentally, the words are badly mistranslated in the text.[1] The motto is rather menacing, certainly, but it is, after all, a threat of very general application.

Still, there were doubtless hints and warnings of varying gravity, and it was Wilde's way to carry on being outrageous or funny rather than heed them. Whether this justifies the claim that he was 'conducting, in the most civilised way, an anatomy of his society, and a radical reconsideration of its ethics' does seem a bit doubtful. Ellmann twice brackets Wilde with Blake and Nietzsche; along with them 'he was proposing that good and evil are not what they seem, that moral taboos cannot cope with the complexity of behaviour. His greatness as a writer is partly the result of the enlargement of sympathy which he demanded for society's victims.' It is true that Wilde was at his best a generous and a gentle man: he would take off his coat and give it to a naked beggar, and he was properly appalled by the meanness and cruelty with which society treated the unlucky or the criminal. But he himself would presumably have denied that these or any other virtues had any relevance to art. To call *The Picture of Dorian Gray* a critique of aestheticism that went 'far beyond Whistler and Gautier' is not necessarily false, and it may not even be false to say that 'by cunning and eloquence Wilde restored art to the power that the romantic poets had claimed for it, able once again to legislate for the world': but Wilde might have thought it odd, and so will many of his readers.

The best of Wilde, outside the theatre, is to be found in such essays as 'The Truth of Masks', 'The Critic as Artist' and 'The Decay of Lying', which are not simple in tone, but do seem to place a barrier between art and action, or legislation in any normal sense of the word. I risk the rejoinder that the implied legislative programme was meant to serve the interests not of action but of contemplation, described by Wilde as 'the proper occupation of man'. All the same, the state of the world was manifestly hostile to contemplation, and therefore required action: a requirement on which Wilde reflects at some length in 'The Soul of Man under Socialism'. One way of finding out whether one agrees with Ellmann's estimate of Wilde as an ethical force is to reread this essay,

---

¹ Since the book will obviously be many times reprinted it is worth pointing out such errors. The aesthetician Baumgarten is called 'Baumgartner' in text and index (pp. 31, 85, 596). The daughter of Herodias (Salome or Hérodiade) is called 'Herodias' (p. 320). 'The cultivation of art apart from life is to build a fire that cannot burn' (p. 300) is a sentence gone astray. I have also thought fit to read 'tabus' for 'tabs' in a sentence I proceed to quote, and to emend the punctuation of the last sentence of the book.

the rather camp arguments of which are here rehearsed with what seems like unqualified approval. For Ellmann was determined to prove that Wilde was a sage, a heroic figure, ahead of his time – the portent of a future ethic, as well as the agent of his own destruction.

What we are here told about Wilde's family may help us to form more mundane estimates. His parents were distinguished and some-what bizarre. His father was a famous Dublin doctor, a man of many interests and evident vitality, who fathered three bastards in addition to his legitimate family, and managed to conceal the identity of their mother or mothers from everybody, including even Richard Ellmann. Wilde's mother was a nationalist poet, good-hearted, flamboyant, and with a bravura dottiness that Wilde must have inherited. She called herself 'Speranza', and claimed a previous existence as an eagle, telling the youthful Yeats that she therefore needed to 'live in some high place, Primrose Hill or Highgate'. Her elder son Willie was a witty scamp, fa-mous in the Dublin pubs. Asked what he was working at, he would re-ply: 'At intervals.' Max Beerbohm said he was very like Oscar, with the same 'coy, carnal smile'. He was completely unreliable and irresponsi-ble, but unlike his brother got into scrapes rather than catastrophes.

Oscar lacked Willie's malice, and his underhand ways, and also had more conscience about work. His career at Oxford left him little time for reading, but despite a failure in Divinity and a period of rustication he took a double First in Greats, aided no doubt by his famous skill as a fast reader (it is said that he could read a novel in three minutes). To have done so well at university, in the perfectly ordinary sense of the phrase, gave him much satisfaction, for at this stage, and possibly later as well, he retained some conventional values. However, as Ellmann puts it, he 'created himself at Oxford', and he did it not by writing Greek proses but by fine talk, fine clothes and a risky degree of impu-dence. The strain of prudence was, however, not extinct, and it showed up when he drew back at the last moment from conversion to Rome, fearing he might lose a legacy by going ahead with it. He contented himself instead with membership of a very fancy Masonic lodge.

Ellmann duly documents these and other contests between incli-nation and prudence, in which, as time went by, prudence had fewer and fewer successes. Yielding to Bosie's false persuasions at the time when he could have withdrawn his action against Queensberry was a crucial defeat for prudence; taking Bosie back after prison was another. But even in the days of his triumph – on the American tour, and in the days just before the disaster, when he had two successful plays in the West End – Wilde was always finding or putting himself in positions where such contests were inevitable. Ellmann often, and rightly, reminds us of his virtues – he was only occasionally overbearing or coarse, and he was always generous; delight in his company was universal, and we see its signs wherever the biographer follows him – at his mother's salons, in Whitman's house, at Mallarmé's *mardis*, in cafés with the young Gide and Pierre Louÿs.

His power to inspire affection was extraordinary, and it depended on more than wit and fancy: he made people love him. But he also gave envy some wonderful opportunities, and knew that he was doing so. 'Of course I knew that there would be a catastrophe, either that or something else,' he told Gide after his release from prison. 'To go any further was impossible, and that state of things could not last ... there had to be some end to it.' He may not have expected that his admirers would so firmly disown him, or that the envious could be so malignant. But like his biographer, he came to see that the shape of his life was determined by its end, and was therefore tragic.

Macaulay in a famous passage spoke of the British public savaging Byron in one of its 'periodical fits of morality': 'He was excluded from circles where he had lately been the observed of all observers. All those creeping things that riot in the decay of nobler natures hastened to their repast; and they were right, they did after their kind. It is not every day that the savage envy of aspiring dunces is gratified by the agonies of such a spirit and the degradation of such a name.' Ellmann catches Macaulay's mood, and it becomes our own, as we read the book – indeed it must, in some measure, whenever we think of Wilde. It is the fate of a very few writers to have led lives so remarkable that we think first of their fates and only then of their works. Merely to have written *The Importance of Being Earnest* must constitute a claim to immortality: yet when our thoughts turn to Wilde we are likely first to remember how he was tormented by a crazy nobleman, spat on at Twyford Junction, alienated from his children, and left to die in exile. After that, we may have some thoughts about epigrams, green carnations, lilies and decadence, and only then of the books and plays.

Ellmann has not sought to diminish the pity of it all, but he has tried, sometimes, perhaps, with rather too heavy a hand, to remind us of the writer, and to persuade us that decadence may be the other face of renovation. 'He belongs to our world more than to Victoria's. Now, beyond the reach of scandal, his best writings validated by time, he comes before us still, a towering figure, laughing and weeping, with parables and paradoxes, so generous, so amusing, and so right.' It is deeply satisfying that Dick Ellmann should have ended his work with that generous sentence.

29 October 1987

FEAST OF ST THOMAS

....

Eliot's New Life by Lyndall Gordon
The Letters of T.S. Eliot edited by Valerie Eliot
The Poetics of Impersonality by Maud Ellmann
T.S. Eliot and the Philosophy of Criticism by Richard Shusterman
'The Men of 1914': T.S. Eliot and Early Modernism by Erik Svarny
Eliot, Joyce and Company by Stanley Sultan
The Savage and the City in the Work of T.S. Eliot by Robert Crawford
T.S. Eliot: The Poems by Martin Scofield

'The idea that Eliot's poetry was rooted in private aspects of his life has now been accepted,' says Lyndall Gordon in the Foreword to her second volume of biographical rooting among these aspects. This acceptance, which she evidently approves, has undoubtedly occurred, as a root through the enormous heap of books about the poet, now augmented by the centenary of his birth, will quickly demonstrate.

By the time of his death in 1965 people had long been curious about this very famous man. Collections such as the one made by Richard Marsh and Tambimuttu for his 60th birthday in 1948 contained much pleasant anecdote, and there were respectful reminiscences in Allen Tate's memorial volume of 1966. Meanwhile, off the page, there was some gossip about such matters as a putatively vast pornographic poem, and about Eliot's first marriage. I once heard J.B. Priestley explaining that the Eumenides in *The Family Reunion* were a direct representation of Vivien(ne), which I couldn't understand since in the play only Harry sees them ('*You* don't see them, but I see them,' he claims), whereas Priestley's point was that Vivien would storm unexpectedly and embarrassingly into parties where everybody could see her. As for the poem, it seems to have been a fitful series of mildly obscene verses included in letters to such friends as Conrad Aiken. Gossips are not on oath.

While these oral versions of biography paid tribute to the celebrity of the poet, the poetry was usually treated as quite impersonal. It had come, in the post-war years, under heavy academic protection: this was a time when potent professors wanted to exclude biography from the institutional study of literature. Eliot's own doctrine of poetic impersonality had contributed to the formation of this austere doctrine, and though quite often subjected to more severe scrutiny than literary journalism normally attracts, the early essay 'Tradition and the Individual Talent' remained influential, and suited the New Criticism well.

As Gordon suggests, we have moved on from there, not just because we like gossip better than professorial personality purges, but because many people have come to think that the impersonality business was nonsense anyway. This is roughly the position of Maud Ellmann's brisk first book. Eliot called Pound's *Cantos* 'a reticent biography', and she thinks we should apply the same description to Eliot's work. According to her, early Modernism, despite the contrary pretence, was always individualistic, and steeped in Bergson. Now Eliot certainly went to Bergson's lectures, and was for a time much affected by his very fashionable philosophy: but he soon changed his mind, as is clear from the satirical assault on Middleton Murry, a Bergsonian surrogate, in 'The Function of Criticism' (1923). And of course he was well aware that impersonal poetry was produced by persons: but this doesn't make the impersonality argument bogus, as Ellmann supposes, or entitle us to think that it has sinister ideological implications – that Eliot 'inveighs against personality for much the same reasons that he ostracises the Jews from his Anglo-Catholic utopia'.

Eliot notoriously remarked that 'only those who have personality and emotions know what it means to want to escape from these things,' which implies a claim to poetic or spiritual election, and this is no doubt what gives rise to the notion that poetic impersonality has, in the long run, some nasty political implications. But one ought to reflect that among the poet's preferred models are Aristotle and Dante, Pascal and Baudelaire; impersonality and intelligence, as he understood them, are the achievement of heroic personalities, and it is hard to see that they *necessarily* imply political wickedness. What Eliot himself says about the topic in 'The Perfect Critic' still seems innocuous: 'In an artist . . . suggestions made by a work of art, which are purely personal, become fused with a multitude of other suggestions from multitudinous experience, and result in the production of a new object which is no longer purely personal.' Many artists – Milton and Picasso, to name

two at random – might have subscribed to some form of this statement, without suspecting that to do so might, on such evidence alone,
get them called fascists, or even Anglo-Catholic utopians.

Even in the years when the impersonality approach generally prevailed there were many books about the more polite and discussable aspects of Eliot as a person who had, for example, thought a bit and read
a bit. Some writers tried, as Eliot himself never did, to work his critical
observations up into a coherent theory; others, like Grover Smith, read
what he had read, so far as this could be ascertained, and examined
his sources with what looked like, but cannot quite have been, exhaustive care: for recently there has been a boom in such research. A pro-
cession of students combs the archives in New York, Cambridge and
elsewhere. The poet's early philosophical studies and his work on F.H.
Bradley have been very carefully examined; and those early slogans,
Impersonality, Tradition, Dissociation of Sensibility, Objective Cor-
relative, have been dissected again and again. One might even say that
no other English critic except possibly Coleridge has had his ideas and
his reading more intensely studied. The reason for all this activity isn't
merely that there are so many more aspirants looking for something
interesting to investigate, though that is not wholly irrelevant. It may
be true that too much has been written and published about him, but
it is also true that there is a lot to write about.

At the same time, however, the poet's life, and especially the first
half of it, has been examined with a persistence that is beginning to
seem prurient: it certainly goes well beyond what Eliot, or any other
private and reserved person, would have thought tolerable. The Letters offer several instances of his rage at intrusions into his privacy,
and one remembers him forcing the withdrawal of John Peter's article from *Essays in Criticism* because it suggested a homosexual element
in his relationship with Jean Verdenal. Lyndall Gordon reports a conversation with Mary Trevelyan which makes him seem mildly amused
about this imputation, but his first reaction was quick and indignant.
After his death the sanction of his disapproval no longer worked, and
almost anything goes.[1]

---

[1] Frederick Tomlin, in his memoir of a long, respectful and predominantly
churchy acquaintance with the poet, describes his reaction to Peter (*T.S. Eliot: A
Friendship*, Routledge, 1988).

Now that so much has been said it seems impossible not to say more, and even Valerie Eliot is obliged to take part. The sufferings of both partners in the poet's first marriage have been amply described, sometimes, as by Peter Ackroyd, with reasonable delicacy, but research continues to discover more painful details. What will not be fully uncovered until 2019 (Gordon's date; Mrs Eliot says 2020) are the letters Eliot wrote to Emily Hale. He had known her since 1912, but most of the letters were written between 1927 (Gordon's date; 1932 according to Valerie Eliot) and 1947. We learn from Mrs Eliot that in the Sixties the poet, 'in a private paper' whose privacy has now gone the way of all privacy, said he had discovered, a year after his marriage to Vivien, that he was still in love with Miss Hale, though 'it may have been merely my reaction against my misery with Vivienne' – we are told that he gave her name the two extra letters when exasperated – 'and desire to revert to an earlier situation.' He attributes the muddle to his timidity and immaturity, and to his worries about a choice of profession – for academic philosophy was still a possibility.

When she heard about Eliot's second marriage, Emily Hale presented his letters (numbering about a thousand, says Gordon) to Princeton University Library. He had wanted these letters preserved, but Mrs Eliot says he was irritated by Hale's act, calling it 'the *Aspern Papers* in reverse'; and when the Princeton Librarian informed him that they were to be sealed until fifty years after the death of the survivor he got somebody to burn all Hale's letters to him. There would appear to be an understandable difference in the attitudes of Mrs Eliot and Gordon to the Princeton letters. Gordon is far from wanting to minimise the importance of the triangular relation between the poet, his first wife and Emily Hale: indeed she makes it central to her account of Eliot's life. It was on Vivien's death in 1947 that he broke with Hale. It is true that at various times he abandoned other friends with equal abruptness (as, when he remarried, he dropped Mary Trevelyan, who had twice proposed to him), but it seems clear that Hale was not just another friend, and any doubt on the subject is likely to be dispelled by Gordon's researches. She is able to quote in full a letter of Hale's, written in 1947, which says she had understood that Eliot had intended to marry her if Vivien should die; during one of his visits to the United States, when they had actually discussed the prospect, he had spoken of a *mariage blanc*. And Gordon has seen, in another restricted Princeton archive, a copy of her sad last letter to Eliot, written as late as 1963.

Indefatigable and resourceful, Gordon has interviewed many witnesses, and had the cooperation of Maurice Haigh-Wood, Vivien's brother; she draws on Vivien's diaries in the Bodleian, the copyright of which, as we learn from the *Letters*, belongs to Eliot's widow. And, familiar with virtually all the archives, she has read a great many of the letters. Her acknowledgments make interesting reading. Mrs Eliot, who helped with the earlier book, is absent from the list.

Emily Hale is Gordon's heroine. Her book has the pattern of a morality: Hale was 'the higher dream' and Vivien 'the sense of sin'. Out of the conflict between these forces come 'the great works of Eliot's maturity, as he converts life into meaning'. Vivien, we gather, 'was Eliot's muse only so long as he shared her hell', and Hale as heavenly muse took over the role in *Ash Wednesday*, 'a dream of sexual purity to set against Vivien'. The *vita nuova* referred to in Gordon's title was announced in a vision inspired by Hale, and it involved a vow of celibacy.

It has long been known that it was with Emily Hale that Eliot visited Burnt Norton, probably in 1934. But Gordon adds much detail about their relationship, and about many other aspects of the long years between the poet's marriages. Even if we may doubt that Hale was his Urania or his Beatrice it seems clear that they were rather close. But I'm bound to say that there is something disturbing about Gordon's handling of all this. Her religiose attitude to the facts, a sort of muckraking sublimity, affects her prose as well as her argument, and the whole pseudo-allegorical and hagiographical enterprise is vaguely disgusting, though I ought to add that it might seem just right to readers of different disposition.

Volume One of Mrs Eliot's edition of the letters takes us up to 1922, when the poet was 34 and had suffered seven years of marriage. It is not, on the whole, an enlivening collection. Quite a lot of it is familiar in one form or another from earlier books, and the depressing events, as well as the successes, of Eliot's first London decade are fairly well-known to all who have any interest in the subject, so there is sometimes a sense of *déjà lu*.

Mrs Eliot's brief and slightly odd Introduction, already mentioned in connection with Emily Hale, explains that she had persuaded Eliot to sanction such a publication. In the nature of the case, a lot of correspondence had been destroyed or lost, especially from the poets schooldays; these lacunae are, as it were, filled by the inclusion of letters by other people, including Eliot's mother and Vivien, whose letters are very nervous and lively: she seems to have been a more vigorous and disconcerting correspondent than her husband. There is also a letter from Alain-Fournier, and a number from Jean Verdenal, the dedicatee of *Prufrock and Other Observations*, '*mort aux Dardanelles*'. Their relationship wasn't of the kind improperly suggested, but it was close and involved some elegant youthful posing. *Ce n'est pas facile de se faire comprendre, et puis d'ailleurs ce n'est pas mon métier* is the kind of remark that would appeal to Eliot, who was fond of Byron's lines about not understanding his own meaning when he would be *very* fine: he quotes them in a letter, and again, a decade later, in *The Use of Poetry and the Use of Criticism*. Verdenal also complains about the way small artists form gangs for mutual support and start short-lived movements – a remark that might, at the time, have been less welcome. The mother's letters are eloquently maternal, calm but worried. Some are to schoolmasters; the boy wasn't robust and as the editor reminds us had to wear a truss, which can't have made things easier at school.

Some of the jollier letters are to a Boston cousin, Eleanor Hinkley, through whom he had met Hale. She had an interest in the theatre, and with her Eliot can go in for the sort of joshing he kept up in one way or another throughout his life. More important, though in essence well-known, are the letters to Conrad Aiken, later dismissed by Eliot as stupid, but a principal confidant of the earlier years. The jesting is intermingled with worry about intellectual constipation, 'nervous sexual attacks', and fantasies about Saint Sebastian, including a version of the poem already known from Mrs Eliot's edition of the manuscripts the poet gave to his American patron John Quinn: though rejected, these verses bear his true voiceprint. It was to Aiken that he could speak of fantasies of flagellation and the murder of women. He also speculates, in what at least by hindsight we can call a characteristic manner, on the necessity of pain: 'what is necessary is a *certain kind* (could one but catch it!) of *tranquillity*, and *sometimes* pain does ~~buy~~ bring it.'

Aiken was also the recipient of this meditation: 'The idea of a submarine world of clear green light – one would be attached to a rock and swayed in two directions – would one be happiest or most wretched at the turn of the tide?' This fancy probably owes something to some strenuous lines in *Antony and Cleopatra*:

> This common body,
> Like to a vagabond flag upon the stream,
> Goes to and back, lackeying the varying tide,
> To rot itself with motion.

This is a good illustration of one of that 'multitude of other suggestions' which 'result in the production of a new object' without eliminating the personal: if you had to guess which distinguished poet wrote that little reverie you might well think first of Eliot. He also had a way of assimilating some particular line or passage that has provided him with what he calls 'a bewildering minute'. In *The Revenger's Tragedy* that expression refers with excitement and disgust to the sexual act: its transfer to the impact of poetry is presumably not insignificant. In the same way, the Shakespeare passage is the comment of chilly Octavius on the fickleness of a populace which switches support from him to the burnt-out lecher Antony. Lyndall Gordon rightly remarks on the psychological importance of these letters to Aiken, but they have interest, too, for students of poetry.

Mrs Eliot includes a series of letters from the young man to his Harvard professor J.H. Woods, which seem to have eluded Gordon. These have a certain dry interest. Eliot, at 26, was at Oxford, and engaged in the serious professional study of philosophy. He kept in touch with Woods, who had taught him some Indian philosophy at Harvard. At Oxford he was working through Aristotle's *Posterior Analytics* with Harold Joachim, reading the *Metaphysics* in Greek, and at the same time struggling with Husserl, whom he found 'terribly hard'. He offered to send Woods his notes on the *Posterior Analytics*, the *Ethics* and the *De Anima*. Although his 'fatal disposition towards scepticism' interfered, he said, with his appreciation of Joachim, he was clearly working very seriously at philosophy. And it might be conjectured that the commentaries written since his thesis on Bradley turned up have not taken enough notice of his Aristotelian studies. They ought at least to be remembered when his famous dictum 'there is no method except to be very intelligent' is trotted out, for it occurs in a context extolling Aristotle, and specifically the *Posterior Analytics*, as a great example of what he means by intelligence.

Much has been written of late concerning Eliot's views on, and indebtedness, to F.H. Bradley. Richard Wollheim, an authority on Bradley, has argued that the famous quotation from *Appearance and Reality* in the note on 1.412 of *The Waste Land* is misleading because out of context. Either Eliot is using it because its decontextualised sense fits his purpose, or because he had simply forgotten the context – in later years he professed not to understand his own book on Bradley. Wollheim detects a progressive loss of interest in philosophy. Eliot more than once spoke of his incapacity for abstruse thought (though this may not be wholly serious – the diligent young birdwatcher, possessor of Chapman's *Handbook of Birds of Eastern North America*, and closely acquainted with the water-dripping song of the hermit-thrush, tells Eleanor Hinkley that he is not sure whether some birds he sees are sparrows, for he knows nothing about ornithology).

He certainly had to decide between a steady job as an academic philosopher, probably at Harvard, and a rougher career in London, where he would have to support his poetry by lecturing, reviewing, and to the dismay of his mother, school-teaching, which she thought beneath him; in the end, it came to banking and publishing. But the philosophical years must surely have left some traces. It has been suggested that Josiah Royce, another Harvard philosopher, was more important than is usually realised, having a congenial theory of tradition and community; some think Russell, who was very close to Eliot in the early London years, cured him of Bradleyan idealism, so that Bradley's continuing influence depended finally on Eliot's admiration for his prose style. Not everybody agrees, and it can still be maintained, as by Lewis Freed in his book *The Critic as Philosopher* (1979), that Eliot's critical theories are Bradleyan almost through and through. Now, however, we have Richard Shusterman with a new view of the whole matter. He believes that Eliot is much more interesting as a philosopher than even his supporters think, and that the easy dismissals on the part of such detractors as Terry Eagleton and Christopher Norris are founded on political prejudice and uninformed assumptions. Shusterman emphasises the Aristotelian studies, and the attack on Descartes in the unpublished

Clark Lectures of 1926, which deplores that philosopher's upsetting of Aristotelianism. As to Bradley, he was thoroughly anti-empiricist, whereas Eliot was from the outset expressly not so: indeed he adopted, around 1916, the analytic empiricist realism of Russell, and did not abandon it till his conversion in 1927, when he moved to 'a non-realist hermeneutical perspective'.

Shusterman's efforts to map Eliot's thought onto 20th-century philosophy may be too systematic, or too opportunist – he makes little allowance for accidental resemblances, claiming, for instance, that Eliot anticipated the thought of Gadamer. What Eliot calls 'the historical sense' is much the same as Gadamer's 'effective historical consciousness', and he is also said to share some of the later thinker's idea of aesthetic activity as a form of play. Moreover their ideas about tradition and community look rather alike. More interesting is the idea that his study of Aristotle's *phronesis* led the poet back towards a native American pragmatism, recalling William James at Harvard but also providing critical anticipations of Richard Rorty.

The truth is no doubt messier than these formulations suggest – say, that Eliot after a time was content to assimilate rather than extend his philosophical learning, but that the philosophical layer of his mind continued to influence an application to matters not manifestly philosophical. Shusterman's is an interesting book, but he seems to forget that even very intelligent people may have cluttered minds, and may be incapable of sustaining the kinds of prescient synthesis he discovers in Eliot's.

The decision to stop doing serious philosophy and take his chance in London was much influenced by Vivien and by Ezra Pound, who almost single-handed launched his protégé into the literary scene. Russell – despite his over-zealous and finally damaging interventions in Eliot's marriage – was probably the main influence on the social side, so important to Eliot. But the tale of Eliot's settling down here is long and tortuous. Arriving from Germany at the outbreak of war, he tells Hinkley (September 1914): 'I feel that I don't understand the English very well . . . it's ever so much easier to know what a Frenchman or an American is thinking about, than an Englishman.' A neutral in an embattled country, he felt partisanship for neither of the conflicting parties. By October he is saying he doesn't think he can ever feel at home in England 'as I do for instance in France', though he admires the English more 'in certain ways'. By 1917 he has come to loathe the snobbish English middle class ('its family life is hideous') and informs his Harvard professor that the English lack of respect for education is amazing.

However, as the war nears its end he can say that he gets on better with Englishmen than with Americans, who 'now impress me, almost invariably, as very immature'. Occasionally regretting his loss of contact with 'Americans and their ways', and also the 'spiritual decadence of England', he nevertheless urges his brother to come here and escape the appalling gregariousness of American life. 'You are unfortunate in having a consciousness – though not a clear one – of how barbarous life in America is. If you had, like all other Americans, no consciousness at all, you would be happier.' In London, he tells Henry, he would have to 'fight very hard . . . in order to survive', but that would surely be better than having friends notable only for their *'immaturity of feeling'*. Mrs Eliot rather wickedly prints a letter to the poet from a distinguished and aged kinsman who says he finds it unintelligible that Eliot 'or any other young American scholar can forego the privilege of living in the genuine American atmosphere – a bright atmosphere of freedom and hope'. It's a remark the poet might have found somewhat wanting in consciousness.

His dwelling on the rarity of this possession reminds one of the cold put-down in *The Family Reunion* when Harry fails to be moved by the news that his brother has been concussed in an accident:

> A minor trouble like concussion
> Cannot make much difference to John.
> A brief vacation from the kind of consciousness
> That John enjoys, can't make very much difference
> To him or anyone else.

To Eliot most people, and by this time all Americans except his brother, resembled John. He would presumably have excepted members of the social circle he had entered, but they did make life difficult.

It is damned hard work to live with a foreign nation and cope with them – one is always coming up against differences of feeling that make one feel humiliated and lonely. One remains always a foreigner – only the lower classes can assimilate.

It is like being always on dress parade – one can never relax. It is a great strain. And society is in a way much *harder, not* gentler. People are more aware of you, more critical, and they have no pity for one's mistakes or stupidities. They are always intriguing or caballing, one must be very alert. They are sensitive, and easily become enemies. But it is never dull.

So much for Bloomsbury and Garsington, and it must really have been hard going. Clive Bell found Eliot's 'studied primness' deliciously comic, and Virginia Woolf was a great tease. But this was his chosen milieu, and although Eliot could call himself 'Metoikos' (meaning 'exile') as late as 1945, he had obviously acquired the censorious Bloomsbury habit. Russell, he discovered, 'has a sensitive, but hardly a cultivated mind . . . in some ways an immature mind'. Lowes Dickinson is 'very common'. But Americans are of course far worse, witness Aiken and Max Bodenheim, an American Jew who made the mistake of supposing he could pick up a living in London as easily as he had done in America. 'He received his first blow,' Eliot contentedly tells his mother, 'when he found that no one had heard of him. I told him my history here, and left him to consider whether an American Jew, of only a common school education and no university degree, with no money, no connections, and no social polish or experience, could make a living in London.'

His pride in his own achievement is understandable. It called for extraordinary industry as well as talent, and at the age of 31 it was with much satisfaction that he told his mother he had been asked to write for the *Times Literary Supplement* – 'the highest honour possible in the field of critical literature'. Yet despite such signal distinctions he continued to be poor: Vivien had to darn his worn-out underclothes, and although the family was generous with hand-outs, he never had enough money to stop worrying about it. At one rather amusing moment, near the end of the war, he says he would be willing to go into the (US) Army 'if I could have a rank high enough to support me financially' – an élite stipulation if ever there was one.

These embarrassments did not prevent the metoikos from quite quickly becoming an insider in the London literary world. He was offered the editorship of the *Athenaeum* but after careful financial consideration, declined. He belonged to the party which scorned Squire's *London Mercury*: 'you must understand that writers here are divided into at least two groups, those who appear regularly in the

London Mercury and those who do not. The *Mercury* has no standing among intelligent people . . . It is socially looked down upon.' It gives one some notion of what he meant by 'society' that literary and social scorn should be so commingled. He was at home in that small world, to the extent of having not only confederates but enemies. Gosse, for example, hated him. Yeats, he fancied, disliked him. Katherine Mansfield was a thick-skinned toady. Of Middleton Murry, toward whom he had once felt quite warmly, he says: 'I think something conclusive must be done to Murry.' A month later he is thanking Murry for an exceptionally pleasant weekend, but, as we have seen, he was quite soon to do something fairly conclusive by making him the representative of the Inner Voice in 'The Function of Criticism'. Above all, he was *papabile*. Herbert Read remarked that by the time he was given the *Criterion* 'Eliot was our undisputed leader.'

There is a good account of his complex early relationships with London writers in Erik Svarny's *The Men of 1914*. One can hardly miss a certain ruthlessness, even some opportunism, in the Eliot of these years. For all his personal unhappiness he was remarkably successful; he knew how to make alliances and deal with misalliances, and how, amid all the hustle, to sustain his really important literary relationships, which were with Pound (sometimes sharply criticised) and Wyndham Lewis, for whom his admiration seems never to have flagged. He had other friendships – for example, with Brigid Patmore, Mary Hutchinson and Sydney Schiff, people less involved in the literary struggle, and perhaps for that reason recipients of some of his most interesting letters. All in all, he seems to have made himself as much at home as it was in his nature to be.

Yet the letters testify, if we needed reminding, that these were also wretched years, plagued by overwork, illness and marital misery. Eliot himself suffered with his teeth, his chest, with repeated attacks of influenza and the sense of breakdown. Vivien was more or less permanently sick, sometimes quite horribly – 'lying in the most dreadful agony, with *neuritis* in every nerve, increasingly – arms, hands, legs, feet, back', and in such pain that she feared for her sanity. Everything conspired to augment their unhappiness – cold weather, hot weather, his mother's failure to visit and then her visit, moving house or staying where they were, the ill-fated Bel Esprit plan to help him by the subscriptions of well-wishers, an insult in the *Liverpool Daily Post*'s report of the matter.

Apart from nursing Vivien, Eliot had to prepare lecture courses and to read, very quickly, writers he had no interest in, such as George Eliot. He knew he was writing too much for literary journals, but needed the money. In September 1922, the nervous collapse associated with *The Waste Land* only recently past, he told John Quinn that he found himself 'under the continuous strain of trying to suppress a vague but intensely acute horror and apprehension'. Vivien at least understood what an achievement it was to edit the *Criterion* when 'tired out by eight hours in the City', meanwhile filling hot water bottles and making invalid food for her. He also had a sense of his own guilt to contend with, telling Pound, in 1922, that his mistakes were 'largely the cause' of Vivien's 'present catastrophic state of health'. And while there was all this to deal with there were also poems needing somehow to be written.

Such a man, in such a plight, could plausibly suppose himself different not only from the *Massenmenschen* but even from his gently bohemian, quite well-off writer friends: and so, after all, still metoikos, always an exile – not merely in the sense of being physically *dépaysé*, like Turgenev and James Joyce, but in the more general sense *dépaysé* anywhere, suffering an exile of the spirit right here in the London that so fascinated him, as the exile of one of his spiritual heroes, Baudelaire, was undergone in his native Paris. How much suffering, and how much guilt, is enough?

For all his social uncertainties and worries about money, Eliot seems to have been remarkably secure in his sense of class and calling. Yet it was still necessary to be separate. There was an apparently instinctive withdrawal from others, shown not only in the abrupt way he sometimes ended relationships, whether male friendships or *amitiés amoureuses*, but in a coldness which could affect even an obituary notice. He needed isolation, not as a *prince d'Aquitaine* pose, but because it was entailed both by his idea of poetry and his idea of intelligence. Some social success was obviously necessary, but so was a deep reserve and a deep self-esteem. He found Joyce to be 'a quiet but rather dogmatic man' who had '(as I am convinced most superior persons have) a sense of his own importance'. And Eliot was certainly a superior person.

It happens that the letters have little to say about Eliot's early life in St Louis, a city which, if only because of its river, grew increasingly important to the poet in the second half of his life. The scholars have looked into his early background, and although Herbert Howarth wrote well about it in *Some Figures behind T.S. Eliot*, Robert Crawford has made a substantial addition. His patient Oxford D.Phil. thesis is intended more generally to illustrate Eliot's preoccupation with the primitive and the city, but its opening chapters are about St Louis and the Mississippi. He illustrates them with gems from the *St Louis Globe-Democrat*, such as the daily advertisement of a Dr F.L. Sweaney, which promised relief to fatigued brains and bodies. The youthful poet carefully copied the drawing of the bearded doctor's face, together with the exhortation: 'When others fail consult . . . ' Did the doctor form one of the multitude of suggestions incorporated in Sweeney? Does the young poet's interest indicate a consciousness or fear of debility? We must make up our own minds. And there may be an additional clue in an early story, printed in the school magazine, in which a man is almost eaten whole by vultures. Eliot, we may conjecture, was closing in on his subject.

Crawford also has a lot to say about Gloucester, Mass., another place of obvious importance to the poet. And as he goes he finds much to say about Eliot's reading in ethnology, even documenting his loss of interest in it, dated by an admission that he did not bother to read Malinowski. The book is a little dogged in manner, as the genre of dissertation requires, but it provides some hard information as well as many conjectures, which might be useful and can certainly do no harm. Stanley Sultan's book can be said to do likewise for the period of *Ulysses* and *The Waste Land*. Scofield's is for the most part a modest exercise in reading the poems. All such books, and there are lots of them, with the centenary likely to produce more, are bound to repeat much that is available already, but beginners will not suffer from using them.

Finally, it is curious that we seem to be keener than ever on centenaries. They are part of the *Aberglaube* of a secularised tradition, taking the place of religious feasts. Of course they are commercialised, but still fairly innocently so, and they serve to affirm, or on rarer occasions to disconfirm, canonical values: which of course makes it all the more apposite that we should celebrate Eliot on 26 September, continuing, if we choose, for the ensuing octave, in the manner prescribed by the best ecclesiastical authorities.   29 September 1988

PAUL DE MAN'S ABYSS

....

Wartime Journalism, 1939-1943 by Paul de Man, edited by Werner Hamacher,
Neil Hertz and Thomas Keenan
Critical Writings 1953-1978 by Paul de Man, edited by Lindsay Waters
Paul de Man: Deconstruction and the Critique of Aesthetic Ideology
by Christopher Norris
Reading de Man Reading edited by Lindsay Waters and Wlad Godzich

Paul de Man was born in 1919 to a high-bourgeois Antwerp family,
Flemish but sympathetic to French language and culture. He studied at
the Free University of Brussels, where he wrote some pieces for student
magazines. When the Germans occupied Belgium in 1940 he and his
wife fled, but were turned back at the Spanish frontier and resumed life
in Brussels. The Germans closed the Free University in 1941, so frus-
trating one possible career; but de Man's uncle, the socialist politician
Hendrik de Man, helped him to a job on *Le Soir*, the biggest newspaper
in Belgium, which was then under German control. Hendrik de Man
had supported the King's decision to surrender, and for a time persuaded himself that the German takeover, though not quite the revolution he had looked forward to, was a revolution none the less, and
might bring about what men of good will had wanted so desperately in
the pre-war years – an end to decadent pseudo-democratic capitalism
and a new era of socialism, even if it had to be national socialism.

Until November 1942, when his contributions abruptly ceased,
Paul de Man wrote copiously for *Le Soir*. He later claimed that he left
the paper as a protest against German control, though the paper was
already under German control when he joined it – it was known as *Le
Soir volé*, and its present management say it was 'stolen and controlled
by the occupier'. The signs are that at least in the early days de Man did
not regard German control as a deterrent; of course the German bosses
are quite likely to have turned much nastier in 1942, as they did about
many matters. In addition to the hundreds of pages he wrote for *Le
Soir* de Man wrote some reviews in Flemish for another German-con-
trolled journal. He also did a lot of translating – including a Flemish
version of *Moby-Dick* – which had no connection with war or politics.

After the war he was briefly associated – his opponents suggest feloniously – with an unsuccessful art publishing venture. In 1948 he went to America, where he worked in a New York bookshop and made useful contacts – for example, with Dwight Macdonald and Mary McCarthy. Soon he was teaching at Bard College. Remarried – his opponents say bigamously – he went to Boston and taught at the Berlitz School. He registered for the PhD at Harvard, became a teaching assistant in Reuben Brower's famous course, Humanities VI, and was recognised as a remarkable teacher, the kind that makes and keeps disciples. In spite of Brower's advocacy he failed to get tenure; in 1960 he moved to Cornell, and thence to Zurich and Johns Hopkins. He ended his career at Yale, where, throughout the Seventies and early Eighties, he was the most celebrated member of the world's most celebrated literature school. He died in 1984.

As academic curricula vitae go, de Man's was certainly unusual, and an account of his publications might seem to make it more so, for his first book, *Blindness and Insight*, appeared only in 1971, when he was 51, and even then, it is said, he published only because Yale drew the line at bookless professors. There were to be only two more essay collections before his death, but now we have two posthumous volumes, and there may be more to come. Considering the ever-increasing density and strangeness of his work, and its ever-increasing fame, it would take a very tough dean to say de Man had under-produced.

The corpus is now augmented by a volume he would not himself have wanted to see. This collection of his wartime writings looks like what it is, a heap of ephemera, ill-printed and hard to read in the photocopies. They testify to the exceptional industry and ability of the young literary journalist – he wrote a long succession of literary chronicles and reviewed large numbers of books in various languages – but it is unlikely that any degree of later eminence would have induced anybody to republish them had not their discovery caused such a tremendous bother. The editors, friends of de Man, decided, probably rightly, that in view of all that had been said and written about them on hearsay it would be as well to make them wholly accessible. The editors have not obtruded themselves; they neither justify nor condemn.[1] And they seem to have been thorough. Here are 170 pieces from *Le Soir*, ten in Flemish from *Het Vlaamsche Land* – these with English translations

– plus 100 brief notices written for a book-distributing agency in 1942-43, and a few earlier pieces from student magazines, one of which is here palpably misdated (4 January 1939 for 4 January 1940).

Keen to extenuate nothing, the editors also include a facsimile of page 10 of *Le Soir* for 4 March 1941, which is headed *Les Juifs et Nous*, and consists of one violently anti-semitic piece on Jews in general, and another claiming that French painting between 1912 and 1932 was *enjuivé* as a result of a plot by Jewish dealers, so that an influx of foreign blood had deflected French art from its natural course, making it morbid and corrupting both to painters and their public. A third essay condemns Freudianism as a further instance of Jewish decadence, and the fourth and last is de Man's now notorious article on the Jews in modern literature. Dissociating himself from vulgar anti-semitism, for which he nevertheless holds the victims themselves partly responsible, he accepts the view that Jews had a lot to do with the disorders of Europe between the wars: but since national literatures evolve according to their own strict laws, they remained largely unaffected by the Semite invasion of other aspects of European life. There were no first-rate Jewish writers anyway; de Man lists some second-rate ones (he doesn't include Proust) and concludes that if the Jewish problem were solved by the creation of a colony isolated from Europe the consequences for 'us' would not be deplorable. It must be added that the page on which this article was printed is decorated with boxes containing comments about Jews from such authors as Ludwig Lewisohn, Hilaire Belloc and Benjamin Franklin, who is said to have wanted Jews, described as 'Asiatics', excluded from the United States by the Constitution. This last citation is spurious.

Some commentators, including Geoffrey Hartman, say that by the standards of the time this was pretty lukewarm anti-semitism. Jacques Derrida – a Jew and a close friend of de Man's – finds it inexcusable, but demands that it be dealt with justly. He repeats that the article deeply wounded him, but discovers in it some redeeming qualities: for example, 'to condemn "vulgar anti-semitism", *especially if one makes no*

---

[1] The same editorial team has compiled a volume in which 38 contributors respond to the wartime writings (*Responses*, University of Nebraska Press). This book is to be published later in the year.

mention of the other kind [i.e. 'distinguished anti-semitism'], is to condemn anti-semitism itself *inasmuch as* it is vulgar, always and essentially vulgar.' Certainly these interrogations should be carried on justly,
but this is all too manifestly a desperate plea. Others have suggested
that this article is virtually a unique aberration in de Man's contributions to *Le Soir*; yet others have conjectured that at this stage he was
unlikely to have known much about what was already going on in 'col-
onies' within Europe – the Final Solution wasn't ordained until January 1942. But as even the charitable Geoffrey Hartman feels obliged to
remark, and as a reading of this collection makes obvious, neither of
these excuses is plausible.

By now these wartime writings have been passionately scanned,
especially by Jacques Derrida in the long article quoted above, which
was published in *Critical Inquiry* last year.[2] Here there is room for only
a few observations. First, there is certainly more than one anti-semitic
piece. An article in Flemish (20 August 1942) about contemporary German fiction deplores the way some Expressionist writers came into
conflict with 'the proper traditions of German art which had always
before everything else clung to a deep spiritual sincerity. Small wonder,
then, that it was mainly non-Germans, and specifically Jews, who went
in this direction.' Again, it is surely odd to find in a piece on Péguy (6
May 1941) a short, but not all that short, account of the Dreyfus affair
which omits to mention that Dreyfus was a Jew; de Man is seemingly at
a loss to understand why the straightforward case of an officer wrongly
accused and reinstated by due course of law should have caused such
a furor. He admires Péguy, a Dreyfusard, for quarrelling, at the cost of
his job, with other liberal-socialist Dreyfusards. Christopher Norris, in
a page devoted to this curious essay, remarks that 'any mention of the
Dreyfus affair must of course raise the question of anti-semitism,' but
fails to add that de Man's mention of it rather pointedly did not; Derrida likewise omits to notice the omission in his *Critical Inquiry* piece,
also preferring to emphasise that de Man was here writing admiringly
of a Dreyfusard. In fact, the drift of de Man's piece is best expressed in
the words *au fond, il ne s'agit pas de grand'chose.*

[2] 'Like the Sound of the Sea deep within a Shell: Paul de Man's War', *Critical Inquiry*, Spring 1988. Derrida at the time of writing had seen only 25 of the essays
from *Le Soir*.

Even if we recall that the affair lasted over a decade, that the opponents of Dreyfus forged and suppressed evidence, and that the victim spent a long time in prison, it might still be maintained that the level of anti-semitism over all these articles is fairly low. But to confine attention to specific references is misleading, for a survey of the whole collection makes it apparent that anti-semitism was at least not entirely inconsistent with de Man's ideas about the national spirit and the need for cultural development to take place on national (and at any rate in some measure xenophobic) lines. Like his uncle, he was, it appears, ready to believe that the 'revolution' brought on by the *événements* of May 1940 had introduced a new and promising epoch of German hegemony in Europe. Flemish is a Germanic language, and it may have seemed opportune and possibly just, even for a writer of de Man's French formation, to score off France, the dominance of whose language and culture was inveterately resented in Flemish Belgium. Yet there is an obvious difference between the French and the Jews. Given a spell of German discipline, the French might yet pull themselves together: but what hope was there for the Jews with their non-European, 'foreign blood'? At the rather abstract level of discourse preferred by the young de Man, there was not much need to be as specific and insistent as some of his fellow contributors, either about Jews or about the flowering of the German spirit demonstrated in the conquests of 1940. Just as he refrains from further overt reflections on the Semite invasion, he silently declines to comment on the continuing progress of German arms, on the Italian alliance (though one article praises the successes of Italian nationalism), on the Russian campaign, the fighting in the Balkans and Africa, the entry of Japan and America into the war. Perhaps he regarded these matters as outside his cultural brief, though the fall of France had not quite been. Yet the military and political developments of 1941 and 1942 must have been of keen and at times disquieting interest to one who had taken the German victories of 1940 as final. For de Man had at first written, understandably, as if in 1940 the war was over, saying more than once that the difference between the two world wars was that the first was long and the second very brief, so that only in the first did people settle down to observable wartime behaviour. Since the Germans had won so completely, any future was going to be a German future, whether one liked the idea or not. But by the time he stopped writing for *Le Soir* the case was some-what altered, with the Wehrmacht surrounded at Stalingrad, beaten in Egypt, and facing future battles in the west against forces enormously augmented since the American entry into the war. Meanwhile the Final Solution was well under way.

All these events, perhaps along with an increase of supervisory rig-our in the office, may have been his inducement to leave *Le Soir*, but there seems to be no evidence for this except de Man's own remark quoted above. And he is said to have offered on occasion rather unre-liable versions of his wartime career – for instance, that he worked in England.

In student articles, written during the phoney war or *drôle de guerre* period, de Man argued that the war had been inevitable, and that after the annexation of Czechoslovakia it could no longer be main-tained that Hitler merely wished to correct the injustices of Versailles. As an anti-imperialist, he said, one must choose the less objectionable of two imperialisms – namely, the British. But when the war was won we would have to deal with all the problems left over from the Thirties – unemployment, for example; and that would require a vast reform of European (and imperial) politics generally. May 1940 changed his mind, and a year or so later we find him claiming that the invaders, far from being the barbarians of propaganda and of leaders in the pre-Occupation student paper, are highly civilised. He rejoices at reports that the French are working alongside their victors in a *solidarité puri-fiante*. Soon he is recommending some German hand-outs explaining National Socialism, and observing that the Germans have made much more generous armistice terms than the French had allowed at the end of the first war.

He sometimes speaks of the irresistible force of a nation's desire for unity, recommending Belgians to study the Italian example and com-menting with severity on the record of the French. Ever since Richelieu they had striven to divide Germany. And they had made a bad mis-take by refusing to collaborate when they might have done so on equal terms: for they must now choose between doing so on terms much less favourable, and passively submitting to England. He admires the traditional qualities of the French (expressed in the customary terms as clarity of intellect and expression), but rarely loses a chance to compare them unfavourably with the Germans. Under Hitler, he contends, there flourished a pure literature, very different from recent French writing. The Germans would give the French, at this decisive moment in the history of their civilisation, what they now most needed: order and discipline, and presumably purity also. However, in April 1942 he complains that the French do not appear to be responding satisfactorily to 'the reforms at present in progress'.

Opinions of this sort surface from time to time in pieces of which the ostensible purpose is simply literary criticism, and the contention that in the mass these articles are just neutral accounts of books and concerts, leaving only one or two collaborationist obiter dicta to explain away, is simply absurd. Taken as literary criticism, they seem to offer few hints of the writer's future interests, though in saying so I find myself slightly, and unwillingly, at odds with both Lindsay Waters and Jacques Derrida. Some of de Man's judgments are routine – he thought very highly of Charles Morgan, for instance, as the French did in those days. He speaks well of Valéry, and that does remind us of the links between his later thought and his early interest in Symbolism. But his views on history, if he remembered them later, must have seemed embarrassingly undeManian. So with romanticism: an essay from the hand of the scholar of whom it is commonplace to maintain that he changed everybody's attitude to that subject says that romanticism was pretty feeble in France, but strong in Germany because deep in the German national spirit, indeed *la consécration définitive de la nature nationale* (21-22 November 1942) – a version of literary history which he was later to condemn.

Unlike some commentators, both friendly and hostile, I see nothing very reprehensible about his failure to talk about this body of work (as distinct from parts of the work itself). Generally speaking, few writers, of whatever kind, and even if conceited enough to think anybody else would be interested, would volunteer to bring their juvenilia to judgment, even if they didn't contain opinions later seen to be embarrassing or perverted. However, this writer's subsequent fame – and the continuing row between deconstructive admirers and more conservative academics – ensured that people *were* interested, some hoping to use the wartime pieces to discredit de Man and the movement associated with him, the rest needing to defend themselves and their hero. So the significance of these juvenilia is strenuously debated.

Few would deny that at least some of the wartime writing is odious, that of a clever young man corrupted by ideas, and corrupted by war (for in wartime the intellect grows as sordid as the conflict), or merely opportunist, or a mixture of all these. To work for *Le Soir* and *Het Vlaamsche Land* was manifestly to forego any right of dissent. To appear on that anti-semitic page was, as almost everybody would agree, an act amounting to full collaboration. The repeated triumphing over the defeated French, having a possible origin in Belgian domestic conflicts, was presumably not done under direct external compulsion. And it is hard to find indications of concealed dissent in this collection, though some have tried to do so. The simplest explanations may be the least damaging in the end: the young man, on his return from attempted flight, found reasons for thinking it intellectually honest as well as expedient to collaborate with the victors. Others, especially in France, did likewise, until, their reasoning invalidated by events, they saw they must cease to do so; and it could be that de Man gave up his job for similar reasons. One wonders whether, had the Germans occupied Britain at the end of 1940, there would have been no clever young people willing to say in collaborationist newspapers (and wouldn't there have been collaborationist newspapers?) that this was at least not altogether a bad thing.

Lindsay Waters's long and interesting introduction to *Critical Writings 1953-78* amounts to an apologetic intellectual biography of de Man. He dwells on the forces – the failures of democracy, the desire for national redemption, the longing for action – which induced intelligent people in the pre-war period to succumb to 'the fascist temptation'. The comparison with Heidegger is here as elsewhere – and doubtless justly – used in de Man's favour. But the main argument is that in his earliest work de Man embraced an 'aesthetic ideology' – its political manifestation is a rather mystical nationalism – of just the kind he was later to attack with such contemptuous subtlety. This implies that the youthful errors were intellectual rather than ethical, though Waters is in no doubt that antisemitism, a rather more than merely cerebral blunder, was an essential constituent of German nationalism, and he has no way of excusing de Man's endorsement of it. However, he finds in these 'marginal texts' the seeds of much later work: they display de

Man's abiding interest in 'inwardness, interiority', so 'there is a fair degree of continuity.'

This connection seems rather tenuous, but Waters goes on to give a convincing account of the later career, from the early Sartrean phase through the decisive encounter at Harvard with American New Criticism, and the revisionary studies of romantic thought, to the decisive 'turn' to rhetoric and the concord with Derrida, which were the features of de Man's last and most influential phase. His rather exotic academic career in America was a genuine European intellectual adventure, typical of what the writer himself, in a letter of 1955, called 'the long and painful soul-searching of those who, like myself, come from the left and from the happy days of the Front Populaire' – which, though it takes us back to a date before there is any substantial record, is plausible enough, as is the highly metaphysical mode of the soul-search.

In support of his argument for continuity, Waters also supplies what many disciples have been demanding: a selection of uncollected essays from the years before the publication of *Blindness and Insight*, with one uncollected late piece at the end. Many of these items are reviews, some long celebrated, like that of Michael Hamburger's Hölderlin translations. Some – on Montaigne, Goethe and Mallarmé – were originally in French. All have that air of quiet, even tolerant authority which, despite occasional severities and bursts of ill temper, was of the essence of de Man's personality. In an essay called 'The Inward Generation' he remarks of certain 'near-great' writers of the pre-war period – Malraux, Jünger, Pound and Hemingway – that they had all been 'forcefully committed politically, but their convictions proved so frail that they ended up by writing off this part of their lives altogether, as a momentary aberration, a step towards finding themselves.' The whole passage has concealed autobiographical interest. It attributes the course of such careers to the collapse of an aesthetic inherited from Symbolism, and used as a protection from real problems: but the war brought these into menacing actuality, and the political was now a matter of life and death. The political and aesthetic beliefs of such writers make them 'vulnerable targets for today's conservatism – more vulnerable, in fact, than they deserve to be, because their predicament was not an easy one'. Although he distances all this by talking about 'the political and aesthetic beliefs of the Twenties', it seems obvious enough that de Man here had himself in view: and in essence this is the best defence that could be offered. Reviewing books by Erich Heller and Ronald Gray, he remarks that both authors 'too readily call "German" a general feature of the romantic and post-romantic intellect', just as he had done himself.

The most intense of these speculations concern Mallarmé and Hölderlin, whose question *wozu Dichter in dürftiger Zeit?* seems to have haunted de Man: he quarrelled over it with the august interpretations of Heidegger. There is a measure of self-absorption about even the least of these pieces. They look forward as well as back, and one of their merits is that they often demonstrate how much can be said in a review or a relatively brief essay: which explains why de Man was so slow to publish a book, and why all his books are collections of essays.

It seems that Christopher Norris had almost finished his book on de Man when the young Belgian scholar Ortwin de Graef uncovered the articles in *Le Soir*, so he comments on them in a postscript. He finds that they contain 'many passages that can be read as endorsing what amounts to a collaborationist line'. It would have been enough to say 'many passages that endorse a collaborationist line', but in general Norris is under no illusions. Before he knew about *Le Soir* he had already noticed National Socialist sympathies in the articles for *Het Vlaamsche Land*, and even in a pre-Occupation piece for the student newspaper. These pieces 'uncritically endorse such mystified ideas as the organic relation between language, culture, and national destiny' – ideas de Man would later 'deconstruct with . . . extreme sceptical rigour'. You can tell how shocked Norris is, for 'mystified', a favourite term of de Man himself, is his usual epithet for ideas he dislikes, and 'rigour' is what deconstructors ought always to use in the necessary business of 'demystifying' them.[3] So he won't excuse the wartime writings as 'youthful aberrations': but de Man is nevertheless a hero and somehow to be excused, if only by a 'totalising' account of his interior life, 'totalising' being a very mystified practice and tolerable only in these very unusual circumstances. Norris outlines the problems of Belgian national politics and the life and opinions of Hendrik de Man, by means of which the young man could, with fatal ease, have got hold of mystified ideas; and argues that the course of his subsequent intellectual travail can be in part explained by the disenchantment that followed their demystifying.

Others, less charitable, have declared that deconstruction is a means of destroying the value of any historical record, or at least blurring a past, as if de Man's work were 'nothing but a series of oblique strategies for pretending that it never happened, or at least that there existed no present responsibility for past thoughts and actions'. This is Norris's account of a view that he of course rejects. It has been expressed with much indignation by Stanley Corngold and others – the holocaust, and de Man's own past, they say, conveniently vanish – but it is dismissed, in my view correctly, as founded on a false idea of the relation between deconstruction and history, admittedly a very dark topic. The alternative reading, vigorously expounded by Norris and more or less the same as that proposed by Waters, is that de Man's later life was dedicated to the purging of the false ideology that had once possessed him – in short, an aesthetic ideology, related to an organicism equally responsible for romantic error and for German nationalism with its attendant evils. Looking with 'principled scepticism' at these youthful beliefs, de Man perceived that they must all fall together, as romantic fallacies he had now seen through.

Some may think it strange to regard Nazism and anti-semitism largely as intellectual errors, corrigible by the mere taking of further thought. And although defences of de Man are decently animated by affection for a dead and admired friend, these attempts at biographical exculpation, these rakings through his evolving, exacting, rather melancholy writings, often seem to lack any serious understanding of how even people of high intelligence are sometimes induced to behave, especially when they may be under stress of a kind the exculpators have

---

[3] Norris has recently published yet another set of rigorously demystificatory exercises in *Deconstruction and the Interests of Theory* (Pinter, 250 pp., £25, November 1988, 0 86187 7128). They show, among other things, that he is not unwilling to be rigorously demystificatory about the very Theory which ought itself to be so, especially when it is put to right-wing or 'irrationalist' purposes, or does its own demystifying with insufficient philosophical rigour. The chapters exhibit a considerable range of interests – from Bloch and Adorno on music, de Man on Kierkegaard, and Rudolf Gasché on de Man, to Pope and Shakespeare post-structurally considered. Norris himself emerges as a demystified left-wing rationalist.

the good fortune to know nothing about. De Man himself has some tortuous but interesting observations on excuses in an essay on Rousseau's *Confessions* (in *Allegories of Reading*, 1979). For example, he distinguishes between confession and excuse. The former is 'governed by a principle of referential verification', whereas the latter lacks the possibility of verification – 'its purpose is not to state but to convince': thus it is performative whereas confession is constative. He is interested in the curious interaction, in Rousseau, of the two rhetorical modes, but at the same time he is willing to say that Rousseau was clearly dissatisfied with his performance as judge of himself, and unable to get rid by excuses of a recurrent sense of shame. For the childish theft of a ribbon is only a beginning: it is followed by other faults that likewise call for excuses, such as the abandoning of one's children. (De Man, we are told by some of his accusers, abandoned his own wife and child, but I do not know whether the known facts really permit this inference.) The critic's interest is expressly not in any simple way biographical or ethical: it is firmly expressed as devoted to an entirely rhetorical problem. It nevertheless passes belief that anybody could write an essay such as this without reflecting on his or her own life, and it may surely be assumed that de Man did so.

It is true that such considerations are not strictly germane to rhetorical theory. Norris quotes an admiring judgment of Minae Mizumura: 'The shift from a concern with human errors to a concern with the problem inherent in language epitomises [de Man's] ultimate choice of language over man,' adding on his own account that it is here – 'at the point of renouncing every tie between language and the will to make sense of language in humanly acceptable terms – that de Man leaves behind that existential pathos that persists in his early essays'. This apathetic purity is what his disciples admire and emulate, though the need to defend the master must sometimes hinder them from quite so scrupulous an avoidance of pathos: the enemy, after all, was representing him as a devious, opportunist, dishonest human being. Furthermore, even if one breathes the air of pure theory, it must sometimes seem strained to argue that it is always impossible to say what one means, even if the statement you wish to make is that it is always impossible to make such a statement; or to combine this belief with the belief that one can and should intend to say, and say, what will make sense of de Man's life as a whole.

Norris is sometimes critical of his subject – for example, of the way in which his views on undecidability are given what sounds like inappropriately decisive and even authoritarian expression. This is his explanation: de Man's style has 'a rhythm that alternates between claims of an assertive, self-assured, even apodictic character, and moments of ironic reflection when those claims are called into doubt'. This is true: de Man almost always achieves this kind of internal tension, the undecidability of his own writing reflecting the unavoidable undecidability of language itself. He was always looking for the point where necessity encountered impossibility, or intention its fated undoing. He is the great impresario of the rhetorical impasse. The title of his first book, *Blindness and Insight*, reflects its thesis, that in critics the two must exist in inseparable tension. In the late essay 'Resistance to Theory', to be found in the book of the same title, he argues that 'rhetorical readings' are theory and not theory at the same time, the universal theory of the impossibility of theory. It would be easy to extend the list of such paradoxes: de Man's quarrel with the aesthetic is the quarrel of an aesthete, his refusal to accept customary distinctions between literature and philosophy is philosophically-oriented, the denial of any differences between literature and non-literature is highly literary. Some such aporia – another favourite word – is the goal of deManian meditation, a kind of substitute for the obsolete satisfactions of closure, now known to be impossible because of the very nature of texts.

Norris, it must be said, is very clear about de Man's positions. He hasn't enough patience to give a fair hearing to anything that he can dismiss as mystified, but one hardly reads him with any hope of that. Within his own ballpark he is lucidly competent. He makes bold use of digressions. The point of a long one about Hillis Miller is to demonstrate that two colleagues, both deconstructionists, may have, within their sympathy, very different attitudes and styles. There is another on Adorno, registering with approval his view of the negativity of knowledge, in order to confer on de Man the increment of this particular virtue of Adorno. The object is to confute those who accuse de Man of nihilism; they are just as wrong as those who accuse him of quietism. The real problem is to discover in him anything, outside rhetoric, that can be stated unequivocally as a belief; and Norris's book does help one to grasp the nature of that problem.

For a while, given the extraordinary veneration in which he was held, it must have been difficult for admirers to write about de Man without referring first to the man and his death, and then, for it emerged almost before the period of mourning was over, to the wartime writing. One impressive thing about *Reading de Man Reading* is that apart from the fine leading essay by Geoffrey Hartman, mentioned above, the contributors go about their rhetorical deManian business without such allusions. Hartman writes as a Jew, and as one who knows more than most about wartime anti-semitism. He admires the intellectual power of de Man's late work: 'the only peculiar thing is that a philosophical mind of this calibre should turn against the pretensions of philosophy and toward literature.' And now he wonders about the *purity* of these deconstructive essays. 'Hegel or Heidegger or Kant or Proust are not sources but materials only: there is neither piety in this critic for their achievement nor any interest in strengthening their hold on us, consecrating their place in the canon.' He clearly thinks of de Man, the philosophical critic, as having made an extraordinary effort of self-dehumanisation, as if the kind of interest Hartman speaks of were somehow base or inauthentic. Nevertheless he speculates that there may be hidden, in the later essays, 'the fragments of a great confession', and that one might 'link the intellectual strength of the later work to what is excluded by it, and which, in surging back, threatens to diminish its authority'. And when de Man asserts that 'what stands under indictment is language itself and not somebody's philosophical error,' we are to understand that this is a reflection 'by de Man on de Man', for 'the later self acknowledges an error, yet it does not attribute it to an earlier self . . . because that would perpetuate its blindness to the linguistic nature of the predicament.' In short, the conscience of the rhetorician is such that it forbids the exercise of conscience in the person.

This gives one a fair notion of the complexity of the problem. Some of de Man's admirers have properly assumed that their business is finally with his mature writings, with the power of his rhetorical procedures; and their ability to continue them is well illustrated in the remainder of this book. Among the most impressive are Neil Hertz's essay on de Man's essay on 'Wordsworth and the Victorians' (in *The*

Rhetoric of Romanticism) – a deManian interrogation of de Man, like
Carol Jacobs's 'Allegories of Reading Paul de Man' (*'Allegories of Reading* is an elaborate allegory of the impossibility of the fundamental
condition of allegory' which 'necessarily relapses into the figure it de-
constructs'). Like the master, these critics have become connoisseurs
of the symmetry between the impossible and the necessary: as he himself pointed out, 'the impossibility of reading should not be taken too
lightly.' Hillis Miller speaks of the 'austere rigour that makes de Man's
essays sometimes sound as if they were written by some impersonal
intelligence or by language itself, not by someone to whom the laws of
blindness and the impossibility of reading also apply, as they do to the
rest of us'. On such matters it may, he feels, be best to keep silent, as he
says de Man does.

But blindness and impossibilism, a love of the aporetic, seem,
among initiates, to promote not silence but an endless linguistic fluency. This is in a way strange, for the prevalent deManian tone might
be called depressed; every critical victory, to be recognised as a victory,
must be a defeat. You may win the local skirmishes of deconstructive
reading, but you have to lose the war. There must, it seems, be a peculiar pleasure in encountering language allegorised as something resembling the great Boyg, with no defence that can be used in that formidable encounter except language itself, now allegorised as a weapon
treacherous and very easily broken. In a rare jocular moment de Man
himself compared undecidability and aporia to getting stuck in a revolving door, which is perhaps a better figure. Anyway, a definition of
reading which claims that hitherto it has never been attempted, and
now that it has turns out to be impossible, might well have seemed dis-
piriting, but it turns out to be positively exhilarating. One might compare these writers to the early Christians, who thought they were the
first people ever to read the Jewish Bible properly, were caught in the
aporia of an end-time that could not end, and managed to feel pretty
exalted about it.

Norris speaks of the essential inhumanity of de Man's views on
language, summarised in a neo-Nietzschean manner as 'a wholly impersonal network of tropological drives, substitutions and displace-
ments'. 'To call de Man's position counterintuitive,' he says, 'is a massive
understatement.' Yet it is just this bleakness, this disclaimer of human

authority over language, that attracts de Man's luxuriously ascetic followers. They mourn the man but rejoice in his 'inhuman' teachings.

The theory that theory is self-defeating, that it cannot possibly control or comprehend the workings of figural language, is part of the master's charm, but it is also a strange foundation for the ambitious institutional and political programmes now being quite stridently proposed by some – for instance, Jonathan Culler in his recent book *Framing the Sign*. Norris, no less committed but rather more critical, is less confident of the imperialist possibilities of theory, though he would like some sort of concordat with Marxism. De Man himself, with his 'extreme and principled scepticism', would possibly have thought this out of the question, as it must be if the inevitable terminus is that revolving door, where language moves in, impossibly, on an understanding of language, and is at once thrown out. The noble course is not to submit to the bewitchments of language, and to recoil from the Acrasian temptations of the aesthetic 'ideology'. But people outside the cult are probably less principled and more prone to mystification. Trilling's students, when he introduced them to the abyss of the Modern, gazed into it politely, said 'how interesting!' and passed by. Others may do the same to de Man's abyss, and carry on thematising and totalising because it is their pleasure to do so, even if it is shamefully human to do so; and they have a long history of resistance to puritanical imperatives. As a rule they will do so without reference to the youthful errors of Paul de Man, and the insiders should now be happy to stop worrying about them and get on with their necessary and impossible projects.

16 March 1989

OUR FAULT

....

Our Age: Portrait of a Generation by Noël Annan

The title of this large, attractive book needs explanation. It isn't to be understood as a claim to deal with the times of all of us who are now alive. First, there is a chronological limitation. 'Our Age' is used in a sense defined thus by Maurice Bowra: 'anyone who came of age and went to the university in the thirty years between 1919, the end of the Great War, and 1949 – or, say, 1951', by which date all who had served in the war had returned to the university. So constituent members of Our Age need to be over sixty and could be over ninety. Secondly, there is an obvious social or educational restriction, since a very large number of people who would qualify by reason of age fail to get in because they never went to a university. Moreover it is distinctly preferable to have been at Oxbridge, and to have made a mark there, so the number of the eligible is really quite small.

Lord Annan makes it clear that he speaks of, and inevitably to a great extent for, this small élite, into which one got by being exceptionally clever, or well-born, or usefully connected, especially with that intellectual aristocracy which occupied the commanding academic and cultural heights in a previous generation – a class upon whose constitution and habit of intermarriage the present author long ago enlightened us. It is from such a cultural establishment that he himself speaks. He remarks that although there are allusions to his own life and work (and he has governed large institutions, sat on innumerable high-powered committees, and known the great and the good), his book is not a memoir. It is only 'the impression I as an individual have formed of the part of my own times that I know something about, and it has no other validity'.

Yet he speaks in two voices, one detached, disinterestedly critical, the other attuned to many of the presuppositions of an establishment he now sees as slipping into the past, propelled there by death and by political and cultural changes beyond its control. There are passages where one can't be sure whether he is voicing his own opinions or reporting those of Our Age in *style indirect libre*, but that ambiguous degree of identification seems appropriate enough. Fortunately the presuppositions include one that permits or even encourages the commentator to look askance at his peers, and another that requires him to be honest, candid and as lively as the case, sometimes a rather hard case, allows.

The panoramic scope of the book is such as to make one wonder that one man, however various his experience, could know so much about so much. Yet for reasons already hinted at there is a certain narrowness of view. For example, he can be critical about the public schools, especially as they were in his own day, when the syllabuses were so confidently and absurdly archaic, the rules and punishments so arbitrary and severe. (Incidentally, I am glad to learn from Lord Annan that the Latin verb meaning 'to be beaten' has an active not a passive form, and discover by follow-up research that *vapulare*, the verb in question, crossed over into English as the rare 'vapulate', though, when used at all, it tends to mean 'to flog' rather than 'to be flogged', so confirming the hint that there inheres in the process of verberation / vapulation the possibility of a measure of complicity.)

All the same, the author confesses that he was happy at Stowe. After a lifetime of more general experience, and despite his persistent advocacy of broader and more technological approaches to education, he still finds it natural to identify people by public-school typologies that many might consider somewhat privileged, somewhat arcane. Thus Lord Eccles is described as 'opinionated, self-assured, a Wykehamist with the manner (so Etonians said) of a Harrovian'. Even if you find this account over-subtle you will still grasp that its subject is a very different sort of person from Richard Hoggart, 'the grammar school extramural lecturer' who at the *Lady Chatterley* trial succeeded, to the amazement and amusement of Our Age, in putting down 'the Treasury counsel from Eton and Cambridge'.

The single most irritating thing about this book is the constant prosopopoeic repetition of the expression 'Our Age', which is always saying this or that, being found guilty of that and the other, contributing one thing, spoiling another, virtually running the show and having a lot of fun while doing so, being powerful yet negligent. However, all this does add up to a fairly full portrait of the imaginary person.

Our Age, who has so much to say in this book, was a gentleman, with the virtues and vices of that condition; if there was Schlegel in him there was also Wilcox. One thinks of Margaret Schlegel's naive resolve, under Wilcoxian influence, to be less polite to the servants: but although Annan reports many gentlemanly activities with an air of detachment or even disapproval, he does not find it necessary to use the word 'selfish', and there are no cads in his book, at least nobody is so described, as some are in Forster's.

Thus we are told dispassionately about the Oxford set, the Children of the Sun, the Brideshead generation, especially Brian Howard and Evelyn Waugh, who is given special status as an important Deviant from Our Age; and also about Cambridge – about the Spies, of course, who escape being described as Deviant, but also about certain slightly less notorious gentlemen. There was, for instance, 'the absurd, insanely touchy Oscar Browning', a member of Our Age, though old enough to have been famously snubbed by Tennyson. Browning was, for quite usual reasons, forced to leave Eton and retire to King's, 'where he entertained the undergraduates and helped dozens of young sailors, soldiers, errand boys and others down on their luck.' The correspondence of Browning, preserved in the modern archive at King's, shows rather a strong if vicarious preference for the Navy. His habit was to send off his young proletarian friends to enlist in that service as Boys. Many of them wrote him interesting and on the whole affectionate letters from various remote stations, sometimes asking for money or for a new guitar to replace one broken in a storm, but sometimes saying they had frankly had enough of the service he had got them into, and would he kindly buy them out. There seem to be no letters thanking him for doing so.

If Browning and Guy Burgess, who 'had the appearance of a man who had just stepped off the Golden Arrow after a night in the Rue de Lappe', were gentlemen, there was a difficult Cambridge figure, another Deviant, who wasn't, perhaps because his father sold pianos. This was F.R. Leavis, for whom, not for the first time, Annan expresses an acute distaste, well-documented and in my view entirely understandable, though there no longer seems to be good reason to carry on about it at such length.

Still, it is natural enough for a Kingsman of Our Age, and so having an inevitable touch of Bloomsbury, to talk unsparingly about relationships and persons; and one of the strengths of this book is that the author's career and his alert, receptive personality are such that he has known lots of interesting people, most in their way rather important, whether because they were clever, or powerful or merely charming. There is a parade of dons, civil servants and politicians, all taking some part in the running of Our Age's great show, which included the introduction of Modernism, innovations in philosophy, sociology, anthropology and of course science. There was also the fighting and conduct of two wars, with a bout of pacifism in between; there were repeated disastrous failures to modernise the economy and the educational system. There was, moreover, the loss of empire; and the general if fairly gentle decline of Britain.

Although Our Age was obliged to take part in, even to manage, all this important business, it is here described as an age of ignorance – sexual ignorance especially, which is known to be productive of disaster. Homosexuals, rather numerous in Our Age, suffered partly from the ignorance of others, but also from their own, for public schoolboys, having been deprived of feminine society in their adolescent years, were the less able to enjoy it later, and were therefore prone to fall into what were still guilty courses. This can hardly be the whole picture, and anyway the whole picture changed in the Sixties, a decade Annan rightly though unfashionably thinks rather well of. In recent years he detects a new puritanism, not wholly bad. The official line on Aids is not that we should be chaste, merely that we should be prudent. Of course not all official lines are quite so permissive. Three years ago I spent a couple of months in Geneva and was impressed by the posters which said, *Soyez prudent: STOP SIDA*, the space in the O of STOP being filled by a condom. However, before I left they had been replaced by very similar posters saying, *Soyez fidèle, STOP SIDA*, with a wedding ring in the hole instead of a condom. Annan, one supposes, would approve the earlier version, but maybe the later one also, for, inveterately liberal as he is on such, matters, he shows some concern about the way things are going, and expressly approves of Bernard Williams's neo-Aristotelian ethics; temperance, and for that matter fidelity, might be called, in Williams's terminology, 'thick concepts', like mercy and honour.

The prevailing tone of the book is genial, but there are occasional severities in its treatment of persons. Among its heroes are Isaiah Berlin and, with a good deal of qualification, Michael Oakeshott; on the Left there is the author's contemporary Eric Hobsbawm. Others' heroes – Raymond Williams, for instance – are sometimes harshly dismissed ('a nonconformist spellbinder, rhetorical, evasive and vacuous'). These judgments are made by an author whose discipline is the history of ideas. Like Berlin, he is 'hostile to the pretensions of technocrats and revolutionaries', and he borrows Berlin's favourite quotation from Kant: 'Out of the crooked timber of humanity no straight thing was ever made.' Consequently a natural geniality is tempered by a slightly morose anti-utopianism, as if the experience of Our Age had shown that most initiatives go awry and come to rather little in the end. Like that of wild horses, Our Age's is a record of failure.

The most depressing part of that record is the political. Annan thinks of politics as having very little to do with ideas or morality; unlike some of their opponents, the Conservatives, though some genuinely if vaguely wanted to do something about unemployment and poverty, were sophisticated enough to know this. There is, regrettably, a kneejerk reference to kneejerk 'progressives'. The Left is credited with an unacceptable mythology, enshrining such errors as the belief that in the Thirties virtually all intelligent men and women leaned to the left. Left-wing politicians and trade-unionists generally get fairly rough treatment. In the interests of balance, the author remembers, and continues to feel, his youthful disgust at Chamberlain's 'insolent self-righteousness', for which not even his interest in the arts could compensate.

Some readers, who harbour quite similar feelings about the present prime minister, may be surprised by the closing chapters of this book, in which she emerges as on the whole an admirable figure with some venial shortcomings, such as a lack of concern for the arts. She was, we gather, much needed. Britain was, in 1979, even more evidently in decline, and if it was Our fault, we have paid the price: 'Our Vision of Life Rejected' is the title of a late chapter. Not getting into Europe at the very beginning is the worst mistake of all, and that seems to have been Our fault. There were others: all the educational muddles of the epoch are here expertly described, including Crosland's fatal spending spree on polytechnics, the refusal of the UGC to behave sensibly when dealing between the cutting government and the wailing universities, the dimness, indolence and selfishness of dons, now at last forced to learn 'Bitter Realities' from the Education Act of 1988 – one dismal failure after another of organisation and imagination. Clearly by 1979 it was time somebody should take things in hand, and, to adapt what Marvell said apocalyptically about Cromwell, 'if these the times, then she must be the man.'

So the Thatcher administrations come quite well out of this enquiry. Since there had to be a Falklands war it was as well that somebody competent was around to run it ('no man could have handled the war better than she did'). 'The most remarkable leader Our Age produced' sought remedies for the decline Our Age had helped to produce. Her methods were not truly congenial to Our Age; now a little weary and ready to comply, it was still too hedonistic to sympathise totally with her spirit. Yet it could not but admire her resolution. She was subjected to criticisms Annan regards as inept and puzzlingly violent; he tries to explain them as due to her personality, to her manner and style, perhaps to her lack of 'magnanimity' – but that, he thinks, may be an exclusively masculine quality anyway. She preaches self-reliance and some of her critics seem unable to distinguish that virtue from greed.

Thatcher, as well as being fairly sound on education, was also right about the miners, right about the GLC, right about the poll tax, right about the bias of the BBC, wrong only on some minor issues such as Cheltenham. Eventually, after a roll-call of her intellectual supporters we at last hear the question: 'But had Margaret Thatcher turned the country round?' Well, possibly not, it seems. Crime, unemployment, miserly administration of social benefits, cardboard cities in filthy streets, disordered schools, high inflation, unprecedented deficit, wanton privatisation, low manufacturing capacity, prohibitive bank rate, the oil wasted, the police suspect, the health service jeopardised, the . . . All this rapidly in a page or so, and not firmly attributed to any failure of will or performance on the part of government.

This partiality, however qualified, is surprising in an author who surveys the rest of his immense field with such independence of judgment. Nothing escapes his interest: achievements and failures in economics, philosophy, anthropology, history, literature, are knowledgeably and briskly surveyed. There are inevitably some off-the-cuff judgments that provoke disagreement, even some misunderstandings – for instance, an apparent failure, or lack of space, to distinguish structuralism from post-structuralism. There is, on page 89, a sentence of twenty or so words that contains three factual errors: but to borrow a quotation from Forster, they arise from 'inattention rather than arrogance'.

A few more niggling points: if it is true that Our Age behaved sensibly in 1939 by giving intellectuals more suitable jobs than fighting, it was presumably true only of those who were accredited members of Our Age; perhaps it could not be helped that the unknowns evaded consideration. Can it be right to say that 'when the Crown failed to indict *Inside Linda Lovelace* it became clear that literary censorship ... had gasped its last'? Rather did it find other and simpler means than the 1959 Obscenity Act when it proved too fair to defendants. Oddest of all, because uncharacteristically provincial, is the statement that 'there had been no butchery in the battles of the Second World War'; also pretty weird is the remark that 'people welcomed the extension of rationing' in the post-war years because they saw it as 'a way to dish the rich for eating in restaurants and getting preference in shops'. Apart from the fact that the rich continued, undished, to eat in restaurants, the rest were too busy getting preference for themselves, in their own shops, to bother much about the eating practices of their betters.

Still, these may have been the reactions the gentlemen of Our Age attributed to the People who were its contemporaries but didn't belong to it. An impression one retains from this covertly sad but vigorous and highly-coloured book is that Our Age had a pretty good time during the half-century or so when our world was in their charge; that despite remarkable achievements in science, technology and even art, they failed because, as Annan puts it, they were more interested in knowing *what* than in knowing *how*. In the end their burden had to be assumed by a deviant from their manners and standards, one who really seemed to care about *how* as well as *what*, and had a go at turning the country round. Almost their last act must be to approve of this person, even though they cannot help noticing that the country quite soon (if it had ever really turned) faced about once more and continued on what they now know to have been all along the primrose path, the road to ruin.

11 October 1990

COLD FEET

....

Essays on Renaissance Literature. Vol. I: Donne and the New Philosophy
by William Empson, edited by John Haffenden
William Empson: The Critical Achievement
edited by Christopher Norris and Nigel Mapp

William Empson maintained that there was a right and a wrong moment to bring theory into the business of intelligent reading, and that the professionals chose the wrong one, but he could not do without theory altogether. His book *The Structure of Complex Words* (1951) contains quite a lot of it; so it is not surprising that a generation of literary theorists, not wishing to remain totally out of touch with the best critic of his time, has decided to appropriate *Complex Words*, a work hitherto much less influential than the very early (and prodigious) *Seven Types of Ambiguity*. Christopher Norris comes right out and calls *Complex Words* 'a work of critical "deconstruction"'. His collection is meant to demonstrate that Empson can be accommodated in modern theory. It can now be shown that he was in many ways anticipating the interests and procedures of a newer criticism, though Norris in his Preface cautiously denies any intention to annex Empson's criticism to any one prevailing trend: 'one could take it as a hopeful sign,' he remarks, 'that "theory" is coming of age when it manages to find room for a strong but problematical figure like Empson, a critic whose thinking goes so markedly against some of its basic precepts and principles.'

As a rhetorical concession this is prudent and ingenious, but it gives some measure of the size of the task. Norris knows very well what Empson thought of these precepts and principles. He once sent the great man some essays from the new French school, including Derrida's famous lecture 'Structure, Sign and Play', later treated as a manifesto by his American followers. Empson wrote back to say he found all these papers, including the one by Derrida, or 'Nerrida' as he preferred to name him, 'very disgusting'. Norris, or Dorris, as Empson might have called him in his later career as a theorist, laments, not without reason, that his correspondent showed no signs of having understood what he had found disgusting. On the whole the current tendency is to compare and contrast him not with Derrida but with de Man – Norris spends time on this comparison, and Neil Hertz, in the collection reviewed here, has a whole essay about it. One can only imagine what Empson would have said about that, or what names he would have found for these in so many respects unlikely mates. True, Empson and de Man shared a certain hauteur, and a certain iconoclasm, but the political adhesions were different, and so were the critical dialects, one conscientiously bluff, the other rarefied and prone to gallicism.

That *Complex Words* is what Norris calls it, 'Empson's great theoretical *summa*', is the view also of his contributors William Righter, Alan Durant and Colin MacCabe, and Jean Lecercle, whose lively piece includes a remark to the effect that the poem 'Camping Out' mentions a girlfriend cleaning her teeth into the lake. Empson, so keen on biography, would have liked him to know that this was no girlfriend but a sister.

Norris's own essay takes up a good third of the whole book and best explains what is going on. There are, as he rightly remarks, more misunderstandings of Empson's critical positions than is defensible. For example, Empson's loose association with the American New Critics of long ago has given rise to the notion that he agreed with their anti-intentionalism, although for forty years he went on explaining with increasing force and irritation that the purpose of criticism was to follow the movement of the author's mind. He saved some of his more brutal insults for W.K. Wimsatt, co-author of a famous article about 'The Intentional Fallacy'. In the end, I think, this particular bogey distracted him from what he did best, and in *Using Biography* he seems to have given up movements of mind in favour of fancies and speculations he wouldn't at earlier dates have thought relevant.

However, you would expect that this strain in his thought, alien not only to the old New Criticism but to the new New Criticism, might give Norris some trouble. He gets out of it by what I take to be a change in his own position, so that theory, now come of age, can henceforth permit some attention to what was intended. Again, it is a congenial consideration that Empson thought that the New Critics adapted his methods in a sneaky way to import Christianity into the argument: indeed, he believed that the decay of criticism was directly due to this intrusion of what Norris calls 'surrogate or ersatz theology'. This accounts for his habit, sometimes baffling to the agnostic opponent, of condemning criticism he disagreed with as 'neo-Christian'. The prefix suggests that indignant denials of Christian faith were merely evasive and would do you no good: you could be neo-Christian without being Christian. I think that historically this has something to do with a certain fashion for Christian criticism, and a more general worry about poetry and belief, at the time of Empson's return from China; this fashion, led by such as C.S. Lewis and practised by such as Fr Martin Jarrett-Kerr, seemed interesting to others, who may thus have seemed, willy-nilly, to be crypto-Christians.

One point of importance in this, as usual good, but as usual digressive, essay concerns Empson's refusal to distinguish between the truth of poetry and the truth of science. He rejected the 'pseudo-statement' theory of his mentor I.A. Richards, and as time went on had many tussles with the problem of figurative language, which often apparently says the thing that is not. He came to think of most contemporary literary criticism as a dreary professional attempt to avoid decisions about truth-statements made in poems. And of course he suspected a Christian plot. Norris is quite right to say that 'what comes across most strongly is his deep-laid humanist conviction that the best – indeed the only – way to make sense of complex or problematic novels and poems is to read them with a mind unburdened by the self-denying ordinances of modern critical dogma.' But of course there are other forms of prejudice. Problems arising from arguments about truth and prejudice were to lead to noisy arguments about Donne.

I believe firmly that Empson was a great critic, but have to regard as wasteful his advocacy, over many years, of an eccentric view of Donne. To understand that view, here documented in full and supported by John Haffenden's conscientious and adulatory commentary, one point at least is essential. Empson found it all but impossible to believe that any intelligent and honest person could be a Christian. A lot of his work is devoted to showing that even writers who would have been amazed to hear it nevertheless did at some level of sensibility or intellect see through the horrors of the Christian religion; Milton is the most obvious example (*Milton's God*, 1961), but the very devout Herbert is another.

Donne he had early taken as his model, regarding him, he says, with awe and love, and trying to write poems like his. That Donne became a famous parson was not too grave a problem, since he took orders against his will, because no other way of making a living was open to him; he wrote most of his poetry, and all of his erotic poetry, before he did so. (Empson doesn't show much interest in the sermons and devotional writings.) He cannot have accepted such absurd doctrines as the Trinity, and such horrible notions as Atonement, or believed in a religion that permitted you to torture your theological adversaries and burn them alive.

A minor instance of Empson's reflex of disgust at Christian thinking comes up in Norris's introduction, worth mentioning only because it shows how that reflex could block understanding. I had remarked, in a book he reviewed, that in Mark 4.11-12, a famous crux, Jesus is plainly reported as saying that he uses parables to ensure that the people will miss his point: in order that 'hearing they may hear, and not understand'. Empson professed to think that I, in his peculiar view a palpable neo-Christian, was reverently offering this as a piece of divine wisdom; as Norris puts it, he 'was quick to discern the hints of a quasi-theological dimension'. My supposed misrepresentation was dismissed by Empson in the interests of 'a forthright appeal to common sense'. Norris applauds Empson for what in any lesser figure would be dismissed as a mere failure of attention.

Critics who disagreed with Empson about Donne got specially harsh treatment. The poet came from a devout Catholic family which was all too familiar with the penalties of recusancy; and it cannot be denied that he was very well read in theology, which Empson regarded as double-talk, a means of hiding from good men the insane wickedness of the God they were obliged, under state penalties, to worship. So no one will say that Donne was indifferent to religion. However, it can be maintained that he saw through Christianity and made up a religion of his own, the tenets of which can be reconstructed from some clues in the poems, and involve the idea of woman as a rival and superior Logos. This religion of love transcended Christianity, and was very modern in that it (more or less secretly) accepted the doctrine of plurality of worlds and the possibility of life on other planets: so it depended heavily on the New Philosophy of the time. Empson believed that Donne imagined lovers rejoicing in a liberty unknown under the political circumstances of the time, but available in America, and conceivably on some inhabitable planet in the newly opened up universe.

Though nobody had taken quite this line before, Donne and the New Philosophy has long been a stock literary-history problem. Empson went carefully into the question of Elizabethan Copernicanism. In 1576 Thomas Digges published a book by his father with an addition accepting Copernicus; it was often reprinted, though without alteration or further addition. Since Digges went on doing advanced astronomy, Empson took this continual reprinting of an unchanged text as evidence of censorship. This is possible, though merely conjecture. But in any case it is probable that a well-connected young man, with an immoderate thirst for learning, would know quite a bit about Digges, and about the novae which, after 1572, upset the traditional idea of the incorruptible heavens. Moreover, Giordano Bruno, the main proponent of the idea that there were other inhabited planets (which gave rise to awkward theological problems, especially concerning Incarnation and Redemption), had made a stir in England. He was well known, for example, to Sidney, and doubtless to London groups of freethinkers, like those around Ralegh and the 'wizard' Earl of Northumberland.

Haffenden talks about the 'School of Night', dominated by such figures as Thomas Harriot, magician and atheist. The School of Night is conjectured to have been an organisation devoted to this kind of modern study; here it is offered as undoubted historical fact. The term derives from a dubious reading in *Love's Labour's Lost*, and good authorities treat it sceptically. Haffenden says nothing of this in his text, consigning evidence against it to the backnotes. But even if there was no group called the School of Night there were certainly people who behaved as its members are thought by some to have done. Harriot had a special reputation as the original thinker; not much is known about his thought, but one has a rough idea of the kind of thing he would go in for. At that time the patterns of learning were not as they later became, and an interest in scientific cosmology was perfectly consistent with astrology, alchemy, skrying and magic in general. Marlowe, it was reported, thought Harriot a better magician than Moses.

Empson, wanting to make Donne as like himself as possible, argues that he would have been very interested indeed in the work of these groups, though he seems to take little account of their interests other than in the new astronomy. The great mage John Dee, a central figure, was a scholar and had one of the great libraries of the age; he was famous not only for editing Euclid but for extraordinary feats of magic, alchemy and fortune-telling. So one ought not to think of these people simply as intellectual revolutionaries dedicated to the advancement of modern science in its early phase. And Donne's poetry uses far more alchemy, angelology and scholastic philosophy then it does up-to-date astronomy. He would be aware that there were exciting new ideas around, but that would not be a reason to give up all the old and more familiar ones, and on any unembattled view he was far from doing so.

In this respect Donne's position is indeed somewhat like the young Empson's. The study of Donne in the Twenties was conditioned by the mistaken idea that he strongly resembled the Symbolist poets, an idea given up when, with the help of Grierson's edition, people perceived that the poems, although difficult because of their extraordinary intellectual ingenuity, normally had perfectly clear arguments one could follow if one could come to terms with the unfamiliar allusions. These, as I say, were more often to scholastic philosophy, angelology and indeed the old Ptolemaic cosmology than to Copernicus. When Donne talks about spheres he is quite naturally thinking of the Ptolemaic ones, one to each planet including the moon, with the earth at the centre; round these spheres an angel or intelligence drove the planet, rather, as the contemptuous Scaliger was later to remark, like horses in a pound. This sense of 'sphere' was not altogether suitable for Empson's argument, so he had to insist that Donne also habitually used it to mean 'planet'.

Empson badly wanted to keep hold of the belief of his youth – that the ideas of the New Philosophy were central to Donne's poetry – and this book contains repeated affirmations of that belief. I have to say that, however ingenious and entertaining the arguments, nothing here persuades me to alter the opinion tersely expressed and supported by citation in 1951 by J.C. Maxwell, a scholar whose name is absent from the index of Haffenden's collection: namely, that the impact on Donne of New Philosophy has been much exaggerated. At a time of worrying cultural crisis, Donne was needed to represent an earlier worrying cultural crisis – the earth was no longer at the centre of the creation, there was a general ferment of religious and philosophical ideas, and so on. The truth seems to be that Donne was interested in Copernican theory exactly as he was interested in other forms of learning: exciting as they may have been, there were considerations that limited their force. In 'The Second Anniversary' he gives a list of baffling intellectual problems and closes it with a dismissive couplet:

> In heaven thou straight know'st all, concerning it,
> And what concerns it not, shalt straight forget.

Empson abhorred the notion that somebody could be quite passionately interested in learning, yet at the same time remain somehow uncommitted to it. And well he might be, for it is an old Christian idea, and Donne had a severe Christian education. The sin of *curiositas* was a desire for human learning strong enough to impair performance of the higher duty of saving one's soul. It was possible for very learned men such as Augustine and Milton to condemn it; and it was sometimes stated in very repressive forms, as indeed it is in *Paradise Regained*. That Donne should have such an opinion even in a mild form was unacceptable to Empson because he would feel contempt for anybody who held it. So he fights throughout for a Donne who was not only profoundly interested in all this new science, but gave it his real assent and even used it as the foundation of a new religion to supplant disgusting Christianity.

Haffenden backs him up loyally whenever he can, saying, for instance, that Donne might have known Kepler's *Somnium* long before it was published in Prague, because Kepler corresponded with Harriot and Donne *may* have known Harriot; the possibility is admittedly slight, especially since nobody outside Prague, according to Kepler himself, saw the *Somnium* until 1611, a year after Donne's skit *Ignatius his Conclave*, which could otherwise have been indebted to it . . . Oh well, says Haffenden, 'it is not unimaginable that Kepler had got the date wrong'. This is a way of introducing supporting evidence even when you know it to be false, a practice now common in our courts of justice but still not admirable. There is more of this kind of 'not impossible' argument. It is even suggested that when Donne wrote the *Conclave* he might well have included an allusion to Bruno's *De Immenso*;

as it isn't there now he must have discreetly crossed it out later.

The real point is not, I think, affected by arguments as to whether Donne knew or read this author or that. It is to decide how, if he knew quite a bit about these matters, which is plausible, he responded to them. One answer is that they mostly got into his poems as witty and conceited arguments or illustrations, demonstrating the same degree of commitment as his repeated allusions to the conduct of angels and alchemists. Haffenden, taking his tone from the master, would condemn this position as an instance of 'superficialism' – or worse, as implying that Donne was a liar. This is a curious objection. Empson, in his poetry, was often himself given to conceits and to a wide range of allusions which are not to be taken as simple statements of truth ('All those large dreams by which men long live well/Are magic-lanterned on the smoke of hell').

This difficulty about belief and figuration in poetry is central to the problems posed in this book; it is as if Empson, with Haffenden in attendance, had devised a special philosophy of rhetoric for this poet, the favourite of his youth. To make it clearer how this arrangement affects the reading of the poems I had better give a sample or two, explaining first that Empson, who hated what Helen Gardner made of the texts, and often attacked her with asperity and justice, also wanted readings that suited his view of the matter best, just as he rightly says she did. The quarrel extends to many poems, but I must select, and the best place to begin is probably the Elegy 'To his Mistress Going to Bed', disagreement about which caused Empson to be remarkably nasty to not one but two Merton Professors, Helen Gardner and John Carey.

The poem is an impatiently erotic series of exhortations to a woman to hurry up and undress:

> Off with that girdle, like heaven's zone glistering
> But a far fairer world encompassing . . .
> License my roving hands and let them go
> Behind, before, above, between, below.
> Oh my America, my new found land . . .

The textual difficulty comes near the end, when he is talking about the last garment:

> cast all, yea this white linen hence.
> Here is no penance, much less innocence.

Such is the version in the belated first printing of the poem in 1669; the poem had been omitted in the edition of 1633, presumably on moral grounds. There is manuscript authority for a different reading: 'There is no penance due to innocence.'

Empson wants this to be the true version; the poem is saying that there is no guilt in sex, that the woman represents freedom, like America; he also compares her to an angel, and a good angel; bad ones 'set our hairs, but these the flesh upright'. Moreover he says, in a theological figure, that women are the source of grace to the elect. In short, he could not have written a line saying the woman wasn't innocent. Empson supposed it had been altered, at first carelessly, by somebody who substituted 'much less' for 'due to', whereupon somebody else changed 'Here' to 'There', to make sense. The reading given by Helen Gardner he can't accept, since it is out of key with the rest, which can be fitted into Empson's general view that the young Donne was serious about sex; in any case it would be a blunder for the lover in these circumstances to tell the girl she wasn't innocent, while on the whole claiming that in going to bed with him she would indeed be behaving very correctly. Critics who favour the Gardner reading, he thought, are likely to be the sort that deplore young people doing such things.

In short, Empson needs the manuscript version. He could be right, though it is not very likely. This is, for all its undoubted erotic force, an odd poem; as Barbara Everett once pointed out, it might be thought a record of failure, since the only participant who is undressed at the end of the poem is the man ('To teach thee I am naked first'). What Empsom seems to have left out of consideration is that there is quite a lot of Donne that takes a Juanish view of women; for instance, the question of what women are to be loved for is taken up in a witty, macho way in the next elegy, 'Love's Progress'. Since virtue is specifically named among the qualities for which we are told they should not be loved, we can be sure innocence was not, in the warmth of pursuit, thought essential or relevant. 'Innocence' might well be read as an ironic citation from the lexicon of conventional attitudes to sex; as in 'The Dream', 'shame' and 'honour' are said to have no place in the play of love.

My point is simple. One could reasonably prefer the reading Empson hates without having any of the reasons for doing so that he always angrily alleges. But he really needed his enemies, and enjoyed working hard to catch them out. One consequence is much textual quibbling, for instance, in his studies of 'A Valediction: of weeping'. All will agree that it is a superb poem:

> Let me pour forth
> My tears before thy face, whilst I stay here,
> For thy face coins them, and thy stamp they bear,
> And by this mintage they are something worth,
>> For thus they be
>> Pregnant of thee;
> Fruits of much grief they are, emblems of more,
> When a tear falls, that thou falls which it bore,
> So thou and I are nothing then, when on a divers shore.
>
>> On a round ball
> A workman that hath copies by, can lay
> An Europe, Afrique, and an Asia,
> And quickly make that, which was nothing,
>>> *All*,
>> So doth each tear
>> Which thee doth wear,
> A globe, yea world by that impression grow,
> Till thy tears mixed with mine do overflow
> This world, by waters sent from thee, my heaven dissolved so.
>
>> O more than moon,
> Draw not up seas to drown me in thy sphere,
> Weep me not dead in thine arms, but forbear
> To teach the sea what it may do too soon;
>> Let not the wind
>> Example find
> To do me more harm than it purposeth;
> Since thou and I sigh one another's breath,
> Who e'er sighs most is cruellest, and hastes the other's death.[1]

The opening seems straightforward, but the first edition says 'falst' instead of 'falls'. Grierson preferred 'falst' and so does Empson, who says the variant 'raises large issues'. If the correct version is 'falls' the line means 'that image of you that is on the tear falls with it'. In the last couplet of Shakespeare's Sonnet 130, 'My mistress' eyes are nothing like

---

[1] This is a modernised version of the Gardner text.

the sun', you make a bad mistake it you take 'she' to be the subject of 'belied' rather than a word for 'woman':

> And yet, by heaven, I think my love as rare
> As any she belied with false compare.

In rather a similar way it might be thought that some copyist mistakenly wrote 'falst' because he thought 'thou' was a pronoun subject, not a noun. Empson will have none of this, regarding 'falls' as dull, perverse and pedantic: 'She' – Gardner – 'is doing what Theobald did to Shakespeare, altering the text to make a duller and simpler kind of poetry'. 'Falst' has the backing of Grierson in the original Oxford edition, though his gloss seems to me rather to fit 'falls': 'as your image perishes in each tear that falls'. However, Empson argues that 'falst' is essential to the idea that the lady has a 'real presence' in her reflection. I cannot see why you couldn't believe that while reading 'falls', thus avoiding not pedantry or harshness but nonsense. Empson sometimes gets himself into cantankerous fights without necessity; here his argument is as obscure as it is contemptuous.

One final instance: 'The Dream'. Here the poet is dreaming about his mistress when she arrives and wakes him. She joins him in bed and later, to his regret, leaves, presumably out of caution. He consoles himself with the thought that she will return. Empson scolds Gardner for printing

> Thou art so true, that thoughts of thee suffice
> To make dreams truth . . .

when the first edition has 'thou art so truth . . . to make dreams truths', and Empson wants this. Here I agree entirely: the reading has good authority and is much more striking. John Carey and Gardner, I also agree, got this poem as a whole wrong, and are chid for it, but so does Haffenden, when he says the lover chides himself as 'weak'; what he says is that 'love is weak' if it takes any notice of fear, shame or honour.

Empson is right about 'so truth', and about two other disputed readings in this beautiful text; but he feels obliged to argue that getting them and the poem right depends on our understanding that the lady is really God or rather better than God. At first the man thought his visitor was an angel, but then realised she couldn't be, for she has read his mind and angels, unlike God, are not empowered to do that. So

> I must confess I could not choose but be
> Profane, to think thee anything but thee.

So, concludes Empson, she must be God, or his superior. But this hardly seems a necessary conclusion: the lover is saying that it would be profane to think her God, so he must settle for her being just her. An alternative reading is: 'I must confess, it could not choose but be/Profaneness to think thee anything but thee.' Rather remarkably, Empson likes this; and here, having been right about the drift of the poem, he is wrong on a detail because he wants support for his theory about a new religion. He thinks Donne changed the original reading because he 'got cold feet', and says that on purely textual grounds 'it . . . profaneness' has more authority. The textual argument is very involved, and Empson went into it pretty thoroughly when attacking Gardner's edition; but he could not have claimed that his textual choices were not, like hers, influenced by their coming to the poems with a set of prior assumptions about them and their author.

The battle is fought through these pages, and in very fine detail, but the conclusion has, I think, to be that following one's nose – a practice Empson recommends for critics – can occasionally cheat one into following false scents. It remains impressive that one true poet should so wish to identify with a predecessor, should wish to credit him with the attitudes the newcomer finds most admirable, and wherever possible to clear him of all moral and intellectual blame, even if it means that less important commentators will sometimes be traduced. All Empson's writings about Donne are labours of love, and have their own inwardness. Not many professional critics nowadays love poets in this manner. Empson's new admirers do not love him for loving a poet, only for having had the prescience or luck to anticipate some of their theories. For on the whole it is for the theoretical elements of *Complex Words*, rather than the individual and devoted study of complex words in poems, that they seek, according to their lights and without necessity, to rescue Empson from critical oblivion.

22 July 1993

DARK FATES

....

The Blue Flower by Penelope Fitzgerald

Penelope Fitzgerald's *The Blue Flower* is a historical novel based on the life of the poet, aphorist, novelist, Friedrich von Hardenberg, a Saxon nobleman who wrote under the name of Novalis and lived from 1772 to 1801. He figures largely in all accounts of the German literature of the time, and Georg Lukács is not much more extravagant than other critics in calling him the *only* Romantic poet. He spoke of the need to romanticise the world by the action of intellect and imagination; in this novel he parodies his teacher Fichte, crying: 'Have you thought the washbasket? Now then, gentlemen, let your thought be on *that* that thought the washbasket!' He also dwelt on self-annihilation, and in his last years made a cult of death.

In this country his reception has been less than tumultuous. Carlyle, liking the idea of self-annihilation, and also finding in him a sympathetic tendency to worship heroes, thought it his duty as a Germanist to introduce Novalis to British readers, and wrote an essay about him in 1829, treating him as a mystic and comparing him with Coleridge. This is held to have been a mistake, to be explained by Carlyle's erroneous view of Coleridge as a mystic, and by Coleridge's obsession with obscure German Idealist philosophy. Carlyle was right to describe Novalis as talented, poetical and philosophical, wild and deep, and right to compare his thought with 'what little we understand of Fichte's', but again wrong, as Rosemary Ashton explains in her admirable book *The German Idea*, in failing to understand that Fichte and Fichteans differed fundamentally from Kant in rejecting the Thing in Itself. You were to think the Thing only as a preparation for thinking that that thought of the Thing.

In Fitzgerald's book the student Novalis and his friends gather in order to *fichtieren* among themselves after the great man's lectures, but Fichte wasn't the only influence; there were others, possibly deeper. The Hardenbergs were a noble but not a rich family (the poet, though formally addressed as 'Freiherr', was short of cash, rode a nag and sometimes had to walk). They had a 16th-century reformer among their ancestors, and they were Moravians, interested in prayer, hymn-singing and simplicity of life. Although he was to find the disciplines of the sect too limiting, the poet retained a powerful strain of pietism, unaffected by his professional interest in the latest chemistry and geology. Familiar with modern philosophical idealism and the Romantic 'organicist' aesthetic, resistant to the rationalism of Enlightenment, Novalis can presumably be thought of as participating in what Isaiah Berlin named the 'counter-enlightenment'.

As Berlin remarks, irrationalists such as J.G. Hamann could turn Enlightenment thought to their own purposes, and it is here slyly hinted that Novalis could have reconciled his interest in Jakob Boehme and Spinozan pantheism with an interest in Hume (for example: it is belief in miracles that is the miracle). Other leading ideas were that matter and spirit were continuous, and that all knowledge, from mathematics to poetry, was of the same basic stuff.

Like Goethe, though probably with more practical success, Novalis had a job in mining, and seems to have found a place in his philosophy for mineral deposits. And as Goethe wanted to find an *Urpflanz* in Sicily, Novalis had a vision of a unique blue flower as the goal of a quest. He admired Goethe, of course, though he found *Wilhelm Meister* artificial, a work of the understanding rather than of the imagination, and wrote his unfinished, posthumously published novel about the blue flower (*Heinrich von Ofterdingen*) to counteract what he regarded as the coldness of that work.

The above ragged and perfunctory account of Novalis is in sad contrast with Penelope Fitzgerald's. She has the gift of knowing, or seeming to know, everything necessary, and as it were knowing it from the inside, conveying it by gleams and fractions, leaving those who feel so disposed to make it explicit. Her first novel was a detective story set in a museum rather like the BM, and it was at once clear, though unobtrusively so, that she knew all about museum administration and its crises. *Bookshop* implied knowledge not only of bookshops but of bookkeeping; *Offshore* not only of life on a houseboat in Battersea Reach but of William de Morgan. *Human Voices* unmistakably suggests an inwardness with life at the BBC, and *Innocence* a close familiarity with post-war Italy, Gramsci and various human deformities. Other novels hint at omniscience concerning Cambridge, and Russia in 1913.

All this is inside information, which never seems to be got up or stuck in for the occasion, as sometimes happens with historical block-busters: and of this rare skill *The Blue Flower* is a remarkable further instance. 'Novels arise out of the shortcomings of history,' runs one of Novalis's fragments, used here as an epigraph. It is a wise remark and explains why familiar ways of writing history acquire something like the narrative qualities of fiction. Fitzgerald, a superbly tactful novelist, has avoided a form of fiction that might be thought to resemble that kind of history. The method used here is episodic, discontinuous: the effect is rather *tachiste*, which enhances one's sense that the book's design or designs are for the reader to make or discern.

The visionary blue flower dominates his imagination, but in the waking life of Fritz von Hardenberg the part of the flower was played by Sophie von Kühn. She is 12 years old when he meets her and at once designates her his future bride and his incarnation of Wisdom. Reluctant parental permission is obtained for their betrothal, but Sophie (as well as not being noble) is tubercular. Much of the story concerns this painful and destructive illness, which kills her when she is 15. Novalis himself, though he lived long enough to get engaged to somebody else, thereafter confessed a wish for death, and did not long survive Sophie, dying at 29 of the same disease. Their relationship, and Fritz's dealings with his own family and Sophie's, are the main business of the novel.

Sophie was, it seems, a perfectly commonplace young girl, neither intelligent nor particularly beautiful, but on Novalis's view of the world nothing is commonplace because all when rightly seen is symbolic. There is no barrier between the seen and the unseen. He claims to love Sophie all the more because she is sick: 'Illness, helplessness, is in itself a claim on love. We could not feel love for God himself if he did not need our help.' His friends can understand neither his blue flower nor his passion for Sophie, though one of his brothers also falls in love with her; unlike Fritz, he is repelled to discover that because of her illness she has become bald. Only another brother, 17 years younger than Fritz, has an intuitive glimmering as to what the flower is all about; he doesn't say, but probably guessed it had to do with death. This boy is the latest version of a type that Fitzgerald has used before, a sort of wise child figure, with a gift for shrewd, pert dialogue, rather like some children in Ivy Compton-Burnett. The Bernhard, as he is called, is sketched with great delicacy and humour, in spite of his dark fate; he died – before Fritz – by drowning, a fate he probably sought. His end is prefigured in the novel though outside its time scheme.

The main narrative is fragmentary and rather distanced. What is so impressive is the sureness and economy with which the setting is established. Great men – Goethe, the Schlegels, Fichte – walk on without seeming in the least intrusive. Allusions to contemporary university life (students could still ask Fichte questions only because he was not yet a professor), to contemporary philosophy, medicine, agriculture, have the same unobtrusive certainty, which also characterises more humdrum matters. If a piano is bought to replace a harpsichord the qualities of this newfangled instrument and the merits of rival makers are touched in with the same assurance as the domestic duties of daughters, the pious habits of a Moravian father, or the privileges and duties of the minor nobility.

The book opens with the confusions of washday in Fritz's noble Saxon household, and we learn as it were by the way that washday was an annual event in establishments possessing enough linen to last out that time – a friend of Fritz's, deriving from less exalted stock, feels ashamed that he has only 89 shirts, so that at his house there has to be a washday every four months. Fitzgerald, who delights in knowing this kind of thing, also knows how winter supplies of wood were delivered, how coaches were sprung, why the wrist-watch was invented and how Christmas was celebrated in pious homes (all confess the sins of the year to father; there is a Saxon variant of Father Christmas called Knecht Rupert). The cuisine of Saxony (rose-hip and onion soup, goose with treacle sauce, *Kesselfleisch* – the ears, nose and neck fat of the pig boiled with peppermint) seems too recherché to have been made up for the purpose, and is unlikely to have been included in the collected works of Novalis; but this curious and retentive writer has not confined her researches to them. She has always had a taste for detail.

Detail, expertly dabbed in, provides in the end a substantial background for the story of a poet which, it is subtly suggested, is also the story of a remarkable moment in the history of civilisation. There are echoes of the great disturbances in France; a brother joins the Army; the universities, notably, Jena, and the cities, Leipzig and Dresden, are just out of view, but the formation of the poet is largely domestic. He is naive and provincial, but innocently intelligent, which enables him to entertain with uncorrupted enthusiasm ideas of all sorts – about nature, its purity and its symbolism, about God and mineral deposits, about the epiphanies vouchsafed to the elect, about the new and the old ideas combining at the great moment when it was possible to proclaim that the world must be romanticised. It is hard to see how the hopes and defeats of Romanticism, or the relation between inspiration and common life, between genius and mere worthiness, could be more deftly rendered than they are in this admirable novel.

5 October 1995

A LIKELY STORY

....

Howard Hodgkin: Paintings
Howard Hodgkin by Andrew Graham-Dixon

Faced with such books as these it is hard not to regret the passing of an age when it seemed easy to write about painting and painters. The grapes of Zeuxis, as Pliny admiringly observed, were so real that birds came and pecked at them. Vasari, a painter himself, believed that in his day art had rediscovered those lost antique skills, built on them, and was now close to perfection. To make representations look deceptively real, and to remain untroubled by considerations of what 'real' could possibly mean, was the aim of the artist, and the function of the critic was simply to admire the technical accomplishments that made the illusion credible.

You could also express an admiring or even a disgusted interest in the personal life of the painter. Writing about Piero di Cosimo, Vasari does more than comment on the strange works of this artist. He adds that Piero lived more like a brute than a man, subsisted on boiled eggs, cooked 50 at a time while he was boiling his glue, studied a wall on which sick persons had used to spit, imagining that he saw there fantastic cities and combats of horses. Moreover he would never suffer his fruit trees to be pruned or trained, and so on. Vasari improves the story by arguing that there was method in Piero's madness: he was so eccentric that people mistakenly thought him a fool, and this assumption prevented other artists from profiting by his example. George Eliot remembered Piero's eggs and reclusive habits in *Romola*. Improving the story yet again: why she has the eggs delivered ready-boiled is a question for Victorianists.

Vasari had got on to something important when he perceived that the lives of painters are likely to be of considerable general interest, as well as being rather easier to write about than their productions. He does describe certain works in detail: for example, Piero's *Car of Death*, with tombs from which emerge figures with skeletons painted on their black body-stockings. He can remark that Piero drew well from life, that he painted St Antony wearing spectacles and reading an excellently represented parchment book, that he displayed to perfection the art of colouring in oils. Vasari was clearly aware that biographical information, gossip indeed, was seductive; as to technique, it was enough to say, without going into great detail, that Piero had lots of it. The excellence of his colouring in oils could be remarked without further analysis. So with Leonardo's 'great and marvellous art' in the representation of the rotundity of the dates on a palm-tree, and the wonderful texture of the tablecloth in the *Last Supper*. If virtually the whole art of painting was perfect representation there was no need to strain for a vocabulary appropriate to anything other than skilled and diligent workmanship.

Everything was bound to get harder when painting found other tasks than mimesis. Picasso said that painters no longer live in a tradition but need to 're-create an entire language . . . from A to Z'. This development could, he admitted, be called a liberation, but 'what the artist gains in liberty he loses in the way of order.' The writer about painting is in an even greater difficulty than the painter himself, for he must learn the elements of that new language yet seek for himself a matching other, which has to consist of words. The problem of translation now looks insuperable.

Despite the variously interpreted opinion of Horace, *ut pictura poesis*, the match between painting and what can be said about it has grown more and more strained. Proust's Bergotte contemplates the 'little patch of yellow wall' in Vermeer's *View of Delft*: 'that's how I ought to have written,' he says, and, after weighing his own works against that patch, falls over and dies. Only a life of perfect writing, made of language 'precious in itself', could equal the beauty of that passage of paint; and yet to equal it, even by such hopelessly arduous effort, would still not be to match it or describe it.

Here is a final surrender of words to paint. There is a long tradition of poems about paintings, but there is really never a contest: the poem is always talking more or less vainly to an interlocutor using sign language – at best offering an oblique and unsolicited tribute. There is evidence of this persistent dialogue of the deaf in John Hollander's excellent book, *The Gazer's Spirit: Poems Speaking to Silent Works of Art*, a learned study of the tradition of *ekphrasis* – poetic description of paintings – illustrated by a 'gallery' of paintings and their tributary poems: Aretino on Titian, Rossetti on Leonardo, Baudelaire on Callot, Donald Hall on Munch, Hollander on Monet and dozens more, including Richard Wilbur's exquisitely meditative imitation of a Baroque wall fountain, a poem that sounds more like the work of art it imitates than any other I know.

The painting of Howard Hodgkin is a first-rate example of the vivid muteness that resists critical attempts at conversation. Vasari himself, after praising this man's power as a colourist, would have had trouble explaining the relationship of the paintings to their titles, which often suggest scenes, persons and ideas that were perhaps the points of origin of the works but have more or less entirely disappeared from the finished product. There are, for example, a number of portraits of husbands and wives, in which not even the couple who commissioned the works could be sure which figure was which. Sometimes the human shapes have virtually disappeared under the paint or, as in *Mr and Mrs Stephen Buckley*, are converted into geometric forms; which doesn't prevent the artist from saying: 'the subject of the picture is simply a family group sitting round a fire in the evening.' Other titles seem to promise that the picture will tell a story: *When Did We Go to Morocco?* Or *It Can't Be True* or *Haven't We Met?*

Of *It Can't Be True* Michael Auping says: 'It is echo-like in its composition. It is composed of a series of tilting frames jostling each other for position within the whole. The eye is teased back to a bright yellow frame in the centre of the painting and stopped short by a series of abrupt strokes that violate its containment.' So far, fair enough; after all a critic needs to say *something* about this dazzling production, and the words seem not entirely unrelated to the painting. But Auping continues: 'What "can't be true" is not altogether clear, unless it is Hodgkin's hesitant acknowledgment that the voyeuristic tendencies that inspired an early work like *Memoirs*' – a small gouache done when Hodgkin was 17 – 'have for a number of years been turning increasingly inward.' A despairing lunge at a biographical interpretation; a likely story. If you can believe that you can believe anything, which could be said of many desperate interpretations, many words addressed to the questioner who sits so sly, so mute.

The gap between title and work is often remarked on by the

contributors to *Howard Hodgkin: Paintings*. This gorgeously illustrated volume is really the catalogue of an exhibition organised at Fort Worth, Texas by Maria Price, whose more than useful catalogue raisonné offers, among much else, information as to how ostensible subjects are eroded, sometimes after much repainting. When the picture has been exhibited in more than one state it can be seen that its originating subject was at first more readily discernible. In *Large Staff Room*, for instance, it was once possible to detect human presences at the table, possible even to relate the image to a particular staff room: but after reworking about 70 per cent of the picture surface was reduced to 'a vast expanse of cadmium red', leaving only a small image of a knee under the table. One is inevitably reminded of Balzac's story 'Le Chef-d'oeuvre inconnu', in which a perfectly-executed foot alone survived the mad, obsessive onslaught of paint. Art critics contrive to say fairly solemn things about the much reduced *Large Staff Room* (the expanse of colour suggests 'a kind of mind space in which the memory – a knee under a table – exists') and if some prefer to call it a leg-pull or visual pun, they don't mean by that to disparage the work – leg-pulls have an honoured place in modern art, and to suspect one may be intellectually preferable to a flight into allegory. Like Picasso, Hodgkin has his own technical alphabet and can do exactly as he pleases, as his brush pleases, according to his humour; it is, after all, the biggest of leg-pulls to kid us into believing that words can be found to explain the beauty of these patches of paint.

What can be done instead, and what convention permits, is to perform certain art-historical rituals: to divide the artist's career into phases (voyeuristic, post-voyeuristic etc), and to identify the painters who influenced him, a long list: Seurat, Pasmore, Bonnard, Morandi, Bacon, Matisse, Vuillard, Degas, Stella, Johns, Pollock and so on. All this Auping does. On other topics, such as Andrew Graham-Dixon's proposition that 'there are a lot of pictures about fucking,' he judges it best to be non-committal; yes and no, certainly many of these works are about bodily pleasures, he says, but they 'may or may not refer to intercourse' ('refer' is anyway too strong a word). Graham-Dixon quotes Hodgkin as saying that he is a representational painter, but at once adds firmly: 'he is nothing of the kind.' It's an issue that comes up again and again, but Graham-Dixon seems to get it about right when he remarks that 'the passage of forms across these bright surfaces is of no more consequence than the passage of clouds across the sky at sunset. They are as insignificant as weather.' Yet among the strange gaudy forms, some distinct, some vague as clouds or weather, it cannot be denied that a good few bear some resemblance to the male organ.

To write as Auping does is perfectly reasonable in view of the sheer difficulty of finding anything really susceptible to being written about. As Susan Sontag remarks, 'the thoughtful – as distinct from the inarticulate – may have good reason to be wary, anxious, at a loss (for words).' She endorses Valéry's obiter dicta, 'One must always apologise for talking about painting,' and: 'A work of art, if it does not leave us mute, is of little value.' 'Of course,' she adds, 'we don't *stay* mute.' The implication is that the necessity of saying something about art reduces its value. This is one of those aporiae Paul de Man likened to getting trapped in a revolving door, but Sontag, as it were noticing the normal exit usually available at the side, emerges to say several valuable things. For example: 'having renounced painting's other primary resource, drawing, Hodgkin has fielded the most inventive, sensuously affecting colour repertory of any contemporary painter – as if, in taking up the ancient quarrel between *disegno* and *colore*, he had wanted to give *colore* its most sumptuous exclusive victory.' She dwells convincingly on Hodgkin's hesitations between revelation and concealment, and comes close to explaining the obviously intense pleasure she gets from these works; which is an achievement.

Yet the best writing in this book is to be found in a correspondence between the painter and John Elderfield of the Museum of Modern Art, New York. Hodgkin complains of 'the tyranny of words in England' but submits with elegance to this epistolary conversation. Elderfield, an expatriate Englishman, so still under that tyranny, puzzles over the way his correspondent's works 'attach to the external world', finding that they both afford and deny narrative readings. Hodgkin affirms, as he always does, that the subject-matter of his paintings 'is of primary importance – I couldn't make a picture that was not "about" anything' – and is irritated when people describe his pictures as 'beautiful', so suggesting that because 'they look "pretty" they cannot have any content'. He thinks that in England richness of colour is thought to denote 'a fundamental lack of seriousness'. In these letters he says many revealing things about concealment and other matters, repeating in his own terms the lament of Picasso quoted earlier: 'Never under-estimate the heroism demanded of the artist ... at a time when no one tells the artist what to do, except himself.' He writes about Vuillard and, with the greatest admiration, about Degas: 'a classical artist, something I have always wanted to be ... As for being tied to the past, what other home have we got?' Together with his remarks on his own techniques, his preference for wood over canvas, for example, he makes one feel, with deep ingratitude to the critics, that if painting has to be talked about, and it does, the painters may do it best. Yet they may need crit-ics to make them talk, as David Sylvester, the great master of the inter-viewing discipline, has induced Hodgkin to talk in the past.

When all is said the paintings do the real talking in their own tongue, but we still need to have our attention directed to them, our possible blindnesses cleaned, our sensitivity to their weathers refined. Reproductions are one aid: Hodgkin is understandably sceptical about their value and nobody will take them as adequate substitutes for the real thing, but I find that on the images so abundantly presented in these books one dwells with increasing pleasure. The actual paintings now provide an extra delight, an enhanced shock of recognition, as if what had been seen through a glass, darkly, though not too darkly, were now seen face to face. The real thing can now thrive without fur-ther articulate description.

Having been made ready for the experience, no one will care that Hodgkin's Venice is hardly a place, that *Waking Up in Naples* may have something to do with waking up but not, as far as one can see, particu-larly in Naples, that *Egyptian Night* contains an identifiable pyramid yet looks like a sumptuous carpet, or that *Sunset* is a sunset belong-ing to Hodgkin's private meteorology – though if told it's a sunset you might just recognise it as such, which is more than you can do when searching for Patrick Caulfield in *Patrick Caulfield in Italy*. But if you don't *have* to say anything about these paintings your pleasure will be the greater, and so, if we are to believe Valéry, will the paintings.

25 January 1996

UNDER THE LOINCLOTH

....

The Sexuality of Christ in Renaissance Art and in Modern Oblivion
by Leo Steinberg

In 1983 the magazine *October* devoted an entire issue to a remarkable study of genital display in some – indeed in a great many – Renaissance depictions of Christ. Publication in book form followed, and among the reviewers there were some who were embarrassed or shocked and some who were sceptical. The author, Leo Steinberg, kept watch on them and has now greatly expanded his original report. He is agreeably discursive and writes informatively and exuberantly about all manner of marginal topics, but his revision has two main purposes: to multiply the visual evidence – seeking 'the cumulative impact of number' – and to rebut his critics. It seems to him that English reviewers in particular were inclined to be contemptuous or dismissive, so some venerable commentators – the late Lawrence Gowing, Michael Levey, Richard Wollheim, Marina Warner and, singled out for a special treatment, Charles Hope – are, in this new edition, keenly reprehended.

It should be said that Steinberg, a lively and resourceful writer, could not with any justice be charged with irreverence or lubricity. That he greatly enjoyed researching, writing and defending his thesis is clear enough, and fair enough; his satisfaction is of a legitimate, scholarly kind. He has achieved something original, and offered unignorable explanations of a body of rather mystifying evidence that has been almost entirely repressed for centuries (hence the 'modern oblivion' of the title). His undertaking is so extraordinary, so adventurous, that one would expect him, at least now and again, to be wrong, and he must have foreseen opposition from professionally dissident art historians. He got it, and will doubtless expect it again on publication of this new version, though it must be a comfort that for a decade or more his arguments have also attracted much intelligent support. For my part I think he's right about the detail of the paintings, and his explanations of why they are as they are – why they attend so insistently to the genitalia of Jesus in infancy, during crucifixion and in death – are very persuasive.

This revised edition is clumsy to use, for it simply tacks two hundred pages onto the original, occasionally qualifying as well as augmenting it, and replying to its critics. (Steinberg says he was tempted to call it *Double or Nothing*.) It now contains many more illustrations, but of course doesn't repeat the ones that were already present in the first edition, although renewed discussions and refutations often make it necessary to refer to them. But the argument is so absorbing that these minor, probably inevitable irritations are easily forgotten.

There is an immemorial taboo on the topic of the sexuality of Jesus, but it has sometimes been defied. Steinberg demonstrates that from about 1260, painters (perhaps affected by the success of the Franciscans, who had a slogan *nudus nudum Christum sequi*) departed from the hieratically clothed, unsexed Byzantine tradition, and undressed the infant Jesus. Thereafter, for two centuries, they pictured him naked but without genital emphasis. But by the end of the 15th century they not only painted his penis but represented it as 'pointed to, garlanded, celebrated', stared at and venerated. In the following century it was touched and manipulated, and by the 1530s it was sometimes being shown in a state of infantile erection. This theme of erection, though under cover of a loincloth or other garment, was repeated in pictures of the Crucifixion and the dead Christ. There are some extremely fantasticated loincloths in paintings of the Man of Sorrows, as in two 'deeply shocking' pictures by Ludwig Krug (c. 1520) and Maerten van Heemskerck (1532), here reproduced. Some renderings of Crucifixion and Pietà are, I think one must agree, clearly intended to suggest large erections, which may have been intended to symbolise Resurrection.

The purpose of these displays, it is conjectured, was to celebrate the Incarnation – though Steinberg prefers the obsolete term 'humanation'. God became an *entire* man, and therefore a sexual being; his sex, like his dependence on his mother's breast, is a pledge of that full humanity the doctrine asserts. And it will not do to offer naturalistic explanations of his infant behaviour; Jesus is entirely unlike other painted babies in his behaviour and the behaviour he elicits from others. There is no need to stress the humanity of ordinary babies or marvel at it.

In a woodcut by Hans Baldung Grien, dated 1511, St Anne is fondling the infant's genitalia, while he chucks the Virgin under the chin, an amorous gesture with a tradition going back to the Song of Songs (and here signifying their mystical marriage), while Joseph looks understandingly on. Steinberg (who throws in a catalogue of what he calls 'chin-chucks' stretching from antiquity to Proust and Nabokov) will have nothing to do with the notion that these images simply reflect the sort of thing that went on in the average household. They are first an affirmation of full humanity, with the reservation that the sexuality of Jesus was not like ours but like that of Adam and Eve before the Fall. He was 'like us in all things except sin'. His genitalia could therefore only with much impropriety be called pudenda. These pictures dwell on that paradox or oxymoron, the sinless generative organ.

Despite much bowdlerising by overpainting there remain many hundreds of images which support this interpretation, some as striking as the Hans Baldung Grien. The practice of celebrating humanation eventually came to a halt as the taboo began to assert itself, in painting as elsewhere. But for a long stretch of time the sexual member had been an image of God's condescension, an image not of virility but of a voluntary divine abasement to humanity.

The member yielded not seed but, at the Circumcision, blood. The Circumcision was described by St Thomas Aquinas as 'a remedy for original sin, which is transmitted through the act of generation'. God further condescended when consenting to enact this sacramental admission of guilt, though of course free of it himself. Steinberg again and again illustrates the conjunction, or, as he calls it, the 'hyphen', formed by the blood from the spear wound in Christ's side and the blood of the Circumcision. The blood from the greater wound, it would seem by established convention, flows directly into the groin of the dead Christ. One bleeding is the type of the other: 'those first oozings guarantee Christ's humanity' and may be thought to foretell or even inaugurate the redemptive Passion.

Steinberg regards the insistent display of the penis, its potentially generative function and its wounds, as a silent counter to heresy, notably to Arianism but also to various forms of Docetism, which denied the humanity of Christ. In the first edition he was glad to find confirmation of this motive in Circumcision sermons of the relevant period, but in the new version he tends to disparage or even reject this extra-pictorial documentary support, perhaps because he wants to cast doubt on what he regards as the deplorable art-historical practice of depending more on documents than on pictures. He has to answer the objections of Charles Hope (*LRB*, 15 November 1984), whom he characterises as a historian of that persuasion, and who is indeed sceptical of Steinberg's thesis precisely because it lacks documentary support. Hope believes that one needs to find out what Renaissance art meant to people at the time 'by reading what they said about paintings and about their faith'. Steinberg's rejoinder is that he would prefer to look at the paintings, and ask why the artists, of all people, felt it necessary to introduce these theological innovations and deal with the resulting representational problems.

In the course of a lengthy response to Hope's criticisms, Steinberg considers his rival interpretation of the Adoration theme: the Magi, it is claimed, are primarily concerned not with Christ but with the Virgin; Renaissance babies are usually nude; the mage may seem to be staring reverently at the Child's genital area but is probably just checking its sex; the infant is at this moment only an adjunct to the Madonna; and so on. Hope particularly objected to the claim that in such pictures as Ghirlandaio's *Adoration of the Magi* in the Uffizi the mage is humbly contemplating the infant penis, unveiled by the Virgin, as proof of total humanation – as evidence that Jesus was born 'complete in all the parts of a man'. Yet similarly intent postures and gazes occur not only in a whole batch of Adorations, but in other Quattrocento pictures, here reproduced, of the Holy Child with reverent donors. And it certainly looks as if the presence of the infant member was considered a particular miracle.

Since conversion or surrender tends to be rare in such disputes, Dr Hope will probably have his answers. But in certain matters of detail, such as the argument concerning what St Anne is really doing in the Hans Baldung Grien woodcut, I think Steinberg is the victor. In a sense this is the argument he needs to win, if his thesis is to survive, so it is well that he wins it. We have the paintings, he says, and if we consent to look at them rather than adopt the unimaginative, unseeing habits of art historians unhappy without the support of the written word, we shall better understand the motives of the artists.

I suppose this contest with Hope was crucial because it really does turn on what opponents might judge the most vulnerable point of the

book – that the author deduces entirely from wordless pictorial imagery a complex religious mystery on which many thousands of words
were written, though never, it seems, with reference to the unarticu-
lated theology of painters. But the deduction turns out, I think, to be
plausible as well as interesting.

The display of the sex of Jesus (*ostentatio genitalium*, Steinberg
names it, on the analogy of *ostentatio vulnerum*, the showing forth
of the wounds) is emphasised in all manner of ways. The *ostentatio* is
sometimes made by the Virgin, holding aside the child's covering,
sometimes by the infant himself, pictured with a hand on his penis, as
in Veronese's *Holy Family with St Barbara and the Infant St John* in the
Uffizi, and in at least twenty other paintings of the Cinquecento – 'a
gesture unknown to devotional art before or since', and later deplored.

Steinberg has a long and brilliant excursus on bowdlerism, the
practice of eliminating or toning down such gestures for the sake of
decency (and for other reasons no less reprehensible), citing Ruskin's
destruction of Turner's erotic drawings as akin to the overpainting of
the loins of naked Christs, or to the painting of a cache-sexe on Man-
tegna's *Madonna and Child with the Magdalen and St John the Baptist*,
still on view in the National Gallery with the genitals cursorily covered,
despite the cleaning of 1957.

A curious, recherché instance of bowdlerisation was commu-
nicated to Steinberg by William Ravenhill, a geography professor of
Exeter University, who read the first edition. In the course of his own
unrelated researches, Ravenhill had examined by beta radiography a
watermark in an atlas by Christopher Saxton, printed about 1590. This
watermark apparently shows the risen Christ bearing a cross above an
eminently visible erect penis, emblem, doubtless, of Resurrection; but
even quite recent reproductions of it contrive to erase or conceal that
member. Another English instance is an alabaster sculpture of the 14th
century which had been buried under the chancel floor of a church
at Long Melford in Suffolk, where it lay until it was discovered in the
1700s. A reason for its concealment may be that it shows the infant's
phallus protruding from a knee-length robe – it was hidden, that is, out
of modesty rather than to thwart 16th or 17th-century iconoclasts. It is
impossible to conjecture how many objects of this sort were destroyed
or defaced, though the number is probably very large; but abundant

evidence has nevertheless survived and is still being investigated, as Steinberg's second edition testifies.

He reproaches himself with having paid too little attention to what he calls the 'reactive modesty factor', a force which he thinks began, around 1500, to combat the representation of the genitals, whether intended as evidence of humanation or for any other reason. The idea may have been that the pudency of Virgin and Child had been insulted and needed defence. This new trend eventually ended the fashion, if one may so call it, of the *ostentatio genitalium*. Perhaps it just went out of date; as Yeats observed, 'the painter's brush consumes his dreams.' But it may, for a long time, have seemed less a painterly fashion than a devotional necessity.

When the Apostle declares that God 'sent his own Son in the likeness of sinful flesh' (Romans 8:3), and when Augustine speaks of the Word assuming 'the flesh of our sin but without sin', we do not, we need not, suppose that they had the penis in mind. But Renaissance image-makers? Those among them who were rethinking the God-man's physique had no choice but to mind it . . . The question before them was how to visualise sinlessness in the '*likeness* of sinful flesh'; and this is no writer's problem.

No doubt more and more recondite and relevant evidence will be accumulated on either side of the question. In an interesting disquisition on what he calls 'remote symbolism' – echoing the advice of Dionysius the Areopagite that symbols should not cleave too close to their referents – Steinberg cites the 13th-century sage Durandus, who said that one can represent the Church as a harlot 'because she is called out of many nations, and because she closeth not her bosom against any that return to her'. He can find no other instance of this symbolism, and supposes that Durandus must himself have invented this illustration of this thesis of the Pseudo-Dionysius, and 'judged it too good to drop'. Perhaps so, and there may be no earlier instances, but there is a familiar example of the church-as-harlot in Donne's sonnet 'Show me, dear Christ, thy spouse', which ends

> Betray, kind husband, thy spouse to our sights,
> And let mine amorous soul court thy mild dove,
> Who is most true and pleasing to thee, then
> When she is embraced and open to most men.

It may be worth noting that Counter-Reformation Catholicism, part of the tradition in which Donne was writing, believed not only in 'dissimilar symbols', as is evident from emblem books, but in the efficacy of a kind of sexual imagery which, though different from that which Steinberg attributes to Renaissance painters, is sometimes amazingly explicit; a famous instance is the orgasmic St Teresa of Bernini. In another religious sonnet Donne asks God to make him chaste by ravishing him.

Perhaps sex cannot be perpetually kept out of religion, if only by way of analogy; as in the old saw about nature, you may try to get rid of it but it always recurs. There is a modern manifestation of this recurrence in Steinberg's dispute with feminist theologians who found sexist reasons to quarrel with his original book.

What Steinberg does admirably is to relate technical practice in the painting of the period – the arrangement of figures, body parts, hands, drapery – to a theological and devotional position. He is very thorough; yet there is probably more work to be done. For example, some critics allege that typical patrons wouldn't be interested in enigmatic pictorial allusions to humanation. Is there anything to be said on that topic? How do we know, how can we be sure they wouldn't? Steinberg could argue that while they might not experience, as the artists did, a pressing need to give visual expression to that doctrine, there seems to be little evidence that donors disliked or complained about the representations, which could have been explained to them as in perfect conformity with a doctrine to which the pious should assent. As for us, we can dissent all we like, but the religious art of the Renaissance will never look quite the same again.

3 April 1997

NO TRICKS

....

Call If You Need Me: The Uncollected Fiction and Prose by Raymond Carver

Raymond Carver was much taken with the idea that every writer creates a distinctive world: 'Every great or even every very good writer makes the world over according to his own specifications ... It is his world and no other.' The idea is hardly original but one sees why he liked it. Carver's world is something like a room in which the television is always on, unless you happen to be subjecting the neighbours to home movies. The ashtrays are overflowing. There may be an alcoholic, active or reformed, lying on the living-room sofa. Is he thinking about the pint of whiskey he has hidden under the cushions; or has he just got home from an exhausting AA meeting? He has a job he does not like and is not getting on with his wife, who may well be at work in a fast-food restaurant. If so he might just go along there and watch the male customers eyeing her shape. Living somewhere in the Pacific Northwest, he is probably thinking of moving house, perhaps just across the state line to Portland, a city often mentioned but never visited, or, more ambitiously and yet more hopelessly, to Alaska. However, he never does seem to move, and if he ever did find himself in Alaska he would still spend much time smoking on the sofa in front of the television. If he has children he cannot think them unmixed blessings. He knows he needs to love them but cannot bring himself to believe the pleasures of parenthood outweigh its pains.

He and his wife only rarely have neighbourly relations with other people; to be asked out to dinner is to face a small social crisis, in which all parties behave with a touchingly awkward, repetitive, unpractised courtesy. The kinds of thing they say on such occasions, as on others, are recorded with bleak and dispassionate accuracy. Out in the inhospitable great world, not far away from the street where they live, are many pitilessly illuminated motels and gas stations, as aptly pictured on the jacket of this book, on which the photograph powerfully, inevitably, alludes to Edward Hopper. Whatever is going to happen around here is likely to be depressing: possibly just a marital argument, more seriously a fire in a neighbour's house or the death of a child. Such happiness as can be expected must be looked for on fishing trips, and even fishing trips are likely to be ruined by the intrusion of a floating corpse. Yet some stories turn out to be funny in unexpected ways.

This latest Carver is a miscellany containing five posthumously discovered stories, five early stories not previously collected, and some essays and reviews. Some of the essays are autobiographical. His father, also called Raymond, worked in sawmills, moved a lot and drank a lot. Carver married young and also moved and drank a lot. He had an ambition to be a writer but his life was so disrupted by the need to make a little money and by the incessant demands of his children that he could never get far with a novel. He had to be content with short stories and poems, and in time came to prefer brevity. 'Get in, get out. Don't linger. Go on.' 'No tricks' is another piece of advice, picked up at a creative writing course, and studiously followed. The prohibition applies to terminal narrative twists, though sometimes he allows himself one, as in the story 'Vandals', in this last book. But it extends to more modern 'formal innovations' as well. They are not needed and they destroy the story's contact with the real: 'It's possible, in a poem or a short story, to write about commonplace things and objects using commonplace but precise language, and to endow those things – a chair, a window curtain, a fork, a stone, a woman's earring – with immense, even startling power. It is possible to write a line of seemingly innocuous dialogue and have it send a chill along the reader's spine.'

Carver came to be exceptionally good at short stories not only because he worked hard at them, but also because he listened to advice, especially from John Gardner but also, more remotely, from Hemingway, Chekhov and V.S. Pritchett. One of the things he learned was the need for arduous revision, draft after draft. Another lesson was that the writer needs to trust the tale. Lawrence notoriously advised the reader to do so, but the writer has to trust it because it will collaborate in the composition of the work if the work is any good. Carver is impressed by Flannery O'Connor's remark that she started work without knowing where the story was going: when she began 'Good Country People' she 'didn't know there was going to be a PhD with a wooden leg in it'. Carver might have a single phrase in his head as a donnée: 'He was running the vacuum cleaner when the telephone rang.' Given time, more sentences attached themselves to this one and finally there is a story called 'Put Yourself in My Shoes', which turns out to be one of the funny ones, though a little sad also.

Here are some of Carver's openings:

> I had a job and Patti didn't.
> Earl Ober was between jobs as a salesman.
> My marriage had just fallen apart. I couldn't find a job. I had another girl. But she wasn't in town.
> I was out of work. But any day I expected to hear from up north. I lay on the sofa and listened to the rain.
> It was the middle of August and Myers was between lives.

The last of these belongs to a story in the present collection, called 'Kindling'. Myers is a drunk, fresh from 28 days in a drying-out facility, during which time his wife has run away with another drunk. He takes a room he has spotted in a small ad and finds himself shyly sharing a little house with a nervous, civil couple, poor but neither kind nor unkind, neither generous nor mean. Myers keeps himself to himself. When not working the man of the house watches television, the wife wants to write, and tries to write about Myers. One day a load of wood is delivered. Chopping it up is a big job and the husband has no time to do it. Myers, without payment, without being asked, cuts the wood, though, as requested, he does nothing about the kindling. He finishes the job and writes some words about the experience in his notebook: 'I have sawdust in my shirtsleeves tonight. It's a sweet smell.' Then he ends his stay.

You are entitled to think the woodcutting did him good, even that he was about to start on a new life, but nothing is said directly about the therapeutic effects of hard labour, or of the causes of Myers's spontaneous generosity: these are precisely the sorts of thing Carver by his own hard labour learned not to say. One of his best stories is 'A Small, Good Thing', in the collection *Cathedral*. A woman orders a birthday cake at the local bakery, but her schoolboy son is knocked down by a car on his birthday and dies in hospital. The baker, wanting payment for the uncollected cake, nags her with phone calls. The woman and her husband confront the baker. There are insults, then a humane reconciliation, and they sit and eat some of the baker's richest bread. It would be useless to try in words other than the author's to give an idea of the depth and humanity of this story, a late one done when Carver was allowing himself to write at greater length, as, in the later years, he decided he ought, citing as a model Chekhov's 'Ward 6'. The title story of the last volume, 'Cathedral', he regarded as a turning point in his career, but the career suddenly came to an end. Perhaps, had he lived, he would have moved on to the novella. One can feel sure that V.S. Pritchett would have admired both these stories, as Carver would have admired Pritchett's favourite among his own, 'When My Girl Comes Home'.

For various reasons the English short story is now a predominantly American form. There are hardly any London outlets, while New York still has a few, which sometimes accept British stories, as with Sylvia Townsend Warner and also, of course, Pritchett. There are many annual prizes for stories. Moreover the form fits better than the novel into the pattern of the creative writing courses that are taught all over the country and often by good writers. Carver says it was a struggle to get his first collection, *Will You Please Be Quiet, Please?*, published in 1976. It took 13 years to write ('the long delay was due in part to a young marriage, the exigencies of child-rearing and blue-collar jobs, a little education on the fly') and the publisher took some persuading, but the prospects for American writers were even then better than for their British contemporaries. Later Carver could claim in an optimistic essay that there has never been a better time than the present for his aspiring compatriots and contemporaries; this is not to say it's easy, but it's far less difficult. 'Short stories are flourishing,' he says, and the readership is increasing.

Naturally no writer on this side of the ocean sounds very like Carver, deep in what is now a naturalised tradition and in a world of his own. One of his stories reminded me faintly of an excellent one by William Trevor called 'Broken Homes', in which a group of adolescents, from broken homes, sent in as an experiment in 'community relations', cheerfully defile and desecrate the home of an 87-year-old woman. The story is the more horrible in that the teacher who sent these 'good kids' to the old woman's house is impervious to complaint; the old woman ends by blaming herself for her failure to communicate with the kids, who covered her kitchen and carpets with paint, released her budgerigars, and had sex in her bed. Carver has stories about cruelty and old age, but he is, perhaps curiously, less interested in emphasising the lurid nastiness of the tormentors. Perhaps a sort of natural piety that shows through in his most serious pieces would have prevented him from imposing such garish humiliations.

Or they may be what his American studies in the craft have taught him to leave out. There seems to be a rule against seeming to be excited by a situation. A good instance is the story 'Vitamins' in *Cathedral*. The narrator has 'a nothing job' and his wife sells vitamins from door to door. He goes on a date with one of his wife's colleagues and takes her to a black bar, where they are menaced by a Vietnam veteran who carries an ear in a cigarette case: 'I took it off one of them gooks. He couldn't hear nothing with it no more. I wanted me a keepsake.' The vet, drunk but cold, coarse and threatening, propositions the girl. The proprietor arrives to prevent bloodshed and they leave the bar, the little affair already over. The girl says she could have done with the money and resolves to go to Portland; the man goes home and disturbs his sleeping wife, noisily looking for aspirin. There is no actual violence in this desperate tale, though the language of the veteran suggests a whole continent of terror, as the conduct of the narrator and the girl sketches a society in despair.

Indeed there is not much violence in any of the stories; instead Carver is very good on anomie and also on certain kinds of pain. 'Will You Please Be Quiet, Please?', the story that gave its title to the collection published in 1976, concerns a rather proper young schoolteacher's discovery that years before his wife had had a drunken one-night stand with a friend. This revelation, though the fact was long suspected, causes severe pain, carefully and reticently explored. Such lesser discomforts as having to be on friendly terms with a wife's ex-lover are equally well managed. Commentators often find themselves talking about Carver's 'clarity' and that is fair enough, but there is always something the reader has to say, and will say confusedly, because of the indefinitely large context it is suggested he or she must supply.

Carver died of lung cancer at 50. Much that happened in this rather short life was unfavourable to the business of writing. First he needed to get an education, but making a living in nothing jobs hindered that. Then there were the children: 'They were born before I was 20, and from beginning to end of our habitation under the same roof – some

19 years in all – there wasn't any area of my life where their heavy and often baleful influence didn't reach.' In an autobiographical sketch he illustrates this misery by an anecdote. In the mid-1960s he is in a laundromat with five or six loads of washing, mostly kids'. He has to wait a long time for a free dryer, is anxious because he is late and has to pick up the kids. His misery is unforgettable; he is almost in tears at being in 'this position of unrelieved responsibility and permanent distraction'. He has a job at a service station, or as a janitor or a delivery man, with the prospect of many more years in this unwriterly posture, so unlike the situation of the well-known writers he admires. And after these destructive years of parenting there was an alcoholic hiatus, ten years of silence, before he joined his present editor, Tess Gallagher, and started writing again.

Carver was sure you could learn to write well, to find out by constant revision what the story you were working on really amounted to, and he more than once records his debts to John Gardner as a teacher, and to Gordon Lish as his editor. Partly by their efforts he became a very famous writer, at any rate in America.

When *Will You Please Be Quiet, Please?* appeared in 1976, Gordon Lish sent me six copies, for he was sure I would want to spread the good news. I duly distributed them among my literary colleagues and waited for a response, but there was none. Carver's British reception has taken a little time. The Robert Altman movie *Short Cuts*, of 1993, based on nine stories and a poem of Carver's, helped to get him wider notice. Among the stories incorporated in the film were 'A Small, Good Thing' – the one about the bereaved couple and the exigent baker – and 'So Much Water So Close to Home', about the girl's body discovered, but not reported, on a fishing trip. These are stories of high quality, as are many of the others. Now one can read almost everything in volumes published by the Harvill Press.

There is quite a lot of verse, most easily found in *Fires* (1984). Americans seem to assume more readily than we do a close affinity between poems and stories. The fact that I am not impressed by the poems may be related to that difference. A collection of prose pieces of varying weight, to be found mostly in *Fires* and in the present volume, are written with the usual care, though not all of them – brief reviews, prefaces to anthologies and the like – seem worth preserving for their own sakes. From this censure the autobiographical material must be exempted. As for the minor pieces, they have been collected as a sort of tribute to the great man, the kind of thing it is seemly to do on the understanding that it is not really that these bits and pieces matter in themselves: what matters is the fact that they were written by the hand that wrote the stories.

19 October 2000

THE SMALL NOISE UPSTAIRS

....

The Body Artist by Don DeLillo

The publishers describe this book as 'lean', which may be taken to refer to its style, though it also serves as a euphemism for 'very short, especially considering the price'. Its immediate predecessor was *Underworld*, about seven times as long (or as fat). That book, as nearly everybody must know, begins with a chapter about a famous baseball game and a boy who retrieves the ball with which the decisive home run was scored. *The Body Artist* is about as long as the *Underworld* ball-game.

DeLillo is a serious and various writer, and we have to take these extremes as deliberately chosen to reflect different aspects of his talent. *Underworld* belongs to the category of the Great American Novel, to which all the really big writers aspire. Structurally it has some resemblance to Pynchon's *Gravity's Rainbow*, and that thought prompts the reflection that Pynchon also wrote an exceptionally fine novella, *The Crying of Lot 49*. If there are two traditions of great American writing it is proper to show up in both of them. One of them may be said to originate with Hawthorne, the other with Melville, one lean and self-absorbed, the other heavy, expansive, determined to contain a world. On the whole the heavyweights have prevailed in recent years; one no longer hears much talk of, say, Glenway Westcott, a lean writer of whom Gertrude Stein remarked that 'he has a certain syrup but it does not pour.' This memory came to me as I read *The Body Artist*. But here the syrup does, slowly, pour.

Underworld aims to put together a complicated image of the desperate condition of the United States in the second half of the 20th century, with some allusion to the rest of the world, since it is still impossible to say everything relevant about life, civilisation and the decaying future by talking about America alone. It has a very basic narrative idea; tracing the history of a baseball is a grander version of the exercise one occasionally had to perform at school: the adventures of a sixpence, or the like. However, DeLillo's idea can encompass a vast array of narrative themes and characters, and I have to admit I don't have a firm grasp on every one of them. Garbage is a principal and much reiterated theme. It is taking over the world: 'What we excrete comes back to consume us.' Baseball has here, as so often, a pastoral simplicity in contrast with pretty well everything else that affects our lives. The seed of the book was probably the fact that the day of the great pennant-deciding ball-game was the day America first heard that the Soviet Union had tested an atom bomb. What is fallout but more cosmic garbage? It signals the end of any hope that even baseball can remain pure and simple. But in fact the game is already contaminated by the presence of some of the more eminent spectators, such as J. Edgar Hoover and his cronies.

After that critical moment it seems that modern history is all downhill. The 1960s are a decade that has 'paranoid breath'. Evil has formed itself into a system; so thoroughly is the world 'systemed under' that we don't even perceive the connection between orange juice and Agent Orange, which the system 'connects . . . at levels outside' our comprehension. Even the quite recent pre-system past is food for nostalgia. A tune can take you 'back to your bedside radio and the smells in your kitchen and the way the linoleum used to ripple near the icebox'. We can even feel nostalgic for the Cold War. 'Many things that were anchored to the balance of power and the balance of terror seem to be undone, unstuck. Things have no limits now. Money has no limits. I don't understand money any more. Money is undone. Violence is undone, violence is easier now, it's uprooted, out of control, it has no measure any more, it has no level of values.'

Underworld is a heroic work, colossal in its assurance, in its temporal and spatial range. Its narrative is propelled by extraordinary imaginative energy, by spectacular feats of dialogue and prose of incessant animation. DeLillo, not for the first time, is writing a great book. Gentler readers may well prefer some of the earlier novels, especially *White Noise*, produced in 1984, back in the good old Cold War epoch; set in a small New England college town, it is dominated by an episode of industrial pollution, a lethal toxic cloud, but it preserves a memory of neighbourly happiness, and is nearly always amusing, sometimes even funny, as well as somehow benign. (In the new book 'somehow' is described as the weakest word in the language, a dishonour Joyce reserved for 'yes'.)

It must have seemed a challenge worthy of a virtuoso to abandon the complex and the extensive, and produce instead an intensive, crystalline novella. The animation of the language, the fervour of the scrutiny applied to a world now grown small, need not be less. All the power of the big-book writer must now be applied to a brief scenario and a setting hardly more ambitious than Jane Austen's.

The 'white noise' of the earlier title is death, and DeLillo always has some of the big subjects in mind. In *The Body Artist* they are, as the jacket copy lets us know at once, space, love and death. A man and a woman are in the kitchen of a large rented house in New England, having breakfast and reading the Sunday papers. He has run out of cigarettes and is looking for his car keys. Instead of coming back with the cigarettes he drives to New York and shoots himself in the apartment of a former wife.

The woman stays in the rented house. A 'body artist', she keeps in trim by day, but at night watches on the Internet the videoed traffic on the outskirts of an obscure Finnish town. Eventually she discovers that the house has a squatter. This strange man speaks a weird dialect of English, having, for instance, no control over tenses, and he is evidently below par in many other ways, but she forms an adhesive relationship with him. He had overheard the husband, a film director, talking into a tape-recorder, and discovered that he could mimic the speech of the dead man. The woman accepts the stranger as a member of the household, and tries to capture on the tape-recorder her attempts to converse with him. But the conversation fails; it lacks the unspoken contribution of presence, on which personal communication depends. These participants cannot share a sense of inhabiting a particular time between past and future. The man develops a kind of chant in which he seems to identify himself with a moment that is neither the present nor the past nor the future. 'He is another structure, another culture, where time is something like itself, sheer and bare, empty of shelter.' Sometimes he repeats sentences spoken by the dead husband, or by the woman herself, either in the past or, less explicably, in the future; for 'this is a man who remembers the future.'

When her guest disappears she mimics his voice on the telephone. She, the body artist, gives a performance in Cambridge, Massachusetts, which expresses all that she has discovered about time. As well as miming the interloper she builds into her act many other allusions, and even runs a video of that two-lane highway in Finland. As far as possible her act eliminates the sense of passing time, and a feeling that it may never end causes the more easily bored members of the audience to walk out. Returning to the rented house, she seems to achieve a separation of fact and fantasy, feeling once more 'the flow of time in her body'.

In saying that much about the story I'm not breaking any rules about plot revelation, for the interest of this book is primarily in its texture. Its repetitive, fragmentary motifs remind one of the old nouveau roman: the unavoidable touch of a hand on a newel post, the arm that hits an overhead light when the woman removes her always grubby sweater, the gait of a Japanese neighbour (later incorporated in the Cambridge performance), the behaviour and the noises of birds at garden feeders.

The opening chapter is where you have to learn to read the book. The kitchen detail, how water from the tap looks first clear, then opaque, the toaster where you have to press the lever twice to get the right shade of brown, the cereal box and the handful of blueberries and the soya granules – it's all calculated to make you think the good old days of *chosisme* have come back. The man is trying to remember something he needs to say, remembers it and doesn't say it. The radio plays, he turns it off, turns it on again, remembers he has just turned it off and turns it off again. The husband and wife are in subtle ways separate (have not been long together) though in others they are more at one. She struggles to get rid of a hair in her mouth, he has cut his chin shaving. Although she knows what he was going to tell her, she insists that he do so, but he doesn't. These are seemingly ordinary failures of communication. 'When he walked out of the room, she realised there was something she wanted to tell him. Sometimes she doesn't think of what she wants to say to him until he walks out of whatever room they're in. Then she thinks of it. Then she either calls after him or doesn't and he responds or doesn't.' What he had meant to do, though without doing it, was to mention a certain noise in the house, caused, as we are to discover when he has left, by the movements of the intruder upstairs.

And so on. Eventually he asks about his car keys and departs. The interest of this scene lies partly in its skilful use of the old 1950s techniques to establish an aura of hallucinated detail, a brightly lit moment, though we don't of course know that the moment is that of a final parting between the pair. But it also cannily inserts a rather more conventional piece of plotting, the delayed significance of the small noise upstairs.

On a second reading this brief novel strikes one as a demonstration, hardly less impressive than the monstrous *Underworld*, of the writer's virtuosity. All the same I dare say many admirers of *Underworld* will find this new novel something of a stumbling block, at least until they see it as what the jacket tells us it is: yet another meditation on time and death, and yet another testimony to the power and scope of this ambitious novelist.

8 March 2001

NUTMEGGED

....

The War against Cliché: Essays and Reviews 1971-2000 by Martin Amis

The main title of this collection may at first seem wantonly non-descriptive, but it turns out to be exact. The first thing to see to if you want to write well is to avoid doing bad writing, used thinking. The more positive requirements can be left till later, if only a little later. Clichés are infallible symptoms of used thinking. Martin Amis has always wanted to be a good writer and he has got what he wanted. He early acquired a habit of vigilance, of stopping clichés at the frontier, and that habit couldn't easily be broken. He is one of the few critics who trouble, even in a shortish newspaper review, to include some consideration of the fabric of a book, the faults of its texture, its clichés.

Over the years Amis has done a lot of virtuous wincing over clichés. John Fowles is a prominent target: 'He managed a wan smile'; 'God, you're so naive.' No expensive talk about Descartes, Marivaux, Lemprière and Aristophanes can procure a pardon for that sort of thing. Other reviewers may commend Thomas Harris for committing 'not a single ugly or dead sentence' but Amis finds enough of them to label Harris 'a serial murderer of English sentences' and *Hannibal* 'a necropolis of prose'. He finds the opposite response of other commentators explicable on the assumption that they aren't listening, and, more generally, because their sense of hierarchy has gone. Some writers really are better than others, though these people lack the power to see that it is so; 'there is a levelling impulse at work.' 'Margot laughed in spite of herself' and 'Bob Sneed broke the silence' are not only dead sentences but an unprovoked pain to all good writers. The fact that Harris, like many others, goes in for the occasional 'fugitive poeticism' only makes things worse. When he says that something is 'truly of the resinous heart' Amis does not know what he means and neither do I, but I catch the poeticism, the theft from Yeats. 'Virtuoso vulgarity' indeed. Amis himself sometimes does a borrowing from high-class literature ('green and pale'; 'promise-crammed'; 'the only end of age') though always when it means something, and where he charitably supposes a decent reader will know not only what it means but where it came from and why it is worth stealing.

And if you quote from memory, get it right. When Andrew Motion, no hero to Amis, says that Larkin's anthology was meant to promote 'the taste by which he wished to be relished' he is adapting a remark of Wordsworth's – 'every author, as far as he is great and at the same time *original*, has had the task of *creating* the taste by which he is to be enjoyed.' But neither Wordsworth nor Amis would have passed 'which ... wished ... relished'. These are small matters, perhaps, but not if you think them symptoms of a destructive illness, as Amis does, or even as just bad manners.

For writers are to be polite in every sense, courteous in manner and properly skilled in literature. To 'have to read the sentence twice, even though you didn't want to read it once' is to suffer undeservedly. Worse still is the wince produced by 'genteelisms': 'a forty-minute hike brought the dog and I to the top of the hill.' A belated disciple of Fowler, Amis abhors Elegant Variation: 'If the President seemed to support the Radicals in New York, in Washington he appeared to back the Conservatives.' This is not only Elegant Variation but Pointless Chiasmus, a crime I have only this minute identified.

The severities may seem to be, but aren't, mere pedantries. It might not be worth carrying on a war against the cliché out of nothing more than an usher's blinkered interest in Fowlerian correctness of language. But cliché is a disease that must be stamped out; it infects the mind and even the heart; it makes it impossible to be honest, and that, for Amis, is an unquestionable duty of authorship. He says in his introduction that he has tried not to go on as he did in his youth, slashing, burning, jeering; such antics, however pleasing to the author and his readers in their nonage, do not become men of substance in middle life – an attitude more humane than that of Housman, who made up epigrammatic insults and stowed them away for future use. 'Mutton dressed as lamb,' says Amis of middle-aged slashing, burning and jeering. This renunciation reflects a firm moral position, but it does not excuse him from duty in the war against cliché and 'scruffy writing'.

No one, except Amis's heroes Nabokov and Bellow, is exempt from censure. Angus Wilson, who gets a bit of a drubbing, was capable of writing 'the admirable Admiral Croft' and 'a revolting revolutionary act'. V.S. Pritchett, for whom Amis has a well-considered and affection-ate admiration (expressed with less qualification in an earlier essay), doesn't understand the elements of punctuation, his being 'tangled, hectic and Victorian'. Moreover he commits sentences here character-ised as 'verbal pile-ups' or 'train-wrecks', over which Amis's pencil, his lifting gear, hovers and is regretfully withdrawn. Iris Murdoch makes a futile attempt to avoid cliché by using inverted commas: 'the wrong end of the stick', 'worthwhile activities'. But you can't slip away as easily as that: 'a cliché or an approximation, wedged between inverted com-mas, is still a cliché or an approximation.' It does not help that Mur-doch was also given to 'train-wreck adjectives'.

An especially favoured site of cliché infection is the adverb. When Don DeLillo has a character say something 'quietly' you know he's drawing on a long tradition of 'said quietly' as a conventional an-nouncement that the remark it follows should be taken as particularly impressive. Ordinary reviewers, and even this extraordinary reviewer, cannot manage without the likes of 'genuinely pleased' or 'brilliant-ly realised', 'brilliantly told'. These are rare instances of Amis himself catching a dose of the disease, and, like much of his rather less brilliant writing, they tend to occur in essays on the authors he most respects, in this case V.S. Naipaul.

Normally he protects his health and virtue by ranging as far as pos-sible from adverbial conventionality. I made a list of recherché adverbs, of which this is a selection: 'beamingly upbeat', 'lurchingly written', 'deeply unshocked', 'embarrassingly good', 'tremendously unrelaxed', 'fruitfully uneasy' (Pritchett), 'pitifully denuded' (admittedly apt, for a Leavisian bookshelf), 'janglingly discursive', 'remorselessly indulgent', 'scarily illusionless', 'hugely charmless', 'promiscuously absorbed', 'cus-tomarily rotted', 'chortlingly habituate', 'finessingly cruel', 'implacably talented', 'bicker halitotically'.

The great thing about these expressions is that the author can be fairly sure they will never be used again, much less become new en-emies of clear thought and virtue. If Amis occasionally allows himself something a bit less 'off the beaten track' (as Miss Murdoch might have said) like 'cruelly burdened' instead of, say, 'crunchingly loaded', or ar-gues that a book has 'aged dramatically' (when he might well judge that adverb, used by another author, to be a vulgarism), or writes that somebody 'espoused … free love', he gets off because of the merit acquired by his 'ceaseless labour' of cliché avoidance over such a 'long haul'.

It has not evaded the writer's notice that there are other, equally subtle ways of thwarting clichés, whether of the page, the mind or the heart. He regards Joyce as the great master of the art of 'hoisting' the cliché 'with its own petard'. 'The summer evening had begun to fold the world in its mysterious embrace': so begins the Nausicaa section of *Ulysses*, described here as 'one of the greatest passages in all literature'. Its heroine, Gerty MacDowell, is, as Amis accurately remarks, 'a beautiful slum of clichés'. Observing that 'Joyce never uses a cliché in innocence', he describes the whole novel as being '*about* cliché'. A moderately unhappy consequence of this purgative achievement is that *Ulysses*, being itself, as a whole, a 'structural cliché', can be boring. The scene in the cabman's shelter is a deliberate insult to the very idea of writing: 'a nightmare of repetitions, tautologies, double negatives, elegant variations, howlers, danglers: "Mozart's *Twelfth Mass* he simply revelled in, the *Gloria* in that being, to his mind, the acme of first class music as such, literally knocking everything else into a cocked hat."' And after many pages of this sort of thing Amis has had enough: 'This writer has the power to take you anywhere (nothing is beyond him); but he keeps taking you where you don't want to go.' It is relevant that '*Ulysses* takes about a week to read, if you do nothing else.' Amis always feels able to acknowledge greatness without denying that it can be boring and make insolent demands on one's time. This combination of unaffected admiration and critical honesty is very attractive.

He thinks it a pity, but not a pity worth spending much precious time on, that the canon is dead and literary criticism, as he knew it in his youth, a thing of the past. All the same, he has visited the canon and here and there shows a dwindlingly acute interest, not in the great men of the age of literary criticism, like I.A. Richards and F.R. Leavis and Northrop Frye, but in what might be called, rather vaguely, the Hazlitt tradition. Yet he is still mildly bothered by the old Intentional Fallacy, and it causes an occasional disturbance of logic: 'Although writers' lives are no more than optional extras in the consideration of their work, the dull fact of Jane Austen's spinsterhood – her plainness, her childlessness, her virgin death – invests her comedies with disappointment, and with a sense of thwarted homing. It also confirms one's sense of the diminishing physicality of her later heroines.' And the virgin Austen is reproved for being cruel to Lydia Bennet. 'The reader begins to feel that artists should know better than that; we expect them to know better than that.' For all its 'eternal humour and élan', *Pride and Prejudice* fails the test as art, and the question is, whether we'd have known this if we hadn't also known about the disappointments of the author's plainness and spinsterhood.

That said, or, as Amis allows himself to say, 'simply put', we have here a literary critic of startling power, a post-literary-critical critic who, incorrigibly satirical, goes directly to work on the book. Often, being right and being funny are, in this book, aspects of the same sentence. Often, as one reads on, one finds oneself quietly giggling, or gigglingly quiet. The precision of the attack is astounding, and is matched by the bluntness of the condemnation. Alexander Theroux is scolded for 'pseudo-elegant variation' when he switches from 'which' to 'that' in mid-sentence. Worse still, the sentence in question is in any case 'a wreck: ugly, untrue and illiterate'.

Even greater names are not spared. An essay on *Don Quixote* begins as it means to go on: 'While clearly an impregnable masterpiece, *Don Quixote* suffers from one fairly serious flaw – that of outright unreadability.' Anybody could make bold to say that, but few could justify the remark so lightly and ably as Amis does in this piece.

Neat tricks of style co-operate in the business of judgment. Meditating a long-past crisis in the management of the English football team, he decides that 'it is all too easy to blame Ron Greenwood. Yet I think we should blame Ron Greenwood.' Greenwood is then thoroughly blamed, mostly for choosing a goalkeeper who 'came cartwheeling off his line to flail at innocuous crosses; all night he looked capable of being nutmegged by a beachball.' Of course that was twenty years ago, before stern charity and moderation of language became the name of the game.

Amis likes games and seems especially keen on tennis and poker, but he spends more time on chess. He does what might by some be described as a 'splendid job' on Bobby Fischer, and a genial one on George Steiner's book about the great Reykjavik encounter: 'There's not one detailed comparison,' he writes admiringly, 'between a middle game and Bach's *Die Kunst der Fuge*. Page after page goes by without any reference to Auschwitz.' All the fine writing (what Amis ungraciously calls 'the old apocalyptic beefcake') is confined to chess itself: 'The dynamic dovetailing of the whole game, the unfolding ramifications of its crystalline armature are implosive in the very first move.' The youthful critic, after properly acknowledging the merits of the book, takes the liberty of advising its famous author to cool it, and to discover the difference between brilliance and dazzle.

The kind of writing this writer belongs to is the novelistic kind, so we expect, and get, more detailed comment on novelists, especially 20th-century novelists, than on poets, playwrights and the like. Here are penetratingly friendly notices of Ballard and Burgess: 'the failure is (vexingly, boringly, ineffably) a failure of language.' Michael Crichton has a bad case of cliché rot ('animals – especially, if not exclusively, velociraptors – are what he is good at. People are what he is bad at. People, and prose.' Crichton has 'herds of clichés, roaming free. You will listen in "stunned silence" to an "unearthly cry" or "a deafening roar".') Evelyn Waugh 'wrote *Brideshead Revisited* with great speed, unfamiliar excitement, and a deep conviction of its excellence. Lasting schlock, the really good bad book, cannot be written otherwise.' Malcolm Lowry is 'a world-class liar'. The response to John Updike is slightly chilly, but loses its cool when required to be respectful: 'enduringly eloquent . . . in a prose that is always fresh, nubile and unwitherable'. (Yes, it does say 'nubile'.) Philip Roth is admired, though Amis seems uncharacteristically terrorised by *Sabbath's Theater*: 'an amazing tantrum . . . You toil on, looking for the clean bits.' Mailer is 'grandiose and crass'. And so on. It's all deeply interesting and interestingly deep, especially when the subjects are the American masters alongside whom, one can't help feeling, this writer would choose to be assessed. Hence the long eulogies on Nabokov and Bellow: 'the world has never heard this prose before,' he writes, all irony discarded, 'prose of such tremulous and crystallised beauty'. Don DeLillo later gets into the side, while Updike still frets on the bench.

There are, however, some good writers on this side of the ocean. The Naipauls and Larkin must be praised. The long central *New Yorker* essay on Larkin is probably the most considered and the most permanently valuable part of the book. It recycles some earlier remarks to great defensive effect. More than any other piece it confirms one's opinion that Amis is the best practitioner-critic of our day – just what Pritchett was in his prime, though without the bad punctuation and the jangling train-wrecks.

Of his pieces on nuclear weapons and global warming I will merely say that they are virtuously impressive. It remains to ask two questions. The first may seem a bit academic. Why did Kurt Vonnegut, as reported in one of these reviews, call the central figure of his novel *Galapagos* 'James Wait' – a name pre-empted long before, and with good reason, by an even better writer? Somebody must know, and I'd have expected Amis would – he himself has played the name game in his fiction – but not a word. Finally, the acknowledgments page states that the 'pieces in this book were compiled by Professor James Diedrick.' We thought they were all compiled by Martin Amis. A double, a *nom de guerre*? An affable familiar ghost? President of the Society for the Elimination of the Cliché? We need to know.

10 May 2002

RETICULATION

....

The Wreck of the 'Abergavenny' by Althea Hayter

There has of late been a vogue for what is sometimes called 'micro-history': the historian chooses some anecdote, some occurrence remote from the mainstream of historical writing, and from it deduces an entire culture, the conflicts or negotiations of power within a whole historical community. Althea Hayter deals with a single event, focusing on a particular moment in history, but she is not a new or micro-historian and is innocent of Foucauldian or any other theoretical ambitions. Nevertheless she explores her subject in such depth that she really does illuminate the culture and society of her chosen moment.

Her interest in the wreck of the East-Indiaman *Abergavenny* arose primarily from the circumstance that its captain was John Wordsworth, brother of the more famous William and Dorothy. His death in 1805 at the outset of what was to have been his last voyage before he retired (at 34) caused convulsions of sorrow at Grasmere, where he had intended to join the family circle. The chief mourner was of course William, whose exceptional sensibility was recognised by all, and who had been hoping to spend his life as a dedicated poet, freed from irksome restrictions by the money John would make on this voyage. William's welfare was the first concern of everybody. His grief was prolonged, and it was some time before he could assuage it with poems; but he was a specialist in the poetry of loss, and a little over a year after John's death wrote the fine 'Elegiac Stanzas Suggested by a Picture of Peele Castle, in a Storm, Painted by Sir George Beaumont'.

This poem confronts the reader at the beginning of the present book, and is, very fittingly, quoted in full in its closing pages. It enacts a characteristic Wordsworthian gesture, the claim to have found consolation in tragic loss. Much of Wordsworth's best poetry is a celebration of 'something that is gone'. The cruel death of his brother joins all the other evidence of loss and emphasises the need to accept it as somehow humanly necessary, and, finally, as God's will:

A power is gone, which nothing can restore;
A deep distress hath humanised my Soul.
Not for a moment could I now behold
A smiling sea, and be what I have been:
The feeling of my loss will ne'er be old;
This, which I know, I speak with mind serene.

Hayter undertakes to describe the sorrows of the family and their friends, among them Lamb and De Quincey and Coleridge; but her purposes are not simply literary or literary-domestic. Much is known and much has been written about the loss of the *Abergavenny*; salvage work is still going on after almost two centuries. She has used this information and added to it the results of her own research. A foreword expresses mild regret that the book lacks references, but assures the reader that 'everything . . . presented as fact is taken from letters, diaries and official records, newspapers and pamphlets . . . with no fictional additions or inventions,' except the ones that figure in the contemporary reports of the wreck. One understands this hint of disappointment at the omission of supporting notes like those that added value to her earlier book, *Opium and the Romantic Imagination*. No doubt it was a publisher's commercial decision; yet it is not really credible that anybody wanting to read this book would be so inveterate a 'general reader' as to be scared off by a few foot or endnotes.

The facts necessarily include a lot of information about the operations of the East India Company and, less directly, about the economic assumptions of middle-class life in the opening years of the 19th century. Oblivious of new-historical talk about the interaction of literature with other 'signifying practices', Hayter does not treat the sinking of the *Abergavenny* as a marginal anecdote that can be made to disclose the truth about such connections; that there are connections is not to be doubted, but the loss of the *Abergavenny*, as here described, belongs not to the margins but to the centre of life in what was now a bourgeois empire.

John Wordsworth was born in 1772, went to sea at 16, worked his way up in the service from sixth mate, and had been captain of the *Abergavenny* since 1801. Like his brother Richard, who became a lawyer, and unlike his brother William, who became a poet, John needed to make a living in a gentlemanly job, and began his sea career immediately after leaving Hawkshead Grammar School. It may have been a peculiarity of the Wordsworth family that whereas the other sons sought employment and preferment in the ordinary way, it was assumed that the poet was owed a living from the outset. In *The Prelude* Wordsworth celebrates the freedom conferred by a legacy of about £900 from his acquaintance Raisley Calvert, which 'set him above want', and which, a polite but insistent legacy-hunter, he did something to solicit. John was expressly committed to the support of his brother and sister: indeed, the principal purpose of this last voyage was to make a large sum of money and devote it to the comforts of William and the family.

As in most walks of life, advancement in the employment of the East India Company depended on patronage. Another Captain John Wordsworth, a cousin of this one's father, had originally got the young man into the Company service. A cousin, Joseph Wordsworth, was third mate on the *Abergavenny*, following his cousin the captain on the way to the top. One did not become a captain in the Company's service simply by individual merit; this was not exactly a career open to the talents. John had also benefited from the support of William Wilberforce, the great opponent of slavery, who had an interest in the Company. Hayter explains that it was quite usual to buy shares precisely in order to acquire the power of patronage. So there was a great deal of what she calls 'reticulation', a word she has employed before as an elegant euphemism for the old boy network. John, though apparently far from brilliant, cannot have been bad at his job, but he would probably not have had it, nor would those other Wordsworths have found berths in the Company's ships, without reticular assistance.

Hayter's account of the operations of the East India Company is beautifully done and full of interest. As befitted a successful joint-stock business, it encouraged competitiveness in its captains. A voyage to China and back might earn the captain as much as £30,000, a huge sum to be had only by beating the other vessels in the convoy, and acquiring, by influence, the much sought after right to go to China via Bengal. The captain was permitted to do some trading on his own account, and John was prepared for this, having collected some capital and even got Dorothy and William to make an investment. The main source of this illicit private profit was the opium trade. The best opium came from Bengal, and the best market was China.

The opium trade was against both British and Chinese law, but nobody seemed bothered about that. This was a time when opium in one form or another was widely used to alleviate the illnesses of the British – even Wilberforce was a user, though not addicted on a Coleridgean or De Quinceyan scale. John seems to have had no objection to making money by selling it to the Chinese, or to bringing home hashish for the use of friends. This is an interesting sidelight on the business ethics of the virtuous Clapham Sect, to which Wilberforce belonged. No doubt the rewards could be represented as reasonable, for the voyage was long and arduous. It is hard for us to imagine what it felt like to live for months on shipboard while arranging for the wind alone to blow you all the way to China and back. Also there was a war on; the big East-Indiamen travelled in convoy and carried almost as many guns as a warship. John Wordsworth had already been in a minor scuffle with some French ships, and won a reward of 500 guineas for his part in the action. Honour was firmly associated with profit, and even military valour was paid for in cash, which is why Captain Wordsworth could say that 'the longer this war continues the better it will be for me.'

It is doubtful whether his crew felt the same way, or that their exertions were proportionately recognised. Without giving the matter much serious consideration the officer class seems to have assumed that they had sole claim to any money that was going. The 'men' were treated to the stick, not the carrot. Discipline was severe and enforced by brutal flogging, a punishment Wordsworth often awarded. Hayter believes he was 'firm but just' and 'not a sadist', and when he says he would like to give 'a tight flogging' to the man who cut down some trees in Grasmere she observes that modern ecological campaigners 'may find themselves in sympathy' with this 'idea of a suitable punishment'. Others may have difficulty deciding whether this form of discipline was not at least equally disgusting. The Navy has managed without it for a long time, though I suppose it may be argued that life on the lower deck is less likely now to drive men to mutiny or to 'improper contradiction', which Wordsworth particularly disliked.

Hayter likes the Captain within reason, though she wonders why, even allowing for the fact that the era of sentiment was not over and it was virtuous in men to weep freely, this morose man, formerly thought the dunce of the family, should have been so extravagantly mourned.

Summing up his character, she says:

Modern readers may find it difficult to see heroic status in a Merchant Navy captain who got his job by nepotism, was not averse to smuggling, and hoped to make a fortune by opium trading. But that would be hindsight; by the standards of his day, John Wordsworth was a man of integrity, an upright honourable citizen, respected and admired by everyone who knew him.

This is an argument that might be stretched to excuse all manner of infamous behaviour as long as it happened some time ago. It would doubtless be naive to ask *how* these happened to be the standards of the day: how it had come about that reticulation, and what is here called 'a relaxed attitude to smuggling', were acceptable as correct gentlemanly conduct. The answer is that financial security was an index of virtue; and that the gentlemen concerned saw no reason to question the convenient assumption that their honourable status constituted an unchallengeable claim to as much spoil, whether legal or just across the border of legality, as they could get away with.

Hayter's account of the very brief last voyage of the *Abergavenny* is a remarkable piece of writing, cool and vivid. The ship sailed from Gravesend to Portsmouth, carrying not only an extremely valuable cargo – there was a huge consignment of silver coins – but troops of soldiers and a number of more rewarding passengers: officers bound for India, women who brought along harps and pianos. Passage in such a ship, partly a warship, partly a freighter and partly a passenger vessel, was quite unlike anything that could now be experienced. Cabins were jury-rigged of canvas, so that they could be rapidly dismantled if the guns needed to be run out. Livestock shared the decks, and throughout the long voyage people were tormented by foul smells, incessant noise and seasickness. Yet among the gentry standards were kept up: formality ruled. They dressed for dinner and the forty places at the captain's table were taken in accordance with the rules of precedence. The captain provided the food out of the passage money. The women were permitted two glasses of wine before withdrawing to their canvas cabins, but the men stayed to drink port until dismissed by the captain. The food was plentiful and mostly meat. There was a drum and fife band to provide entertainment. Theatricals were organised – perhaps an old custom, for we know of a 17th-century performance of *Hamlet* in a ship off the African coast. On a very long voyage there would be time for such amusements.

Wordsworth's ship led the convoy out, and for that reason was the last to turn and seek shelter from the storm that sank her when all the others escaped. The wreck happened off Portland on 5 February 1805. The convoy sought shelter from the weather in Portland Roads, and the *Abergavenny* was trying to do the same when she ran onto the shoal known as the Shambles. Wordsworth was heard to blame the pilot for this disastrous mistake: 'Oh pilot! pilot! you have ruined me.' He probably meant financial ruin, for the ship, though damaged, did not at that moment seem likely to sink, and he need not yet have in mind the danger to the hundreds of lives in his charge, as well as to his own.

The smashing up of the *Abergavenny*, the efforts at rescue and the loss of perhaps three hundred lives are here described with extraordinary and admirable command of nautical detail. Hayter then turns with equal attentiveness to the sequel: official inquiries, questions of compensation, finally the exoneration of Captain Wordsworth from blame for the disaster.

What interests her most is the public response, the newspapers and pamphlets that devoted so much space to the sinking and to the behaviour of the Captain. She is surprised that the papers should have devoted so much space to a civilian shipwreck at a critical moment in the war, with Napoleon's Army encamped at Boulogne, but explains their interest as a consequence of the heavy loss of life and the value of the cargo, which they duly exaggerated. Their reports of the nightmare events on the Shambles were detailed and sometimes correct, but they made fanciful mistakes, saying, for instance, that Wordsworth had a wife and five children, that he was drunk (highly unlikely) or in a state of depression, that he made little attempt to save himself. These rumours proved particularly disturbing to the family at Grasmere. It is not difficult to guess that some might call this sad, quiet man, so ready to withdraw from company, depressed, and he was not likely to be in a spritely mood when he was helplessly watching the destruction of his command. But it seems that in fact he behaved well. When his body was washed ashore it was buried with the others, not, as would have been proper for an officer, in a separate grave; another piloting error.

It isn't easy for journalists 'to get catastrophe reporting right', Hay-

ter concludes, glancing at some modern instances such as the Mozam-
bique floods and Kosovo. 'No calamity is ever described with perfect
truth.' But this fine book must come very close to it. It makes the subject important, not just as a type of catastrophe but as a sensitive exploration of the way it can implicate those who do not directly suffer.
Charles and Mary Lamb selflessly, patiently, served the Wordsworths
by interviewing survivors for news of the Captain. Wilberforce wept.
Coleridge, on hearing the news in Malta, had to be helped to his room.
William Wordsworth, experienced in the business of finding some kind
of happiness in sorrow, eventually wrote a very good poem, which, in
a way, makes the *Abergavenny* a luckier ship than hundreds of others
lost no less calamitously.

6 February 2003

CLUTCHING AT INSANITY

....

Winnicott: Life and Work by Robert Rodman

Modern biographers aspire to tell all, and psychoanalysts writing the lives of psychoanalysts should be better at this than most. But there are those who may doubt the propriety of their revelations and investigations. Even when the subject is a fairly ordinary mortal they feel that he or she has a right to some posthumous privacy; and the psychoanalytical profession would presumably claim to be at least as ardently insistent as their orthodox medical colleagues on the preservation of strict confidentiality. But it seems widely accepted that the fame or notoriety of the subject eliminates the need for such discretion.

It is true that in the early days the profession was small and rather isolated so that something must be allowed to family gossip. Freud, admittedly an exception, since he had no predecessor, had to analyse not only his daughter but himself. Donald Winnicott was the analyst of Melanie Klein's son Eric, so couldn't go to her himself, but his analyst was Joan Riviere, very close to Klein, and his wife was a patient of hers. Readers of this journal may recall Wynne Godley's complaint that his analyst, Masud Khan, was himself a patient and confidant of Winnicott – Robert Rodman even conjectures a homosexual attraction – all the time he was treating Godley in such extraordinary ways. And Godley's stepdaughter was another of Winnicott's patients.

Khan was by any standards and in any company a wild and perhaps even a dangerous character, but Winnicott was nothing of the kind. Though occasionally capable of anger and mildly eccentric, he was noted for his normally gentle temperament. He was described as imitating or reflecting in his own attitude to his patients the role of his famous 'good-enough mother'. But it has become obvious that he was capable of potentially harmful moments of indiscretion. Only the other day I was told of a paper of his in which he cited the case of a literary person and left him clearly identifiable by a good many people. There was of course strong official disapproval of such careless exposure; in his youth Khan had been reprimanded for giving a paper in which he inadequately concealed a patient's identity. That Winnicott 'socialised' with Khan gets him a black mark from Rodman, who thinks it possible that in his more extravagant 'socialising' Khan was following the senior analyst's example.

Although the formal commitment to confidentiality was very considerable, within a small circle of gossiping friends, associates, supervisors – and of course one's own analyst – it must sometimes have been difficult to observe. Anna Freud argued that it was technically wrong for an analyst to accept a patient from his circle of acquaintance, or to have similar interests, or to discuss the patient with others, or to manipulate him, or to permit the patient to identify with the analyst personally. Yet, she added, 'we commit every single one of these deviations from the classical technique when we analyse candidates. Further, we do not inquire frequently enough how far these deviations complicate the transference and obscure its interpretation' (quoted by Jacqueline Rose in *On Not Being Able to Sleep*). Rodman conjectures that while Riviere was Winnicott's analyst she couldn't not have discussed him with her mentor, Melanie Klein. He admits there is no documentary evidence for this, but clearly regards it as close to inevitable.

John Forrester argues, more radically, in *Dispatches from the Freud Wars*, that the founding ambition of the psychoanalytic movement, rightly understood, was to overthrow conventional ethics, leaving no trace except an absolute obligation to tell the truth. He gives in evidence the behaviour of Ferenczi, Jung and others, and the fact that Freud made no objection to incest. Their behaviour, he claims, makes 'love, the most important thing in life, the victim of truth's callous disregard for human beings'. Breaking a confidence might on this view be seen as an act of love.

It is easy enough to see why so many celebrated or notorious practitioners were seen by some as rebels, rule-breakers, enemies of the nascent institution. Though not given to extravagant behaviour – a few foibles and oddities apart – Winnicott was, or could be seen as, a rebel of this kind, as he assumed more and more intellectual independence. It seems he was not a great reader, of Freud or anyone else, and although he could not avoid the ideas of others when they were implicated in, or resistant to, the movement of his own thought, he seems to have developed the themes of his innumerable papers and books largely from his own clinical experience and private musings. Some believe the kind of psychoanalysis he developed – a 'master-plot of human development', according to Adam Phillips – is incompatible with Freud's, and it certainly came to differ critically from that of Melanie Klein, from whom he nevertheless learned a great deal. Indeed Phillips says that his work 'cannot be understood without reference to Klein. It is a continuous, and sometimes inexplicit, commentary on and critique of her work. The importance of the internal world and its objects, the elaborate and pervasive power of fantasy, the central notion of primitive greed – all these ideas Winnicott takes over from Klein and uses them in his own way.' But in the end the institutional rigidity of Klein's system repelled him. As between people enslaved to a doctrine and a method, and people who work things out on their own, Winnicott strongly preferred the latter, and thought the practices of the former likely to inhibit rather than encourage personal development. Like many another genius, he knew how to find – or, as he put it, 'steal' – and use what he needed. Rodman does not fail to consider the significance of this word 'steal', used when most of us would prefer a more neutral expression.

Winnicott is often described as the greatest psychoanalyst of his time – or even the greatest English psychoanalyst – though some, perhaps especially the more doctrinaire Kleinians, reject that opinion, occasionally with contempt. The clearest introductory account of his work, providing reasons in support of the favourable judgment, is Adam Phillips's short *Winnicott*, published in 1988. Rodman's 'first full-scale life', as the blurb calls it, is three times as long as Phillips's book, has more to say about the clinical work, and much more about the life, especially about Winnicott's marriages and his endless, though usually civil, disagreements with his colleagues.

The first marriage, which lasted for years, was sexless, either because Winnicott was impotent or because his first wife was averse from sex; or perhaps both. The second, though not restricted in this way, remained childless. These are private matters, but cannot fail to interest a biographer, least of all a biographer as industrious and astute and professionally alert as the generally sympathetic Rodman. So keen is his scent, so candid his interpretations, that it seems odd to find him turning away from consideration of an affair Clare Winnicott may have had when Winnicott felt he had to wait for his father's death before he could marry her. 'It is none of our business, anyway,' Rodman says. Coming from a biographer who sees practically everything else as his business, this is a strange disclaimer.

Rodman knew Clare Winnicott, and gives a good account of this strong and intelligent woman, perhaps rather forbidding when dealing with her husband's biographers. In general it is not his way to allow anything odd or quirky to pass without comment, but this is probably inevitable in psychoanalysts. For example, Winnicott had a comfortable middle-class, well-to-do background and can never have been short of money, but it seems that in an odd way he was rather stingy. His first analyst was James Strachey, the translator of the Standard Edition of Freud. When Strachey's wife, Alix, was living in Berlin enduring or enjoying analysis with Karl Abraham and making friends with Melanie Klein, James wrote to her almost daily. Among the chatter and gossip one finds an account of Winnicott's reluctance to pay Strachey's fee. Strachey was poor at the time and was obliged to insist on immediate payment at each session. One day he observed that Winnicott lingered on the stairs outside the consulting-room door, where, as Strachey correctly guessed, he was writing a cheque, an act he had deferred to the last possible moment.

He rushed in & pressed it upon me – die Tinte noch nass – threw himself upon the sofa & started off feverishly with 'There's someone whose name I keep forgetting.' And then long talks about why he should forget names – other people whose names he forgets, etc. It flashed into my mind that he'd made some mistake over my name on the cheque, & I nearly risked the coup de théâtre of walking over to the writing-table where I'd put it down, & looking at it. However, I restrained myself. When he'd gone, I went and looked at it. He hadn't signed it!

Strachey evidently enjoyed this proof of his own interpretative shrewdness. Rodman gives examples from later in Winnicott's life of this presumably significant stinginess. After he contracted to pay Riviere, his second analyst, below the standard rate, she wrote him a dignified letter complaining that he had misled her about his financial position. 'There is no speculation on the transference meaning of this behaviour,' Rodman writes, 'that is, on why he wouldn't seem to want to pay his bills.' It would be shallow to assume, as a non-psychoanalyst writing about a non-psychoanalyst might, that it wasn't simply that he disliked paying bills, a reluctance shared by a great many ordinary people, but that he only wanted it to seem as if he did, which is more complicated and might lead to more gratifying interpretations. If one then adds the consideration that in most respects Winnicott was, or seemed to be, careless about money, there is even more to discuss. For example, he enjoyed urinating into the ocean, and that could conceivably be made relevant, though it might strike the laity as having more to do with dispersion than retention.

Winnicott himself attached importance to the fact that his father had so disliked the quasi-sexual excitement experienced by his wife when breast-feeding baby Winnicott that he made her give up the practice. The analyst Marion Milner was one of those who thought that this prohibition had a lifelong effect on the child, in particular during his long struggle to persuade Klein that mothers really matter (objectively, constituting a 'holding environment'). This effort 'was the adult equivalent' of the baby's 'struggle to get milk out of his own mother'. His father's attitude perhaps also contributed to the most celebrated lacuna in Winnicott's work: until very late in his life he assigned no role whatever to fathers. Rodman naturally has much to say about this partial blindness, or, in a piece of jargon he borrows from Winnicott, this scotoma.

Winnicott had qualified as a doctor and then specialised in paediatrics. His celebrity as an analyst rests in large part on his treatment of children. Like Klein, he disagreed with Anna Freud, who believed that children could not free-associate or form transferences. Fortunately there is among the great mass of his writing a short, accessible, posthumous book called *The Piggle*, which gives a detailed account of the analysis of a little girl, between the ages of two years and eight months and five years. It provides a good impression of what Rodman calls 'playful attentiveness'. The analyst plays, is co-operative and certainly attentive, but he is also reticent, unwilling to interfere, clear up confusions, and so on. Yet at the end he claims that the little girl had 'reorganised her entire life in terms of the experience of a positive relationship with the subjective figure of the analyst'. And he said to her, by way of farewell: 'So the Winnicott you invented was all yours, and now he's finished with. And no one else can ever have him.' He told her she loved him, and he evidently loved her.

Winnicott's priority was always the patient; he evidently thought well of his powers but had a horror of exercising them at the analysand's expense. The idea of 'holding' was important to him, as he argued it was to mothers. The development of a child, or of an analysis, was a process easily impeded if there was no holding environment. Reading him one can sense great intellectual and emotional strain. Critical moments, as when an adult patient has regressed to utter dependence, are truly exhausting to the analyst.

It seems right that the general idea of him is of a doctor who had an extraordinary gift in dealing with children. His account of the mother-child relationship is not as stark as Klein's, but it stresses the emotion of the mother – he sometimes defines it as hatred and regards it as a feature not only of the mother's attitude but also of the analyst's in the counter-transference. It is one of the inevitable difficulties that occur in the process of development. On a superficial view one wouldn't expect him to confess so readily to the experience of hatred, but despite his gentleness he admitted to having a strong aggressive streak. Rodman quotes some pretty aggressive letters, sometimes addressed to embattled Kleinians, for which he often apologised later. Aggression was part of the psychic given and coexisted with gentleness. It seems he would sometimes physically hold a patient during a session, a practice deplored by colleagues as very bad 'technique'; his use of it illustrates what he took to be the critical importance of 'holding' but also the independence of his thought and practice.

He is famous for talking about the 'good-enough mother', and for his insistence that to exact compliance from the child is to create a False Self and inhibit the development of a True one. 'Good-enough' sounds placid and conciliatory, but it is a rather stern requirement. The child must have the conditions for 'going-on-being', and providing them is a delicate matter. The reward for success is a True Self, as opposed to the False Self that can be developed in a medium that distracts the infant from the business of development. Expressed out of context, these notions may sound thin and banal, but they are part of what turns out to be a complex and ever developing chain of thought based on subtle clinical observation.

For most of us the best known of Winnicott's ideas is that of the 'transitional object'. He states this idea in what Rodman rightly describes as 'deceptively simple terms'. Winnicott's language is indeed deliberately simple, avoiding most of the meta-psychoanalytical terminology, but its simplicity often promotes an obscurity that is sometimes, I feel, avoidable. Those teddy-bears and scraps of blanket are similarly deceptive, simplicities covering dire necessities. The baby can feel that he or she has invented the object and must at all costs not be prevented from feeling so. It is the means by which the child moves out of subjectivity and omnipotence into a world made by others. The space in which the objects operate is the space in which the personal life, as Rodman puts it, must join 'the vast inherited culture to which an individual may contribute and from which he may draw. The bodily experience with which life begins thus becomes linked to the accumulation of other people's creative discovery.'

This much elaborated and central interest of Winnicott's is an indication of how far his methods differed from the orthodoxies. It has the merit that most parents can observe transitional behaviour for themselves. I remember that my daughter never parted with a torn piece of blanket; that when it grew dirty and smelly we ignorantly took it from her and washed it, but she was heartbroken when we gave it back clean. It was no longer her invention. (I ought to add that her twin brother took no obvious interest in such objects. Perhaps his T.O. was his sister.) Although Winnicott had no children he had many infant patients, and Clare Winnicott still kept the little doll that had served her as a child.

The point here is that in spite of his whimsies and oddities Winnicott's principal thinking belonged to a world ordinary people could recognise without going into such matters as the Oedipus Complex, or Kleinian bad breasts. Sometimes he is oracular: 'without the initial good enough environmental provision, the self that can afford to die never develops.' This is what Rodman calls a 'typical startling Winnicottian extension of thinking into uncharted territory'. But he uses fairly ordinary language, and though often he makes it sound a bit peculiar it also connects with existential and ethical notions with which the laity can claim some first-hand acquaintance.

He was quite like everybody else, except that he made of himself an environment in which a patient might at last be able 'to take the risks involved in starting to experience living'. It is also evident that he was capable of extraordinary dedication, and in spite of a long succession of coronaries exhausted himself in his care for patients, especially the regressive and the suicidal.

He admitted to a transgressive streak and said he was glad that by means of his analysis and self-analysis he had 'achieved some measure of insanity'. He wanted to be liked and praised, but also allowed the patient the right to call the analysis a failure even when it wasn't. And it may be that this willingness to let patients prevail even when the long business ended in what they took to be disappointment, to allow the little girl who made her own Winnicott to discard him and proceed to other loves, serves to explain something of the man himself. He was loved but also mistrusted, he was sociable – sometimes when he ought not to have been. The person was usurped by the analyst, and he was habituated to dissent, rule-breaking, boundary-crossing, and that habit must be relevant to the association with Masud Khan.

Khan, whom I knew quite well, misbehaved continually, but I was not in his business, and had I wanted not merely to laugh at and occasionally admire him but also to fool about in imitation of him, it would not have mattered much to anybody else. As we know, this proved not to be true, could not have been true, of his relationship with Winnicott. Some would say that confidentiality is as important as that requirement to tell the truth so unanimously and virtuously insisted on, but evidently psychoanalytical biographers claim a certain licence. Armed with that licence, Rodman performs admirably. He makes a few slips from which an English editor would have saved him. He places Battersea in the East End of London. He supposes that when Winnicott, writing from his hospital bed in New York, says he will come home like Cathy, he is making an erudite allusion to *Wuthering Heights*. These are evidently just mistakes, and in time to come Dr Rodman's biographer, though with no constraint of confidentiality, will be hard put to it to interpret them as parapraxes.

4 March 2004

RETRIPOTENT

....

Like a Fiery Elephant: The Story of B.S. Johnson by Jonathan Coe
'Trawl', 'Albert Angelo' and 'House Mother Normal' by B.S. Johnson

B.S. Johnson died by his own hand in 1973. He was 40, and the author of seven novels, all of them rather odd in ways that put publishers off because their oddities made them expensive to produce and hard to sell. He bullied the publishers haughtily and often got his way, though at some cost to himself: the books *were* hard to sell. Fred Warburg, responding to Johnson's peremptory complaints about a paperback advance beneath his dignity, explained to him that his 'ideas about how novels should be written are, if not unique, at least held by a tiny, but tiny minority'. Warburg saw Johnson's manic insistence that his novels should contain no lies as a threat that he would produce nothing but a string of varied autobiographies, and he suggested that if, as he expected, he lost money on them, he would hold the author to his promise to remedy the situation by producing 'a brilliant bunch of lies'. But he knew that Johnson would consider such fiction 'a vulgar pandering to an ill-informed public'.

Johnson went his own way, not only in novels but also in film and television scripts. Convinced of his stature, he grew more and more angry about his poor sales. He was proud of being quite well known but could not see why he wasn't marketable. Though always ready to quote, again and again, any favourable comment, he regarded publishers, agents and reviewers as stupid and venal. He was not without discerning admirers, and won the admiration and friendship of Samuel Beckett, with whom he occasionally claimed equality of esteem. But he failed to see that avant-garde novelists rarely become bestsellers, believing that truth would necessarily prevail over fictions (lies). He defended and advanced his cause with much emphasis; one of the children he taught as a supply teacher called him a 'fiery elephant', which is where Coe gets his title (though he thinks the child meant to call his enormous instructor a 'fairy elephant').

It may be true that in the 1960s and early 1970s Johnson was, as

Coe's publishers maintain, 'one of the best-known young novelists in Britain', but his celebrity quickly faded. Now, as this large biography attests, there has been a revival of interest. Coe has worked on his book for years, occasionally lamenting the loss of time that might have been devoted to writing fiction, his main business. While he has been labouring in the huge archive preserved by the author's widow, others have done their bit to bring Johnson back into the conversation. Nicolas Tredell's *Fighting Fictions: The Novels of B.S. Johnson*, a very well-informed book, was published by Paupers' Press in 2000, and Philip Tew's *B.S. Johnson: A Critical Reading* (Manchester), a heavier, more philosophical study, followed in 2001. Tew projects onto Johnson his special interests, which involve many darkly erudite meditations by the philosopher Roy Bhaskar. Johnson is credited with having employed a kind of analysis that permits 'the multiple diffraction of dialectics as dialectics to accord with the complexities, angularities and nuances of our pluriversal world'. I cannot decide whether I think Johnson would have been pleased to know this. On the other hand, Tredell's lucid and respectful commentary might have impressed him. If a reappraisal was called for, Tredell showed how it could be done. However, if Johnson is to become, in his fashion, canonical, it will probably be as a consequence of Coe's more elaborate act of devotion.

The restoration to favour of forgotten books and authors is always a chancy business. It is a myth that time will do the testing; it would be truer to credit chance, and, more important still, the continuation of reasonably well-informed talk. Sometimes it is possible to guess why, in one case and not in another, that talk continues. Many have argued that a book's defiance of contemporary opinion and convention is itself an index of virtue, that some element of 'estrangement' or 'defamiliarisation' is a preservative, and that too easy a compliance with accepted norms is bound to result in oblivion. Literary transgressiveness, often reflecting radical social and political opposition, can thus be taken as a justification for rescue work. It may be, as Roman Jakobson believed, that its virtue lies in its power to protect us from 'automatisation, from the rust threatening our formulae of love and hatred, of revolt and renunciation, of faith and negation'. Since the transgressive has this value it will be worth much effort to recover lost examples of it.

In its nature the transgressive will tend to be 'experimental'.

Sometimes it may be startlingly so, as it was in some French novels, especially the nouveau roman, which had the advantage of Robbe-Grillet's own theoretical comments, and the invaluable support of Roland Barthes and other influential voices. The English avant-garde novel was, at least until quite recently, a bit short on theory, though Christine Brooke-Rose has done what she could to put that right. What tends to be ignored is the degree to which practically all the modern novelists now admired, though not for their technical stunts, have gone in for 'experiment', from James, Ford and Conrad and Joyce to, say, Golding and Ian McEwan. Lawrence saw how much might be done in a novel, how free it could be of constraints, how apt to the business of making it new; the novel was protean, insisting on its own virtually infinite possibilities, experimental in its very nature.

Johnson was fond of Sterne, and aware that from an early moment of the novel's modern career it was possible to use the flexibility and variety of the form to make fun of narrative convention, and even to set up comic resonances between typography and story. You didn't have to tell the tale in chronological order. You didn't have to stick to an 'omniscient' point of view. You could do the most extraordinary things, enabling you to go far beyond the possibilities of straightforward story. But while Johnson admired the treatment of time in *Wuthering Heights*, he shows no interest at all in James, Conrad or Ford. Conrad understood how certain contiguities, certain repeated motifs, could be allowed to interrupt the chronological progress of a story; Ford learned from the French about such matters as the 'progression of effects', defying simple sequentiality.

All such experiment continues an ancient tradition of intercalating elements of a different narrative in a principal narrative – witness the *Odyssey* and the Gospels (Salome and John the Baptist). Johnson's plan to revolutionise the novel came down to the use of 'devices' intended to disrupt ordinary forms of attention by involving the physical book itself, the material base of writing, in unusual ways, as if to take revenge on it for a long history of tyranny. The most striking but by no means the only instances are the hole cut in a page of his novel *Albert Angelo* and the presentation, in *The Unfortunates*, of a box containing a bundle of unbound gatherings to be read in random order. Of these more later.

Johnson was very serious about these innovations, but they kidnap the notion of experiment or estrangement by making it appear that the violation of narrative order in the interests of what he thought of as truth must be blatant. In fact these tricks simply prompt one to ask what the point of this sort of innovation really is. They distract attention from the novel, the true interest of which is independent of them. Johnson must have been aware of this when he agreed with his publisher to label the first and last gatherings of *The Unfortunates* as opening and close, to avoid confusing readers, thereby greatly reducing the randomness he had wanted to prevail, but giving his readers a break. Since there isn't a great deal of development in the story anyway, what is left is not very different from a conventional presentation. The book is interesting and well written, but it has never been the primary topic of discussion, the sensationally loose gatherings in the box having preempted that position.

Johnson was a stubborn man, but he must have had some notion of this. His attention was reserved for the manipulation of the more material aspects of books. If he had known the word, he would have cared as little about 'narratology' (still not admitted to the *OED*) as Lawrence might have done. Some time around 1972 he came once or twice with his agent, Michael Bakewell, to a seminar at University College London, attended by students and lecturers but open to interested visitors. I can't now remember anything he said, but he made himself welcome, and my memory is of a large and genially argumentative presence. He enjoyed the relative informality of the occasion and enjoyed the arguments, taking part in them but less ferociously than Coe would lead one to expect. The seminar included graduate students fresh from Paris, from the classrooms of Barthes and Gérard Genette, who had so elegantly explained 'anachrony' and the way narrative can defy chronology. In Genette's analepses, prolepses, syllepses and the like in 'classical' narrative Johnson could summon little interest, though these words relate to matters that did concern him. He was a little like Casaubon, slaving at his system but taking no notice of what the clever Germans had been doing for the best part of a century; but this analogy breaks down when one remembers that Casaubon's results were meaningless, while Johnson's results were his forceful and idiosyncratic novels.

His basic error arose from his belief that the truth of narratives was incompatible with the usual way of presenting them: that is, in books which by their very technology insisted on a spurious sequentiality. At the same time, he thought that the neglect of all manner of various typographic opportunities, long since exploited by Sterne and now shamefully ignored, was another enemy of the truth. That the material structure of books can affect their contents is of course true. The use of the codex in preference to the scroll made for a decisive difference between the Gospels and the books of the Hebrew Bible; the codex made easily available relationships between pages remote from one another, and these books, with numbered and turnable pages, may have influenced the writers and probably affected the early course of the new religion.

The modern book descends from the codex, not the scroll, and it inherits and develops the advantages of the form. Resonances between remote parts of a story can be achieved without cutting holes in pages: a regressive technique, which is expensive and does nothing that cannot be done without the bother. But Johnson wanted the reader to see through three lines at the end of page 149 of *Albert Angelo* and read on page 153 an account of the fight at Deptford in which Marlowe received a 'mortal wound above his right eye'. The reference to that historical moment is what Genette would call a 'heterodiegetic analepsis', and, horrible as that sounds, the effect it specifies can be achieved without cutting holes in the pages. There was no need of the famous hole, though the hole and the frantic conclusion of the book are what people think about first when they turn their attention to *Albert Angelo*. The conclusion is a rhetorical trick enacting a great burst of candour; Johnson abruptly breaks off the story and says he will now tell only the truth: 'fuck all this lying . . . whats the point in covering up covering up covering over . . . I want to tell the truth about me . . . if I start falsifying in telling stories then I move away from the truth of my truth which is not good.' Telling the truth means holes in the page and typographical variation, chapters in random order, as if the book, to contain truth, needs to be a model of the author's mind, or of the universe. But he can't stop telling stories even in that final section.

Coe is a devoted biographer though not entirely happy in his work, wishing he was not telling the truth about Johnson but writing his own lying novels. He departs agreeably from the normal procedures of the biographer, sometimes a little in the manner of *The Quest for Corvo*. He provides copious quotation from the novels/autobiographies and the filmscripts and football reports, as well as from surviving acquaintances of the author. Now and then he lets the spotlight play on himself, as he visits Johnsonian haunts or trawls through that huge archive.

His main interest is in the novels, and early in the book he provides a useful potted version of each of the seven. It was the more necessary to do so, since some of them have been hard to find; but there is now a new 'omnibus' volume from Picador containing *Albert Angelo*, *Trawl* and *House Mother Normal*. Picador have also in recent years nobly reproduced *The Unfortunates* in its box, and reprinted *Christie Malry's Own Double-Entry*. For Johnson's first novel, *Travelling People*, and his last, *See the Old Lady Decently*, one had best try Amazon.

Coe describes *Travelling People* as concealing under 'a veneer of stylistic adventurousness . . . a conventional enough Bildungsroman' which mingles fiction and autobiography in a manner Johnson soon came to deplore. Each chapter is done in a different style, a homage to *Ulysses*, but this did not save it from its author's condemnation as a story, not the truth. *Albert Angelo* was meant to correct that fault. In its scattered, episodic way it tells the tale of a young architect forced to work as a supply teacher while lamenting the loss of – or, as he prefers to put it, his betrayal by – a girlfriend: an obsessively recurring theme in Johnson's work, so that even the devoted Coe gets fed up with it. But this book made it obvious, if its predecessor hadn't quite done so, that Johnson was a strong writer; he had a wide range of interests and treated them in resourceful prose. His real enemy was not what he thought of as the inevitable falsity of stories but an agonised egotism, the sense that it was essential but impossible to tell the whole truth about himself. Warburg, who preferred novels, was right to think he would be fobbed off with a series of autobiographies. Johnson wanted his books to be entirely about himself, as he sat there in his familiar room writing them. He greatly admired Frank Harris's *My Life and Loves*, until he heard that Harris told lies. He might have admired Rousseau and eventually been disillusioned again. Not that he read Rousseau; his reading was scattered and he didn't seem to understand that his troubles were not uniquely his, that it is well known that autobiography and fiction share a very unstable frontier.

Trawl, the third novel, is hardly a novel at all, though Johnson perversely insisted on saying it was. It is an autobiographical account, 'all interior monologue', of three weeks passed in a deep sea trawler. Amid the discomforts of his passage the author reflects on or trawls his past, his sorrows and betrayals, his experience as a wartime evacuee. When he reaches port, his wife, who was to give him some years of relative happiness, is waiting on the quayside. Coe finds this conclusion 'too pat', and Johnson himself might have thought it involved a certain illicit manipulation of the facts, a concession to story, the enemy of truth. But *Trawl* has magnificent pages and can claim to be his best-written book.

The Unfortunates, the famous novel-in-a-box, was published in 1969. As I have already remarked, the randomness it aspires to is much reduced by the fact that the first and last sections are blatantly identified as such. In between are 25 sections one is invited to read in any order, a muddle in the middle. Johnson had been a football reporter on a Sunday paper, and his story is accordingly of a football reporter who goes to Nottingham to cover a game. A very close friend of his had lived there, though, with a vague gesture to Kafka, this man is said not to recognise the city. Eventually he makes his way slowly towards the stadium. We follow haphazardly, as he laments the death of his friend from cancer at 29. Mourning is randomly interspersed with other remarks on the protagonist's past, and comments on Nottingham architecture. The general effect is excellent; once again Johnson proves that his powers as a writer can withstand his quixotic attempt to overcome the hated restrictions imposed on his truth-telling by the odious convention of binding up paper, each page in its due and boring order, into artefacts known as books.

Formal experimentation continues in *House Mother Normal* (1971), which consists of a series of monologues by the inmates of an old folks' home, each further gone in senility than his or her predecessor. This regress is signalled not only by increases in mental confusion but by typography less and less coherent, the type straying over the page, and with some pages simply blank. As Coe explains, there are ten sections each of 21 pages, and the same event occurs on the same page, and on the same line, in all the sections. Coe argues that this makes the book 'richly polyphonic'. The House Mother has the final word: she describes herself as 'the concoction of a writer' – another sop to Johnson's conscientious objection to making things up.

The most amusing of the novels (and Johnson had considerable comic talents) is the brief *Christie Malry's Own Double-Entry* (1973). Christie is a clerk in a Hammersmith cake factory (as Johnson himself had once been). Having mastered double-entry book-keeping (which I have heard described as the invention that made the modern world possible), Christie applies the principle – 'every Debit must have its Credit' – to his own dealings with that world. Whenever he suffers an injustice he credits his side of the ledger appropriately. Beginning with trifles, he progresses to larger evils. 'Socialism not given a chance' is balanced by £311,398. He ends by murdering 20,000-odd Londoners by poisoning their water supply. The number is selected because it is, roughly, the number of words in the novel. The Offence for which this slaughter provided Recompense was committed by Them. The book rattles along, its lexicon full of mysterious words like *helmnuthoid, retripotent, campaniform, sufflamination, ungraith* and *brachyureate*. There is much enjoyable fun at the expense of the author's own narcissism.

The last novel, *See the Old Lady Decently*, was meant to be the first of a trilogy about the life of Johnson's mother and the contemporaneous decline of Britain. It covers the time between his mother's birth in 1908 and his own in 1933. Published posthumously (1975), it is a complicated book, mixing facts about his mother's youth as a waitress with documents including letters from her father in the army and facsimiles of the official correspondence concerning his death. Despite the degree of organisation implied by the numerical coding of the chapters, Coe can describe the book as 'diverse and fragmentary'. The medley includes concrete poems, extracts from Erich Neumann's *The Great Mother*, and an elaborate account of the progress of a foetus (himself) from conception to birth, so Coe's stricture seems just, if a little severe.

It is part of Johnson's charm that he has so many ways of making the medley interesting. He can explain his worship of the White Goddess and tell bawdy jokes, offering Chaucer as a precedent. The jokes may not be up to much, but in the end it seems right to admire the author's nerve.

For someone who died at 40 he wrote quite a lot, and intelligent people who knew him found him to be intelligent as well as huge and perverse. Coe does him justice, fascinated by his sentimental and generous style of life and his ineradicable conviction of his own slighted genius. He was self-destructive, intense in his friendships, unlucky in love, but perhaps making more of that than most people feel they should. He could, without blushing, apply to himself the lines of Hopkins:

> O the mind, mind has mountains; cliffs of fall
> Frightful, sheer, no-man-fathomed. Hold
> them cheap
> May who ne'er hung there . . .

Like other poets, he had a religious sense but no religion, except for the White Goddess, whom he found in Robert Graves. Having experienced an epiphany, he had a strong though not entirely easy personal connection with this goddess, believing she would ensure that he would never have a happy love, and that he would die at 29. Michael Bakewell, the agent he settled with after insulting all the others, saw him as a tormented character with an ever-deepening sense of the unfairness of the world. Coe catches quite brilliantly his arrogance (of those 'Oxbridge bastards' he could say: 'Not only are your novels not as good as mine, but you haven't even *started*') and quotes from Graves's *The White Goddess* the story of Little Gwion, 'a person of no importance' who accidentally lit on some mysteries, became an adept, and 'began to despise the professional bards of his time because they did not understand the rudiments of their traditional poetic lore'. 'Bryan Johnson, isn't it?' asked Coe. And then he found Johnson's own copy of Graves's book, with that passage underlined. A pleasant reward for a conscientious though temporary biographer, who can now get on with his novels.

5 August 2004

MANUFACTURED HUMBUG

....

John Payne Collier: Scholarship and Forgery in the 19th Century
by Arthur Freeman and Janet Ing Freeman

Shakespeare scholarship in the mid 19th century, one gathers, was not only very competitive but also morally dangerous. It could threaten the virtue, even on occasion the sanity, of its practitioners, a diverse group united only by their lust for Shakespeareana and their unflaggingly competitive spirit. Enthusiastic, self-taught amateurs, they developed professional skills at a time when university professionals took little interest in vernacular scholarship. They mostly earned their livings in other clerkly trades, as journalists, parliamentary reporters or lawyers. In their spare time they collected 16th and 17th-century books and manuscripts, learned booty which was much easier to find than it later became, and pored unsupervised over ancient documents in virtually unexplored public and private collections. They worked heroically and announced their discoveries with extraordinary fervour. They met, to compliment or deceive one another, at certain booksellers, or in the British Museum Reading Rooms, where they might make the acquaintance of the scholarly but not always accessible palaeographers who dominated that library. They anxiously cultivated the aristocratic owners of great private collections, and they published their discoveries at a rate that can only be called abandoned, meanwhile exchanging insults, though mostly in gentlemanly prose. For learned disputes had gentlemanly antecedents, and so had learned fabrications; even Thomas Warton was guilty, and he was the author of the standard *History of English Poetry*, a work some Shakespeare hunters saw as a model for their much desired history of English drama.

The deceits practised by the 19th-century forgers were more sophisticated, though less celebrated, than those with which William Henry Ireland in the previous century had deceived James Boswell and many others, though not the great Shakespearean Edmond Malone (himself guilty of tampering with manuscripts). The men of this new age were scholars, working in a tradition often said to have originated with Malone and achieving, in the 20th century, an extraordinary degree of refinement. They were pioneers, but were too easily excited, and enjoyed too much liberty. As collectors they were prone, as a contemporary put it, to experience difficulty in distinguishing between *meum* and *tuum*. Their scholarship could be too creative; to learn to read secretary hand you have to learn to write it yourself, but the next step should not be to acquire some old paper, mix some plausibly ancient-seeming ink, and forge or alter documents in order to augment the supply of relevant information. But to some otherwise respectable students of the subject such activities were felt to be a legitimate extension of scholarly research.

J.O. Halliwell (1820-89) was one such. Probably best known to modern readers from Samuel Schoenbaum's account of him in *Shakespeare's Lives* (1991), Halliwell was a researcher of fantastic industry and skill. He began his own collection when he was 15, and by 19 was a fellow of both the Society of Antiquaries and the Royal Society. At 17 he entered Trinity College, Cambridge, and when he transferred himself to Jesus College his departure from Trinity coincided with the loss of a large number of manuscripts from the library. These he seems to have sold to Thomas Rodd, a well-known bookseller, who sold some of them on to the British Museum, where Sir Frederic Madden, the most celebrated of those closeted palaeographers, noticed that at least one of the volumes bought from Rodd had originated from Trinity. He further observed that it had evidently been messed about with. Some pages had been renumbered, and the new numbers were in Halliwell's hand.

The museum authorities, with notable restraint, advised him that he should 'abstain from frequenting our Reading Rooms' until the matter had been investigated. Halliwell at once wrote a pamphlet defending himself, while Trinity and the museum authorities considered a criminal prosecution; but for some reason they decided to drop the whole affair, so Halliwell was free to return to the Reading Rooms, and the Trinity manuscripts remained there, too. All concerned seem to have been remarkably relaxed about this incident, the like of which would nowadays cause heads to roll. It is thought by some, though not by the Freemans, that Halliwell also got away with the theft, from his future father-in-law, of one of the two extant copies of the First Quarto of *Hamlet* (1603). Much later in his life he is said to have remarked that if he ever came across something he thought he could look after better than its owner could, he would not scruple to steal it.

The owner of the *Hamlet* quarto was Sir Thomas Phillipps, a baronet neatly described by Schoenbaum as 'a harmful eccentric'. He let it be known that he wanted to own a copy of every book in the world. While examining Phillipps's library, perhaps defective by these standards but amazing by most others, Halliwell fell in love with and married the baronet's daughter. Thereafter Phillipps hated the young man implacably, and did all he could to damage him and his wife. Halliwell nevertheless went on with his work, much of which was of biographical importance. When Phillipps died in 1872, his son-in-law, to comply with the terms of the baronet's will, assumed his name, so becoming Halliwell-Phillipps, the name he is still best known by. On the whole, his might be counted a successful if eccentric scholarly career.

Understandably, he had a practised eye for the forgeries and fabrications of others, and had justified doubts about some of the work of one senior scholar, John Payne Collier. Halliwell was still only 20 when, in 1840, he joined three distinguished figures – Alexander Dyce, Charles Knight and Collier – in founding the Shakespeare Society. Collier was then around fifty, with another forty-odd years to live. He was already quite famous and has never ceased to be so. The broad outline of his long career is well enough known; his major frauds are well documented, and although some points remain in dispute there is no longer any support for the idea that he was not repeatedly guilty of forgery and fabrication.

This new, absolutely enormous, and remarkably lively bio-biography goes with minute care into all the questions raised by Collier's career. Four hundred pages are devoted to a bibliography; the remaining thousand include a fairly circumstantial account of Collier's ordinary life, but are mostly about books and manuscripts and forgeries. The Freemans make it plain that they like and even admire Collier, referring to him throughout as 'John' and pointedly refraining from making a moral fuss about his misdemeanours. These are described in unprecedented detail. The book is a wonderful demonstration of professional care and zeal by bibliophiles who can take all the space they want to express their appreciation of and, within reason, sympathy for, a distinguished predecessor and colleague. It has long been the custom to deplore the confusion he created, especially in cases where some invention of his, so long as it remained undetected, involved major adjustments to Shakespeare's life records. Some therefore call his conduct criminal, others lament the way he added to an already difficult project the nuisance of having to purge the record of his meddling. The Freemans do none of these things. They enjoy the job too much; they are bibliophiles who sympathise with bibliophily even when it is perverted into bibliomania; but they specify the perversions with great accuracy.

Collier's first job was as a parliamentary reporter for the *Times*, and later for the *Morning Chronicle*. In his early years he associated with such dangerous radicals as Thomas Holcroft and John Thelwall, William Godwin and Hazlitt. Crabb Robinson was a friend, and Wordsworth, Coleridge and Lamb acquaintances. His work as a reporter was fairly arduous, and his social activities, along with his scholarly avocation and his own poetry, for which he was very ambitious, meant that he was always busy. Well equipped by his shorthand skills, he recorded most of the Shakespeare lectures given by Coleridge in 1811-12. Later, at the time of the hue and cry against him, these transcripts were called fraudulent. The question is complicated, and it is evident that the reports are not pure Coleridge, but the Freemans applaud Collier for providing something when, without him, we should have nothing.

The authors certify as Collier's 'earliest essay in deception' a fictive account of a Punch and Judy show written for the *Times* from Margate; the deception lies not in the essay itself but in Collier's citing it 16 years later as a factual contribution to the literature of the subject – on which, however, we're told he remains a standard authority. But he could not let the truth alone. His fabrications, 'usually brief and often scattered amidst authentic testimony or text . . . can be far more difficult to identify than large-scale imposture, and are more likely to corrupt or distort'.

His *History of English Dramatic Poetry* (1831) contains a fake petition from Shakespeare's company concerning the use of the theatre at Blackfriars. This, or a copy of it, he claimed to have found in the State Paper Office. In fact, the association of the company – the Lord Chamberlain's Men – with the Blackfriars did not begin till 1609, and this document of 1596, which lists Shakespeare among the petitioners, seemed to establish his place among the seniors of the company some years earlier than had been believed. But the document, ingeniously but fatally circumstantial, also mentioned another theatre, the 'house on the Bankside called the Globe', which did not exist in 1596; Collier here was let down by a mistake of Malone's. The Freemans commend the technical performance of the forger, but here he had forged too thoroughly, as he quite often did.

Even more troublesome was his tampering with the diary of the entrepreneur Philip Henslowe, a prime source of information on the drama of the time. It had been bequeathed by Henslowe's son-in-law, the actor Edward Alleyn, to Dulwich College, whose librarians evidently, and as we have seen mistakenly, trusted the faith of a gentleman, allowing Malone to take it home with him. He kept it for thirty years. When it was returned to Dulwich after Malone's death, Collier moved in, and used his carefully prepared ancient ink to add, in his practised secretary hand, some items that lack whatever interest they might have had if they had been genuine. This fraud understandably causes the Freemans to wonder why he would trouble to invent such 'arcana' and 'risk his reputation for a pittance'. It is a recurrent mystery in Collier's life.

How did Collier, closely observed by envious rivals, get away with it for so long? When fabrications were detected his usual excuse was that other hands were responsible, and that he was himself the victim of fraud. But he had eventually to face more direct and explicit challenges. The story of the Perkins Folio begins in 1852, here described as 'one of the key dates in the entire history of Shakespeare studies'. Since it occupies 160 pages of this book it will be understood that a summary of it must be hopelessly inadequate. According to Collier, he had called at Rodd's shop in the spring of 1849, just as the bookseller was unpacking some items bought at a country auction. Among them was a battered copy of the Shakespeare Second Folio of 1632, which Collier bought on the spot for 30 shillings. (It is important that, on this account of the matter, Rodd had no time to look closely at the book; and in any case he died almost immediately after this meeting.) A cursory examination persuaded Collier that the copy – stained by 'wine, beer and other liquids' and by candle snuffs and tobacco ash – was too badly damaged to be of interest, but a year or so later he had another look and belatedly noticed that it contained thousands of textual corrections made in a secretary hand by somebody he called the 'Old Corrector', presumably the person who inscribed on one of the covers the words 'Tho. Perkins, his booke'.

The importance of this folio arose from the fact that the corrections, if genuine, were made within a few years of Shakespeare's death, perhaps by somebody connected with the theatre. It was interesting, if a little suspicious, that some of the corrections were, so to speak, pre-echoes of emendations made by later scholars, including Collier himself; but the acumen of the emendators would serve to explain that. Collier allowed members of the Shakespeare Society to look at the folio for two hours only, and thereafter it proved almost impossible for any qualified person to get his hands on it. A certain Francis Parry claimed, on the basis of Collier's account of the book, to have been a former owner. He sought opportunities to confirm this opinion, and once met Collier in the street with the folio under his arm, but Parry, who was recovering from an accident and walking with the support of two sticks, was physically incapable of profiting from the encounter. This is not the only instance of collectors bumping into one another in the street, or at the BM, with possibly precious books tucked under their arms.

Meanwhile 'an amateur antiquary' called A.E. Brae, by profession a railway engineer from Leeds, had directly accused Collier of forgery, or 'manufactured humbug', in his reports of the Coleridge lectures as well as in the Perkins Folio. Collier sued him for criminal libel, swearing an affidavit that he had not, in his published specimen transcriptions, 'inserted a single word, stop, sign, note, correction, alteration, or emendation' that was not in the original, which he believed to have been annotated soon after 1632. The case came before the Lord Chief Justice, who expressed his confidence in the character of his friend Collier, but denied that the court had any business with 'mere literary criticism'.

However, the hunt was up, and Collier found he had implacable as well as learned enemies, notably C.M. Ingleby, N.E.S.A. Hamilton, and Sir Frederic Madden at the BM, who was full of expert indignation but refused to go public. Collier had rather brilliantly presented the folio to his patron, the sixth Duke of Devonshire, a famous collector, whose librarian prevented anybody from seeing it. But the duke died, and the seventh duke obligingly lent the book to Madden. Inspecting it at last, the experts were able to show that the annotations had been written in pencil and then inked in; that there had been an attempt to erase the pencil markings; and that the ink used was not 17th-century ink. Once the actual book was in the BM, the job of proving it a fraud was easy enough. In 1861 Ingleby published his *Complete View of the Shakspere Controversy*, an indictment that does not confine itself to the Perkins Folio but includes earlier Collier misdemeanours.

Collier did not reply, though he attempted a sort of excuse in an autobiography written when he was in his nineties. Shortly before he died he forbade his family ever to say anything in his defence. In old age he felt, quite rightly, that he had undermined his own reputation as a great Shakespearean, and in a note written in 1882, a year before his death at 94, he wrote: 'My repentance is bitter and sincere.' His repentance would have been more useful if he had identified his fabrications and forgeries, some of which are still under question. The Perkins emendations constituted, the authors say, 'a secret hoard of inadmissible evidence . . . which could be solemnly quarried (as it was, and still is) by right-minded modern editors'.

Collier's life was strenuous and, these crazy frauds apart, conventionally virtuous. In his youth he wrote vaguely Romantic poems and perhaps played billiards with Keats. Despite an avowed dislike for women he supported a large family by exhausting piecework. At 60, still in quest of a secure income, he tried to get the job of cataloguing the British Museum library, but was thwarted by the great Sir Anthony Panizzi and had to survive as before. His one lapse from professional competence as a parliamentary reporter resulted in the editor of the *Times* being summoned to the bar of the House, while Collier himself was committed to the custody of the Sergeant-at-Arms, narrowly escaping Newgate and finally getting off with a sentence of one day and a reprimand.

He was an almost incomparably hard worker – though Halliwell ran him close – and is justly regarded as basically an accomplished and original scholar. The Freemans think his Shakespeare edition of 1842-44 the best there was before the long-lived Cambridge Globe edition of 1864. In certain respects he anticipated the work of the 'new' bibliographers of the 20th century. He came close to a modern understanding

of the origin of the 'bad' 1603 quarto of *Hamlet*. It sometimes appears
that it was a simple excess of intellectual energy that led him to produce so many fakes – or perhaps some deep confusion between the arts
of discovery and invention. He enjoyed risks and was often absurdly
reckless, but he was wily in his own defence and a resourceful combatant when challenged. He was also, on a sterner indictment, a thief, a
liar and a perjurer. But he made many genuine discoveries, and sometimes their authenticity has had to be defended by the very investigators – the Freemans among them – whose primary business has been
to detect his forgeries. He enjoyed disputation; his polemical manner
was sly rather than vicious, and he knew when to keep quiet.

His is a curious celebrity. His skills command the exhaustive attention of investigators as skilful and diligent as the Freemans, and for
reasons good and bad his name will always be associated with Shakespeare's. Other bibliophiles have required the same kinds of critical
attention, keenest when they were misbehaving – not only the gathering of Victorian delinquents listed in this book, but, in later times, that
bibliographer's delight T.J. Wise. But Collier has a special place among
them, and the Freemans have built him an appropriate monument.

16 December 2004

A VERY SMART BEDINT

....

Harold Nicolson by Norman Rose

Like everybody else, I had read a lot about Harold Nicolson and his amazing marriage, but paid little attention to him as the author of many books, including a biography of his father, Lord Carnock, a best-selling life of King George V, a life of Mrs Charles Lindbergh's father, some novels and some historical studies. Of these works I had read only one, the pseudo-autobiographical *Some People*, first published in 1927 (according to the Author's Note, 'many of the following sketches are purely imaginary. Such truths as they may contain are only half-truths'). Sixty years on, I had forgotten everything about the book except its incidental allusions to Nicolson's admired friend Lord Eustace Percy, a minor character, but of special interest to me because at the time he was my boss. I, too, admired this courteous scion of the great Northumberland dukedom, partly because of the divinatory powers that had enabled him to choose me, from a field of candidates all manifestly much better qualified than I, for a job at King's College, Newcastle, part of the University of Durham, of which he was at that time the rector. He had been a Conservative MP and briefly a young cabinet minister; great things were expected of him, but for one reason or another they didn't happen. The *DNB*'s explanation is he was not 'a good House of Commons man'.

I remember in particular a moment in that bleak year, 1947. The refectory at the college was approached by two separate staircases, one for men and one for women. No ordinary person dared question the propriety of this arrangement. But one day, as we left after eating a horrible lunch together, Lord Eustace surveyed the staircases, saw that the male one was crowded, and said: 'Let us use the zenana stairs.' This struck me as at once brave and exotic, qualities no doubt to be expected of a man who had spent his youth in the Foreign Office, and had an easy acquaintance with the domestic arrangements of Tehran and points east.

Lord Eustace, as he appeared in *Some People*, was the cleverest of

Harold Nicolson's early friends. They shared the hard labour and discomfort of life in Paris under the discipline of Jeanne de Hénault, a famous Diplomatic and Foreign Service crammer, who gets a chapter to herself in *Some People*. She thought so well of Lord Eustace that she proposed him as a candidate for the vacant job of king of France. Nicolson acknowledged his own inferiority to Percy, though since Percy was so superior this did not make Nicolson very inferior; and in later years he sometimes fancied himself as a possible viceroy of India.

Some People, on a second reading, seemed less charming than it was in 1947. I had forgotten how affected it is. Much of it is in French, though perhaps nobody who cares to read it will mind that, and, after all, the young men were preparing to be diplomats in the days when diplomats had to talk French; but there is still an air of slightly uneasy ostentation, increased by various untranslated allusions to classical literature and the habit of rendering quite ordinary Greek words like *hubris* in Greek characters. All the same, this book showed that writing many lengthy and boring official reports and aides-mémoire had not cured Nicolson of wanting to be a writer, or destroyed his ability to amuse. Some of the persons he described have lingered on in the cultural memory: Ronald Firbank, who stood for a careless bohemian style of life that Nicolson, in a nervous kind of way, found attractive, appears under the name of Lambert Orme. Other personages, some grand in their time, may be remembered only by historians. The book was a success and even won the praise of Virginia Woolf, who normally did not allow her intimate connection with his family to sweeten her comments on his work. But some diplomatic superiors thought the book cheeky.

Of course *Some People* was published many years before Nigel Nicolson's *Portrait of a Marriage* (1973), which, with all the attendant volumes of correspondence and diaries, made Harold Nicolson and Vita Sackville-West more famous for their unusual private lives than for their works. A benefit offered by this new biography is that all that gossip has to take its place along with the non-marital rest of a life that was certainly full. Its subject was an ambitious diplomat and an ambitious writer and journalist, never entirely easy in any of these roles, and, although to the disenchanted eye a peculiar person, a man who was in many respects quite like the handful of others who guided our frequently disastrous political destinies through the first half of the 20th century. He was often said by excellent companions to have been an excellent companion, but was, without wishing it, a man many will find fairly hard to like.

A favourite word of Nicolson's was 'bedint', which somehow derived from the German and signified a person of servile status. It may have originated in the Sackville family, which was so grand that even Nicolson, marrying into it, was conscious of his social inferiority and must have feared that he might be so labelled. In its usage, by a necessarily limited circle of friends, 'bedint' could be extended to mean any sort of person the speaker felt it right to despise or patronise or avoid, and might even be applied to a dull member of the royal family. The knighthood Nicolson reluctantly, faute de mieux, accepted late in life was described as a bedint knighthood. It was suggested that after accepting it he should resign from all his clubs.

The need to keep out the bedints meant keeping social fences in good order. Nicolson preferred not to talk to men who had not been at a good public school. He himself, after the usual dismal prep school, went to Wellington, a relatively bedint-free environment, notable for its fierce but unavailing opposition to homosexuality. He quite liked Wellington, and thought it of great importance to go from there to Balliol, the only college that seemed suited to his intellectual ambitions.

He had a good time at Oxford, but somehow didn't quite fit in at Balliol, partly because of the unexpected presence in the college of 'blacks and Rhodes scholars' and, outside it, of impudent women students. As Norman Rose remarks, this 18-year-old already displayed a lifelong prejudice, a conviction that 'mankind was divided into two categories: a racial, social and intellectual aristocracy, to which, naturally, he belonged; and the rest, philistines in taste, who, by definition, were excluded from his gilded circles'. It might be added that his dislikes were not secret: of blacks he used blatantly insulting expressions, and meeting a Jewish lord mayor of London made him say he felt some sympathy for Eichmann. Among other humans he could not bear were the Japanese, Turks, Persians, Arabs, Slavs and Catholics.

What with the frequent anti-intellectual but non-bedint entertainment provided at Balliol by the profusely celebrated 'Sligger' Urquhart, and vacations spent in his father's embassies in Madrid, St Petersburg and so on, Nicolson was reduced to a disappointing third in Greats. One can imagine what a blow that result would have been to a bedint who had somehow made his way to Oxford: probably a melancholy recourse to Gabbitas and Thring. For Nicolson, however, it was no more than a passing irritation. His family decided he must be a diplomat like his father. It was a good career choice, as he would meet few colleagues who were not the sons of peers or at least from very good families and very good schools.

The fact that salaries were so comically low that one needed a private income was something of a problem; the Nicolson family was not rich, though not what many would call poor either. Later there was Sackville money available. Nicolson complained throughout his life of tight finances, even when he had a handsome house, half a dozen servants, and sons at the correct educational establishments. Some people measure their financial status in terms of relative poverty rather than relative riches; if you keep raising your style of life to a level appropriate to the increasing grandeur of your social position you may well find you become, in a strictly relative way, poor. This perception might be reinforced by anxiety about the social proximity of people even grander than yourself; Nicolson even worried about his name, rather plebeian despite the elegantly absent 'h', and thought that if he achieved a peerage he would get rid of it by commandeering some vacant Sackville title.

Except for his presumably more democratic homosexual excursions, he stayed well within the fences he had built, and his failure as a politician was in part brought on by his loathing of the constituents he had to be nice to: 'I fear the "People" means nothing to me except ugliness.' Canvassing was as painful to the prospective MP as dealing with the 'beastly niggers' with whom, as a junior FO official, he had to trail around the sights of London.

Norman Rose, a Jew and inescapably a bedint, keeps calm, almost to the end, about this side of Nicolson, recording without comment Nicolson's automatic insults (Proust, with whom he discussed 'inversion', was 'very Hebrew', the Hungarian foreign minister 'a little oily Jew'; and so was Emil Ludwig). He is relaxed about Nicolson's relations with Oswald Mosley and does justice to his professional performance as a diplomat. In that capacity Nicolson seems to have kept his prejudices under control – for instance, he supported the Balfour Declaration. The Versailles negotiations of 1919 provided what was probably his best moment. He studied the world's leaders at close hand. He respected Lloyd George, a very smart bedint, but thought the rest of them 'ignorant and irresponsible men cutting up the world as though it were a cake'. He supported the League of Nations, deplored reparations and other revanchist decisions, and formed a permanent dislike for what later came to be called 'summit' meetings. The politicians didn't understand diplomacy; it was best left to professionals. The 'spiritually arrogant' Woodrow Wilson he particularly deplored, and the dogmatic Poincaré almost as much.

While observing these great, dangerous men, Nicolson was himself working hard at drawing new European boundaries and writing copious memoranda. An unrepentant imperialist, he nevertheless seems to have understood other points of view, and he had an admirable mastery of detail. To some friends, and some enemies, it must at this time have appeared that although he was sometimes on the wrong side of the question he had serious diplomatic prospects. And there was a burgeoning literary career as well, one to which he appeared well suited, though not, as he acknowledged, a very high flier.

He was a fast worker – 10,000 words a day, 40,000 in a week – even while holding his Foreign Office job and enjoying appropriately aristocratic sports, like shooting, and pursuing gazelles in motor cars. He rapidly wrote books on Verlaine, Swinburne, Byron and Tennyson, always justifiably anxious about their reception in the Bloomsbury circle (where his friendships were generally uneasy), and always keen that they should make money.

The moment came when he had to choose between two uncertain futures. Part of the argument for giving up diplomacy was his wife's strong objection to the tedium of foreign embassies, even Tehran. But then a 'haughty' paper of his annoyed Austen Chamberlain, the foreign secretary – in Nicolson's view, a bedint Birmingham ironmonger like his half-brother Neville – and this at a time when *Some People*, despite its success, was being called 'a cad's book'. He was useful; he knew Germany well, and was prescient about the rise of National Socialism, while continuing to deplore the 'arrogance' of the Jews who usurped the restaurant tables of the Wilhelmine elite. But he was allowed to go.

He was a little sorry, but did not lose his access to the great ones of his day. Rose's book makes the most of Nicolson's acquaintance with many great men between the wars: the feeble Neville Chamberlain; the hopeless Eden; the charming, charismatic Churchill. He was important enough to be on the Nazi blacklist, scheduled for early elimination following the occupation. He lingered on in the Commons, sometimes making fiery, ineffective speeches. Rose thinks the high point of his parliamentary career was his attack on the government's foreign policy after Munich: 'this terrible Munich retreat', he said, was 'one of the most disastrous episodes that has ever occurred in our history'. He spoke as one who, at Versailles, had actually drawn the Sudetenland frontier, and who knew the Germans would soon move into Prague. Later he opposed Eden's Suez adventure as 'an act of insane recklessness'.

By that time Nicolson had long since made what Rose calls the move from diplomacy to Grub Street. His journalism was successful, though he hated himself for doing it. His parliamentary career was a failure; but he was established as what a perhaps too candid friend called 'a national figure of the second degree'. He was faithful to the empire but voted Labour and applauded the Beveridge Report, constantly aware of a conflict within himself 'between the patrician and the humanitarian. I hate uneducated people having power, but I like to think the poor will be rendered happy. This is a familiar conflict.' His dislike of Jews did not prevent his advocacy of the state of Israel.

At Sissinghurst he helped to construct a beautiful image of aristocratic retirement, and he did it by working hard beside his partner in that famously odd, snobbish and happy marriage. Norman Rose is no great writer but he is well informed, judicious and charitable, and he leaves his subject more memorable, though possibly less likeable, than he found him.

17 March 2005

OUTRAGEOUS GAME

....

Never Let Me Go by Kazuo Ishiguro

All of Kazuo Ishiguro's six novels are first-person narratives. For the most part the voices of these narrators are quiet, civilised, rather formal. This is so whether the speaker is the obsessive butler of the most famous of the books, *The Remains of the Day* (1989); or one of the somewhat demented heroes of *The Unconsoled* (1995) or *When We Were Orphans* (2000); or the Japanese, guilty or exiled, of the first two books, *A Pale View of Hills* (1982) and *An Artist of the Floating World* (1986). Indeed this way of speaking seems appropriate to Japanese conversation, to the talk of a society in which manners are always important, and in which they might sometimes take precedence over candour. The characters do a lot of deferring and apologising, and even when they aren't expressly said to be bowing gently to one another you can easily imagine they are.

This new book, *Never Let Me Go*, is different in one respect: it does have a first-person narrative but abandons the formality of the previous speakers in favour of a familiar, chatty style no doubt thought right for the character of a young woman of the place and date specified, namely 'England, late 1990s'. Whatever the virtues of this authorial decision, the texture of the writing becomes altogether less interesting, and this may be a reason why the novel seems to be, though only by the standards Ishiguro has set himself, a failure. I open it quite at random and read the first sentences to meet my eye:

What with one thing and another, I didn't get a chance to talk to Tommy for the next few days. Then one lunchtime I spotted him on the edge of the South Playing Field practising his football . . . I went over and sat down on the grass behind him, putting my back against a fence post. This couldn't have been long after that time I'd shown him Patricia C's calendar and he'd marched off, because I remember we weren't sure how we stood with each other.

The story, slightly science-fictional but set in the recent past, is told by a woman 31 years old and looking back to the time between the present and her adolescence. Everything is expertly arranged, as it always is in Ishiguro, but this dear-diary prose surely reduces one's interest.

We begin in a strange school where the pupils, though kindly and intelligently treated by their 'guardians', are quite cut off from the rest of the world. The guardians are severe only on the subject of health, and particularly on smoking. Perhaps by way of compensation the boys and girls don't have the usual adolescent worries about sex: the girls can't conceive and so the guardians leave the young people to get on with it, merely warning them about disease and advising them that sex can have difficult emotional consequences.

Indeed sex, though they sometimes want it quite badly, usually amounts to little more than a way of being friends, or practising for more serious partnerships later on. Instead of fantasising about it they construct a mythology of rumours about other things – about the lives of the guardians or the activities of certain mysterious benefactors, or the unusual conditions that will prevail in their later lives.

When they are told they have been conceived and hatched as clones, they have that sense familiar from sex education classes – that they already knew, that they'd somehow heard the news before without taking it in. They had been given existence solely that they might serve as depositories of anatomical spare parts for surgical use. Now they develop a version, appropriate to their condition, of the family romance: a futile curiosity about the model or source from which they were cloned. On leaving the rather idyllic life of their school – a sort of clones' Bryanston – they become either 'donors' or the 'carers' charged with looking after the donors, who rarely manage to make more than three 'donations' before they 'complete'.

The sadness of the fate of these children is illustrated by the song which gives the novel its title. The narrator loves an old tape by a singer called Judy Bridgewater. In the cover picture Judy is smoking a cigarette, which is why the tape has to be hidden away. She sings a number called 'Baby, baby, never let me go', which our narrator chose, as a child, to misinterpret as the song of a woman happy with her baby, though fearing it might get ill or be taken away. Once when she is dancing to this tape, carrying a pillow as a token baby, she is observed by an unaccountably distressed adult; she will explain her grief much later. The tape disappears, perhaps stolen by a rather devious friend; later another copy is found in a Norfolk shop. Norfolk is the 'lost corner' of England and serves, in the school myth, as the name for the lost property room, but the real county is regarded, half seriously, as the place where lost things will turn up.

The woman who tells the story does so with a reticence imposed by her apparent limitations as a writer, yet is capable in the end of registering, or anyway drawing attention to, the plight of these victims, demonstrated by the violent rages of one of the characters and the simple exclamation – 'You poor creatures' – of another. Ishiguro is fundamentally a tragic novelist; there is always a disaster, remote but urgent, imagined but real, at the heart of his stories. The dateline of this book – 'England, late 1990s' – cannot mean that the cloning of children for these purposes was practised at that time, only that we live as if, having developed promising techniques, we may also find the will to use them; so that what we need by way of response is not the patience and kindness of the guardians or the acquiescence of the victims but an experience of pity and terror, however diluted by the limitations of this narrator and our own imaginations.

In *A Pale View of Hills*, his first novel, Ishiguro keeps the reader in touch with disaster: the bombing of Nagasaki on the historic scale, and, on the domestic scale, the suicide of the narrator's daughter and the strained, altered relations between men and women, parents and children. A culture involving obsolete obligations of honour and ostentatious demonstrations of civility is giving way to coarser American influences: 'Here was a system we'd nurtured and cherished for years. The Americans came and stripped it, tore it down without a thought … And the Japanese welcomed it all. Welcomed it with a lot of talk about democracy.' But the complainant, confronted with his own dubious record under the old regime, can no more defend his honour than he can turn back the American tide.

Ishiguro's foreboding, his imagination of disaster, is not simply political or historical. It seems there is a sort of calamity built into the texture of life. A mysterious, alienated little girl is almost the central character of his first book. Her devious, unsatisfactory mother, the mistress of an American, exploits her friend the kind narrator, and at one point, rather remarkably, intrudes into her narration so that the two of them are for a moment only one. Such violations of novelistic convention are of course deliberate. There will be more surprises of the kind, especially in *The Unconsoled*, but from the outset the reader is sure that the author is in control, and this security enables him, in the later book, to be even more adventurous.

An Artist of the Floating World is also set in a postwar Japan where the cities and the lives of the survivors are being rebuilt. This time the speaker is a retired artist, locating himself in the opening sentence at the Bridge of Hesitation, as it were pausing, like Japan and its citizens, between two worlds. The Floating World is the old pleasure district, where traditional artists, though content with their educational hierarchies and the deference owed to their teachers, lead their version of the vie de bohème: 'One could get drunk there with pride and dignity.' But the district is now squalid, unrecognisable; the bars closed long ago, the girls departed, and the pleasures remain only in the memory of old men.

Matters are different among the young, observed as they stream, in white shirt-sleeves, from the glass-fronted offices that have replaced the bars. The old man accepts them as a portent of his country's changed yet satisfactory future. People of a certain age cannot avoid having had a certain past in the militant Japan that is now for the most part renounced, and the old painter says he will accept some of the responsibility 'for the terrible things that happened to this nation of ours'. Nevertheless a composer who wrote popular wartime songs feels obliged to commit suicide. Only the young need not feel guilt. In their lives patriotism can take a more innocent form. You have to consider whether this is an opinion or an irony.

Some of the old ways persist: families still make careful inquiries before agreeing to a marriage, each side being bound to investigate the soundness of the other, in the past as well as the present. (If necessary they hire private detectives.) As for modern children, they now ignore stories about samurai and shout for the Lone Ranger. Yet even they know how to be polite. Politeness survives and can sometimes be cruel. Getting rid of an unwelcome person you may say, courteously but firmly: 'You should not detain yourself further from your other business.' That is the voice of this writer's Japan – perhaps, in a way, the voice of Ishiguro.

The Remains of the Day is, of course, much the most familiar of the

novels. As the wandering butler speaks – a perfect piece of ventrilo-
quism – he unwittingly exposes injustice, folly, even treachery not seen
as such, at the heart of the English upper class in a prewar world he
admires. Some of the success of the book must be due to the humour
arising from the disparity between the butler's language and the conditions of which, by its very nature, it gives a falsified report. That he is
travelling, ineptly, in his employer's grand car is in itself emblematic of
his situation in life. Subtle though it undoubtedly is, this is the easiest
of the novels, as its popular success testifies.

Almost as if to reject the rewards of such a success, Ishiguro next
produced *The Unconsoled*, a baffling book about bafflement. In one
sense it is an outrageous game, announcing fidelity to novelistic conventions in order to violate them. Like various tracks, streets and cor-
ridors in the story, it seems endless. The characters are clearly that –
characters in a novel – yet they not only speak in character but in doing
so impede the progress of the main story, and defy and delay extremely
important undertakings of the central figure and narrator, Ryder. They
have interests that only appear to serve his, as their city only appears to
offer him the means of fulfilling his plans.

He is a man with an intolerable and ever increasing burden of responsibility who never gets anything done, who gets lost pretty well
every time he steps out of doors, who cannot find out where he is supposed to be or when, or how to get there; a scrupulous man who miss-
es appointments by hours, a weary man who is awakened as soon as
he falls asleep. A woman he encounters accidentally turns out to be
his wife, and the boy with her, who has a problem with adults, is his
son. He bumps, unsurprised, into old friends. Arriving at his hotel, he
meets a porter, deeply devoted to the establishment, who insists that
despite his age he must carry three suitcases. The porter turns out to
be, or turns into, his father-in-law. The manager of the hotel is a great
talker but of little use; he has a son already a virtuoso pianist but refuses to admit it. Like everybody else he demands favours of Ryder, and
these add to the already impossible burdens he carries. He is a great
pianist who must give a recital, even though he cannot find a piano on
which to prepare his performance. He must also save the city, which
has somehow fallen into a state of crisis. He is expecting his aged parents to arrive by horse-driven coach, and, when he happens to think of

them, is anxious about their welfare.

Everybody in this city seems to have an informed interest in very modern music, though the names of the composers they mention are unknown to the world outside. Ryder is acknowledged to be a great man as well as a world-class musician, but despite his magical acquaintance with their most private thoughts he can accomplish nothing with these people, or in this place. Everything is either next door or impossibly far away. His hotel room turns out to be one he has occupied before. At one point he leaves the little boy, Boris, in a café and rushes off on some quest. After giving an obscure but passionate speech about modern music he remembers that the café in which he has delivered this address is next door to the one where he left the forgotten boy, who now leads him on a bizarre search for his mother's apartment. Left in a hut containing an upright piano, Ryder hears from nearby the sound of the conductor Brodsky digging a grave for his favourite cat.

At last Ryder makes the impossibly impeded, belated journey to the concert hall, and is almost there when he finds his way blocked by an impassable wall. His response to this setback is to go to a Hungarian café frequented by hotel porters. He undertakes to defend their cause in his important, city-saving speech. Then he dances with them, then he sleeps.

In a truly remarkable scene – illustrating the comic possibilities of this kind of writing – he comes once more upon the conductor Brodsky, who has been knocked over by a car. A passing surgeon, wishing to help, laments his lack of equipment, but Ryder opens a car boot and finds him a hacksaw, with which he amputates the old man's leg. ('It might be a little painful.') The operation has surprisingly little effect on the conductor's health, and he makes his way to the concert hall. As it turns out, he had a wooden leg and that is what the surgeon has cut off. Lacking it, Brodsky has some difficulty on the podium, but supports himself by using a folding ironing-board as a crutch.

Enough: these allusions to the novel can only confuse in the wrong way. The effect is very like a dream; and the shade of Kafka, who could also be funny, hangs over the scene. Struggling, hopelessly and anxiously late, towards an end of sorts, burdened by his task, self-imposed yet steadily increased by others, in yet not of the society he must save, constantly misled, negligent of his family, tending to find himself not

where he needs to be and compelled to do something not to his purpose – Ryder's tale is an artist's nightmare, the threat of contingency,
of a world in which he or she must achieve great things but, as things
are, things that are beyond his competence. I see this book as a sort of
super-novel in which a failed novelist, urgently aware of his responsibilities yet lost, failing, is betrayed by the trivialities that interfere with
his overwhelming need to remake the world, in this case by the treacherous means of writing a novel. I have not succeeded in explaining that
this is a wonderful book.

In *When We Were Orphans* the narrator is a famous detective who
must, by finding things out, solve an enormous problem concerning
not only the disappearance of his parents in the Shanghai of the 1930s
but, roughly speaking, the fate of the world. Here again are the im-
pudently improbable meetings, the quite implausible coincidences,
but the atmosphere is now rather less vague. Nothing of this could
really have happened, but it is represented as if it did, as if the detective's story were as 'real' as the Japanese attack on Shanghai. In an Ian
Fleming-like coup de théâtre a trusted uncle turns out to be the head
of an opium smuggling organisation. A close childhood friend, now a
wounded soldier in the invading army, is met and cared for.

Since the climax of the action occurs during the Kuomintang defence of Shanghai some rather specific accounts of the fighting are
called for. Nevertheless, Banks, the detective, can address a random
crowd in a manner much like the butler's in *The Remains of the Day*,
or Ryder's in *The Unconsoled*: 'Let me say that I would not be here now
if I were not optimistic about my chances of bringing this case, in the
very near future, to a happy conclusion.' At which point a jazz orches-
tra strikes up. We are in a world quite like that of *The Unconsoled*, but
in this case a more powerful version of reality keeps interfering with
the dream. In the end the detective does find his mother, but the moment of recognition that good plots require is a negative one, and so is
the result of his undertaking to settle the world crisis that is ripening
in the East. On the whole plot wins; this is not a reprise of the novelist's nightmare which is *The Unconsoled*. That is the book which gives
one the fullest idea, vague though it is and sometimes alarming, of the
world of Ishiguro.

21 April 2005

YEARNING FOR THE 'UTILE'

....

What Good Are the Arts? by John Carey

John Carey, former Merton Professor of English Literature at Oxford, an authority on Milton and Donne and Dickens and others, the very model of a Merton Professor, has also been, for decades, the chief reviewer of the *Sunday Times*, a BBC sage, a sought-after chairman of panels, a man well known for his strong opinions on all matters to do with literature and the other arts. These opinions he expresses with unusual force and directness; his manner, as his blurb says, is 'important and provocative', whether pronounced *ex cathedra* in Oxford or in allocutions to a wider public.

His new book reaffirms his view that there is much nonsense talked about the arts. It is not innocent nonsense, and he is much concerned with the harm done by privilege, by the assumption that it is acceptable to finance the pleasures of the rich by cheating the poor, and by the failure of our society to understand that the arts should take their place among other legitimate human interests like religion, sex, rock music and football. Modern attitudes to these and other related matters are based on selfish fantasies and expressed in self-serving cant. His plan is to blow them away with the breath of common sense.

To answer the question asked in his title he begins at the beginning: since we attach so much importance to the idea, what, in fact, constitutes a work of art? It's a newfangled notion – nobody could have asked such a question before the 18th century. Since then it has been a major cause of trouble, much of it stemming from Immanuel Kant – a man who spent his life in a backwater of East Prussia, cared little for the arts, and knew very little about them. His *Critique of Judgment* says what is, in Carey's words, 'patently untrue', namely that the beautiful may be so called only if the speaker believes that everybody else shares his opinion, and also that standards of beauty are absolute and universal. From the same unreliable source came the notion that art objects must be of no practical use, provoke no emotion and offer no sensuous pleasure. The beautiful can give pleasure only as a symbol of the morally good. Artists whose work satisfies these requirements are called geniuses. 'It is strange,' muses Carey, 'that this farrago of superstition and unsubstantiated assertion should have achieved a position of dominance in Western thought.'

His treatment of Kant is a fair illustration of the way Carey tackles the opposition. He provides a brisk account of somebody's thought and then briskly knocks it to pieces. John Dewey's thinking on art, once summarised, can be seen to have 'the precision of cooked spaghetti'. A more recent American aesthetician, Arthur Danto, is one of those who make the impossible claim that their experience of art is more valuable than any that could be derived from the 'kitsch or sentimental outpourings' which other people enjoy. Behind the claims, variously stated, for 'high art' there always lurks this assumption that what I feel is more valuable than what you feel. But of course, Carey says, it is impossible for me to know how and what you feel. Powerless to enter into the inner experience of others, we are all debarred from valid comment on any claim they may make about the status of this or that object as a work of art. 'Anything can be a work of art. What makes it a work of art is that someone thinks of it as a work of art.'

This has the virtue of simplicity, but there is surely more to be said, if not about Kant, then about the terms 'art' and 'work', the first long associated with skills of every sort and the second with the results of their application; for example, Prospero's 'art' was magic, and what the magic accomplished was 'work', a word also used to describe the alchemical process. It is easy enough to see that many people, each knowing what the others were talking about, could agree that some object or process was a work of art. And indeed the extended use of the term to characterise a vase or a painting is surely intelligible to most people. There can obviously be a consensus, shared even by people who happen to think it ugly, about whether a painting by Botticelli is a work of art. This is a matter of linguistic community, not taste. The arguments start only when the term is used to attribute value to an object, or to devalue it by denying it the status implied by both 'art' and 'work'.

Carey maintains that there are 'no rational grounds' for believing that 'high' art is superior to mass or popular art. Persistence in such an opinion is hardly to be distinguished from claims to belong to an upper class. Among those here castigated for snobbery and irrationality are Jeanette Winterson, Clive Bell and Kenneth Clark. The last-named is treated with particular severity because he had such power to impose his false opinions on the world. For example, he had much influence on the decision, in 1939, to store the paintings from the National Gallery in Welsh slate mines. Carey points out bitterly that no comparable service was done to the people of London, and that is true, but he can't be saying that the population of London should have been consigned to Welsh caves. They couldn't, but the paintings could be. And he surely cannot mean that it would have been better if the pictures as well as the people had been bombed; he is hostile to public art galleries but doesn't suggest blowing them up. He just thinks they don't do anybody good.

In fact he devotes a chapter to the question 'Do the arts make us better?' It is a question expecting the answer 'No!' They may make us better art-lovers, but cannot be asked to produce moral improvement. I think this is the right answer, but it's probably oversimplified, and Carey will later explain that it is not quite true of literature. But the idea that public galleries with free access are morally uplifting and a benefit to the poor (which was the reason, given in one form or another, which got them started) is simply false, the sort of crooked thinking to be expected from men of power like Clark. There is no evidence that anybody else benefits from subsidised national collections, and some evidence against the notion. Remember that the greatest art-lover of his time was Hitler, to whose artistic accomplishments Carey devotes several cautionary pages.

And what would it mean, anyway, to be made better by looking at paintings? The idea that it makes you more civilised is intellectually as well as socially disreputable because it involves acceptance of a false definition of civilisation or culture. And the maintenance of this pernicious myth – art does you good morally – costs money. John Tusa of the Barbican remarks that art of high quality is difficult, and its difficulty is not unrelated to its need for heavy subsidy. 'What sort of difficulty,' asks Carey austerely, 'do those attending operas encounter? What is difficult about sitting on plush seats and listening to music?' His indignation at the subsidy paid to the Royal Opera is vented in a pleasing fancy: he imagines the 'well-swaddled' audience leaving the Opera House after an evening of pleasure, made possible by 'colossal injections of other people's money', and languidly hailing their chauffeurs.

All this wickedness and folly is caused by the selfish misconception of 'high art' fostered by such insidious propagandists as Adorno, Benjamin and Geoffrey Hartman of Yale. It is fair to add that what really infuriates Carey is the coexistence in our world of a class that can afford the already heavily subsidised seats at Covent Garden and the myriad fellow humans who live on $2 a day. In so far as we condone this state of affairs, art seems to be making us worse, not better. Carey agrees with Pierre Bourdieu that having a taste for art is more a mark of class than anything else, although one has to remember that working-class people have been known to enjoy *The Well-Tempered Clavier*, and that some middle-class folk admire *La Traviata*. But for Carey the important question is still the apparent lack of connection between sensitivity to art and sensitivity to human suffering. One of the few commentators he quotes with admiration is Marghanita Laski, who asked how many people who have achieved ecstatic experiences through art have been induced to do charity work that involves 'personal contact with people who are physically disgusting'. They are probably rather few. Art doesn't make people better, and the notion that it can do so is the product of 'lax and baseless assumptions and pious hopes'. So too with the notion that art can be a kind of religion; this is a non-starter: 'As a religion . . . art is simply an idolatrous fake.'

Something might yet be done to make art more useful. The Arts Council might go back to what was perhaps its original intention and fund community arts rather than squandering money on metropolitan 'quality'. Drama and painting in prisons have been shown to have good therapeutic results and consequential social benefits. More generally, we could rethink our own assumptions in the light of what is known of other cultures. There is ample anthropological evidence that art can be communal, uncompetitive, accessible to everybody. We might try to think of ourselves as what we in fact are – lonely left-over hunter-gatherers who long for community. We might get a much more helpful response to our loneliness from fashion, gardening and football, though there the male bonding, valuable in principle, sometimes ends in violence.

One thing is sure: the defenders of 'high art' and its power to do good have so weak a case that they 'deserve credit just for trying'. Not that they get much. Iris Murdoch's argument 'collapses the moment you give it the slightest prod'. Chris Smith, defending Blair's invitation to Noel Gallagher, claimed that the prime minister was also deeply moved by *King Lear*, which is a 'banal and evasive piece of claptrap'. With so much at stake, claptrap is the last thing we need; clear thinking on the whole question is essential. So Carey wonders if the scientists can help by making aesthetics a matter of knowledge rather than opinion. Well, if Edward Wilson's *Consilience* is anything to go by, they can't, and the same must be said of Ramachandran and Hirstein, who attempted, by experiments on rats, to divine the deep structure or universal rule underlying all aesthetic experience. Carey emphasises that these are professors of eminence; 'yet the objections to them seem obvious . . . their theory's hopeless ineptitude illustrates the difficulty of applying scientific research to art, even when fine minds attempt it.'

Semir Zeki's *Inner Vision: An Exploration of Art and the Brain* does give the prosecutor a moment's pause. He is impressed by Zeki's point that the visual system of the brain is millions of years older than its linguistic system, and can absorb information far more quickly. But Zeki makes rather little of this, and in the end his 'adventures among the brain cells' achieve nothing. For it does not make sense to say that the vertical lines of Mondrian are 'admirably suited to stimulate cells in the visual cortex', since 'everything we see is admirably suited to stimulate cells in the visual cortex, otherwise we should not see it.' A typical Carey knockout; and one more bleak conclusion: science can't help us either.

A long final chapter on literature proclaims its superiority over all other arts. It is the only one capable of reasoning and the only one that can 'criticise itself' or indeed criticise anything; it is also the only art capable of moralising. Examples are offered to show that literature can indeed do all these things: *Religio Medici*, *Rasselas* ('one of the wisest books ever written, and can be read in an afternoon'), *Gulliver's Travels*, *Middlemarch* – no very surprising or non-canonical choices, except perhaps Conrad's *Victory*, praised for its conclusion, a 'Liebestod' that ought to leave us 'misty-eyed'. 'Lena's vision strikes a blow for "low" popular art, and for the masses who have no knowledge of great literature, and it shows they are capable of supreme courage and pure, selfless love.' Carey could have chosen to discuss the endings of *The Secret Agent* or *Under Western Eyes*, both of which he touches on, but he expressly wants to give precedence to what is by most critics thought an inferior novel because his reasons for admiring it resemble those for which 'the masses' admire soaps. Unlike the figure of the maniac with the bomb and the shattered body of Razumov, Lena's courage can impinge on the heroism of ordinary life as well as on its commonplace tales of sorrow and disappointment, and its unexceptional pleasures. It is a typical Carey choice, and his case for literature is that it can work in this way.

At this point one is inclined to think a suspicion has been confirmed, that Carey's critical argument is an old one – he is commending this art because it can be useful. He has a yearning for the *utile*. All along one has been waiting for a word suggesting a corresponding interest in the *dulce*, the pleasant, the delightful, about which, suspicious of all claims to rapturous experience (obtainable, after all, from drugs) he has hitherto been agnostic. He discusses J.M. Coetzee's claim that his life was changed when, as a teenager in South Africa, he overheard *The Well-Tempered Clavier* being played next door; an experience reminiscent of its archetype in Augustine's *Confessions*, in which another voice in another garden urged a young man to pick up a book and read it. Augustine was symbolically choosing Christianity; what was Coetzee choosing? 'High European culture'? Carey, for him rather weakly, says Coetzee chose what would improve his 'self-respect'. But he does not deny the experience, which is an experience of art.

Whatever may be said against art snobbery and the obscenity of spending millions on paintings while around the world the poor are starving, experiences of art of something like the kind Coetzee reports are not uncommon; they may contain an element of self-congratulation, even of guilt at the thought of their inaccessibility to the deprived, but they aren't essentially fraudulent and need not resemble in any way the chemical ecstasies Carey deplores. There are transactions with poems, paintings and music that involve the unaided imagination.

The second part of the chapter on literature does deal with the place of the imagination in the work of reader and writer. A passage in *Lord of the Flies*, when Simon's body moves at the water's edge, is justly called 'wonderful'. The rest of the section consists mostly of verse, and the commentary admires the quality of 'indistinctness' – writing dense with metaphor and simile, writing of a kind that virtually begins with Shakespeare. 'Literature's indistinctness ... makes reading creative.'

Carey writes with his habitual clarity about some difficult matters: about poems which inspire in him what Browne in *Religio Medici* called the pursuit of reason into an *O altitudo*, a love of losing himself in a mystery – an experience of which Carey elsewhere seems suspicious. But on the indistinctness of his poets, from Shakespeare to Larkin, he writes with warmth as well as acumen. 'Poetic ideas do not tell you what the truth is, they make you feel what it would be like to know it.' For literature he sets aside his strenuous argument that we cannot know what anybody else is feeling. He does not believe that poetic ideas do this only for him. Networks of association, we are told, link readers. 'They make literature an internal thing, special to *us*' (my emphasis). Some great poems are quoted much as Matthew Arnold quoted his 'touchstones', with obvious assurance that they affect others as they do Carey.

Can it be true that literature alone has such powers, such an obvious appeal to both imagination and reason? At the end of this absorbing and amusing book one feels that the rhetorical successes of the earlier chapters are, at the end, sacrificed and laid as booty at the feet of literature.

23 June 2005

'DISGUSTING'

....

William Empson. Vol. II: Against the Christians by John Haffenden

In 1940 Empson was back in England, having spent much of the previous decade in Japan and China. His arrival in China had coincided with the Japanese invasion and the resulting southward migration of the National Peking University. He went along, rather enjoyed the hardships of the trek, relying on his excellent memory to teach English with little aid from books. In the autumn of 1939 he made his way homeward via the United States. Arriving the following January he settled in his flat in Marchmont Street and considered his future, at least as uncertain at this date as anybody else's.

He was 33 and already quite famous in some literary circles. His most celebrated book, *Seven Types of Ambiguity*, had appeared in 1930 and was by now standard reading for all bright undergraduates, if not always for their teachers. His *Poems* had appeared in 1935, which was also the year of his second critical collection, *Some Versions of Pastoral*, as brilliant and influential as *Seven Types* and with stronger political undertones. With the publication in 1940 of his second volume of verse, *The Gathering Storm*, he could claim considerable eminence and originality as both poet and critic.

Minding the squalor of his accommodation no more at this moment than he would in the future, he survived well enough on a small private income and some reviewing. He was not short of friends, including some as grand as T.S. Eliot, who admired Empson as well as finding him funny ('dirtier and more distrait than ever ... most refreshing to see him'). But the war was coming on; myopia left him unfit for military service, and so, almost inevitably, he found himself in mid-1940 working for the BBC, first in the Monitoring Service, later in the Chinese section of the Overseas Service.

Haffenden's huge second volume begins there, and it is clear at once that his industry and love of Empson and Empsoniana have not diminished. He gives an interestingly detailed account of the BBC at war. Like many of his colleagues, Empson was a drinker, a frequenter of pubs, a lifelong lover of parties, in many ways a strange wild figure, but always a worker, and his work at the BBC was done with serious purpose. He competed resourcefully for space in broadcasts designed for China, or meant to explain China to the British. The strong views he had brought home on the China situation were unlikely to be pleasing to his superiors; he had no time for Chiang Kai-shek or his American supporters, and insisted on the evidence of his own eyes that the Communist armies had, at this stage anyway, been welcomed by the Chinese people. His efforts to instruct and to affect opinion were constantly frustrated by malign bureaucrats and hierarchical committees, but he still seems to have acquired a muted authority; the bosses listened to him, even if they did not encourage him in his deviant designs.

Among his colleagues at the BBC were George Orwell and Louis MacNeice, both of whom he greatly admired; and there were others, their names by now probably forgotten, who brought conviction and real knowledge to Empson's side of the fight. One such, Ralf Bonwit, a formidable, dedicated Japanese specialist, was eventually sent away from London to the Monitoring Service in Caversham, where he worked with Ernst Gombrich and other learned exiles. By chance I came to know him a little and thought him amusing as well as fierce, in these respects if in no others not unlike Empson himself. Empson apparently did not much like him, but valued his intelligence, and as long as they were allowed they worked well together, as they needed to. When Empson left the BBC Bonwit, a man not given to promiscuous praise, said he had been 'an outpost of China' there.

This BBC phase of his life taught him, if he didn't know already, that bureaucrats make it a point of pride to defeat the intelligent, even when they are supposed to be on the same side. Orwell commended Empson's successes in these struggles but saw they could not be other than limited. Empson himself told Sir William Haley: 'I think it really was rather exhilarating for us to feel that we were fighting alone against the forces of evil.' And for the rest of his life he would arm himself against various opponents who, merely by disagreeing with him, betrayed their allegiance to the forces of evil.

In 1941 Empson met Hetta Crouse, an Afrikaans-speaking South African artist who was working in the African Service, and they married at the end of the year. Two sons were born within the next three years – nothing unusual there, but for other reasons this marriage might well have been thought peculiar. Haffenden does full justice to the extraordinary Hetta, tall, beautiful, funny, a hard drinker, and no more than her husband a lover of domestic peace, cleanliness and conventional morality. The marriage was 'open' and Hetta set the pace by having lots of lovers. The poet encouraged her in this, believing in the virtues of the 'Consenting Triangle'. In a long and curious poem called 'The Wife Is Praised', here printed for the first time, he explains this preference:

> Did I love you as mine for possessing?
> Absurd as it seems, I forget;
> For the vision of love that was pressing
> And time has not falsified yet
> Was always a love with three corners
> I loved you in bed with young men,
> Your arousers and foils and adorners
> Who would yield to me then.

And so on, for 25 stanzas, unambiguous about the preferences of the parties, but also firm that the marriage was far from lacking in love. There were times when Hetta's exercise of her freedom may have caused Empson some pain; he missed her badly when she went off to Hong Kong for a year with a lover, and seems to have been a little unhappy when she added illegitimately to the family (possibly, as Haffenden suggests, more because of his sense of obligation to his brother as head of the family than to common or garden jealousy). And it may have hurt that while he worked at Sheffield University, as he did for 18 years, living in conditions of squalor that amazed all who saw them, Hetta rarely paid him a visit. Not that conditions in their Hampstead house were very different from those of the Sheffield 'burrow' – they were described by Robert Lowell as having 'a weird, sordid nobility' – but of course it was much larger, and the company tended to be noisy and numerous, whereas in Sheffield he depended on his middle-class academic colleagues for talk and drinking company and even for baths, and nursing when he was unwell. More comfort was provided by Alice Stewart, a distinguished Oxford doctor and almost a Nobel Prize winner, with whom he had a long, intermittent and affectionate affair.

The Consenting Triangle was not a passing fancy but a serious pre-occupation. An important aspect of Empson's character was his bull-dog unwillingness to give up an idea, and he was always ingenious in discovering in favoured works of literature evidence in support of his own theories, literary, social or psychological. For him sexual freedom was an ethical imperative even if the consequences might sometimes be painful. His belief that artists and people of intellect must break with social convention in order to bring about beneficial change naturally applied to sex as well as everything else.

These leading ideas would spread and colour his thinking about matters that might have been thought independent of them. One such instance is his view of the story Joyce tells in *Ulysses*. It was in 1948 that he first outlined the theory in a letter to his wife: Bloom would like to make love to Molly but hasn't done so for ten years, since his first son died, though he is keen to have another child. If he could get Molly away from Boylan and 'get her to bed with Stephen' he thinks he could manage it provided Stephen preceded him – perhaps when Stephen returned to Eccles Street, as he promised. Joyce was apparently 'shy' about this bit of narrative, and hid the point from his readers. Not from Empson, however, who expounded it several times adding more and more detail in evidence: for example, in two successive issues of this journal in August and September 1982, and finally in the posthumous collection *Using Biography*. He reached a point where he could not believe an unprejudiced reader could help finding what Joyce had rather cravenly hidden; and in any case he would presumably have given up the hope of a triangular arrangement by the time he started *Finnegans Wake*. But we are to understand that his desire for it had been urgent, and Empson studies it with appropriate intensity: the triangular outcome is 'amply foretold'.

Here as always he was ready to take on anybody who dissented, or who failed to understand his unaffected devotion to his favoured writers. Vast though Haffenden's edition of the letters certainly is, there are many more letters and drafts than he was able to include, and they are often, like the published ones, a curious mixture of civility and sneering. Anybody who is Roman Catholic is likely to be insulted. Other varieties of Christian fare no better, and unbelievers who only behave as if they were Christians but aren't are almost worst of all. What honesty required was the abolition of the entire Christian tradition, the great enemy of human decency. It was unwise to disagree with him unless prepared for a long, often jeering response. Only a few answered the insults in kind: Empson's correspondence with Philip Hobsbaum, who was his pupil but disagreed with some of the basic tenets, is full of rude words and anger on both sides. In this case the insults were part of what Empson called 'my long attempt to improve the mind of Hobsbaum', and Hobsbaum, defying his correspondent's rank and reputation, had the cheek to answer back. It was never easy for Empson to have a civil discussion with anybody who took a deviant view of matters he believed to be much more important than an opponent's feelings.

And yet he would never have pulled rank. He was generous-minded, affectionate, a very likeable man; he just thought that people who took what he regarded as 'dirty' or 'disgusting' views (favourite terms of debate with him) should be corrected. His victims were usually confident that his habits in controversy were in some measure aspects of a more general eccentricity: the strangled, oddly inflected voice or voices, the peculiar beard, the use of drink to lubricate all argument, to get something started. People who worked with him or saw a lot of him for other reasons had little difficulty in liking as well as respecting him. If he thought them, like Hobsbaum, professionally competent despite their gross and obstinate follies, he would still back them when they applied for jobs. One belief he shared with some whom he scorned was that a university English department should be so constituted as to offer its undergraduates a wide variety of critical approaches. When he realised that his Sheffield colleagues were professionally all that could be asked, and possessed of a suitable variety of talents, he saw to it that new appointments to the department would not disturb this pattern. It is clear from Haffenden's book that he made friends with at least some of them, and even, as time passed, became increasingly dependent on them.

His views on language, as originally set forth in *Seven Types*, changed as book followed book, but the changes are not radical. The most important influence on his critical thinking came from I.A. Richards, his Cambridge supervisor. The dedication of *The Structure of*

Complex Words (which Empson regarded as his masterpiece) calls Richards 'the source of all ideas in this book, even the minor ones arrived at by disagreeing with him'. The advocacy and practice of Basic English occupied quite a lot of Empson's and Richards's time, but this common interest was less important than their disagreements. Briefly, Richards stood by his views on cognitive and emotive language and the idea of the 'pseudo-statement', which rendered irrelevant questions as to the truth of statements in poetry. Pseudo-statements are 'not necessarily false . . . merely a form of words whose scientific truth or falsity is irrelevant to the purpose in hand'. But Empson refused to distinguish between pseudo-statements and lies. Richards was wrong to say that 'the Emotions of the words in poetry are independent of the Sense.' On that view 'the function of poetry is to call out an Attitude which is not dependent on any belief open to disproof by facts.' And this position Empson rejects. However complex the words he undertakes to study, the critic should always be thinking of an author who really means them; if he doesn't, he may be just as guilty of lying as he would be if using such language in the ordinary way and not in a poem. Empson admits that 'we can enjoy the literary expression of beliefs which we don't hold' but in that case 'we imagine some other person who holds them, an author or a character.' This works even if we think we know the author himself or herself did not believe them; the character does, and we can see what it means to hold them.

This 'cognitivism' of Empson is the root of his disagreements with Richards, and is at least part of the explanation of his larger and virtually incessant quarrel with academic criticism. He came home from China and found criticism in a terrible state of professionalism. Everybody, it seemed, had been corrupted by an essay called 'The Intentional Fallacy', by W.K. Wimsatt and Monroe C. Beardsley. Empson rarely relaxed his pursuit of an enemy: a disagreement with the American scholar Rosemond Tuve, which he began in the closing pages of *Seven Types*, was still exercising him when he drafted another rebuttal in the 1950s. So it was with what he called the Wimsatt Law, which maintained that the intention of an author should be of no concern to the interpreter; if the poet succeeded, all the relevant evidence of intention was there in the poem. Wimsatt regarded the poem as a 'verbal icon': an autonomous verbal structure, an aesthetic object independent of the truth or morality of whatever it says.

This places Wimsatt on the Richards side of the argument with Empson, who found the Wimsatt Law disgusting: it violated his strongly Romantic notion of what poetry is and does; and he thought he saw that the entire profession of literary criticism, on both sides of the Atlantic, had been corrupted by it. In his later years he paid very little attention to what he knew in his bones to be the disgusting nonsense of French 'theory' because he was still engaged in the refutation of the older Wimsattian kind of disgusting nonsense, as practised by adherents of the American New Criticism, by then long out of fashion. It is strange but true that he was long regarded as a founding father of the New Criticism, but that perception derived from its adaptation of Empson's analytic skills; this other matter, his belief that criticism must concern itself with the author in whose mind the poem occurred, his American followers seem simply to have ignored.

Henceforth, in the years after *Complex Words*, he showed again and again where his interest lay. Shocked by the return to fashion of Christianity, which he had supposed long dead among intelligent people, he attacked critics who were Christians and also critics who had picked up bad habits from Christians and whom he named 'neo-Christian'. He had been deeply impressed by Orwell's *1984*, and added to *Complex Words* a note on the 'dreadful book'. The Christian church thrived on such slogans as 'war is peace', as in the double-talk of the Trinity, a teaching which assures us that the Father and the Son are, and are not, identical. 'I have thus to conclude,' Empson says in *Milton's God*, 'that the Doctrine of the Trinity is a means of deceiving good men into accepting evil; it is the double-talk by which Christians hide from themselves the insane wickedness of their God.' And Communism, he claimed, was now almost as bad as Christianity. Orwell's book can be seen to be an attack on both. Many of the critical follies that he noted in his colleagues derived from a loss of ordinary intelligence and human feeling brought about by this brainwashing. 'From now on,' says Haffenden – who discusses these matters very thoroughly and clearly – 'he would seek to vindicate the value of rational humanism over Christianity. The Christians, whether clerics or literary critics, must be hoist by their own propaganda.'

Empson's appointment at Sheffield in 1953, at the age of 47, required him to teach English students for the first time in his life, and to take on the business of examinations and the chores of a departmental head. He applied himself to these duties conscientiously, though his colleague Francis Berry noted his 'endearing helplessness' and spoke in the same friendly verses of 'Chestnuts pulled for him from many fires'. He particularly disliked committees where one has to argue as cunningly as possible for a share of the money; I was reminded of the lesson I myself had to learn as an inexperienced professor at Manchester when, arguing honestly for a new assistant lecturer, I was annihilated by Sir Bernard Lovell, who claimed that if he didn't get the money I was asking for he would have to close down the Jodrell Bank telescopes. Empson at least had the experience of infighting in BBC committees. In my shoes he would not have been intimidated by Sir Bernard, but he might have felt a certain tenderness for the telescopes.

He made his inaugural lecture autobiographical – lively, perhaps flippant, possibly a little fuddled, not a great success. But by the end of his long tenure his virtues were recognised and his eccentricities had become endearing. He wrote a witty, adulatory masque to welcome the Queen on her 50-minute visit to the university of the city of steel (claiming later that this left her no alternative but to knight him). He was, finally, recognised as a sort of quaint hero, a survivor, the teacher who had risked crossing the Chinese Communist lines to give a lecture on *Macbeth*; who had, by now a long time ago, written some superb poems, once almost forgotten but now restored to the attention of all who cared for such things; who even now was involved in what he deeply believed to be struggles on behalf of human decency. Sometimes ill, sometimes experiencing 'isolation and suffering', always dependent on alcohol to get going and keep going, he wrote continually; letters, for he relished combat by correspondence, notes, chapters to replace mislaid chapters, lectures for Sheffield and many other places.

His first book since *Complex Words* was *Milton's God* (1961). Empson explained to his publisher Ian Parsons that along with studies of Donne, Joyce and Fielding his work on Milton was designed to show how 'the neo-Christian movement has greatly upset the natural and traditional way of reading such authors,' and to 'challenge' this heresy. In the event Milton got a whole book to himself. It shows a Milton whose feelings are at war with barbarous Christian theology. Empson could not believe that a writer whose work and mind he greatly admired would simply accept the doctrine of the Atonement and believe in a god who required for his 'satisfaction' the sacrifice of his son, as Christians and neo-Christians professed to believe. Blake had the right idea when he said that Milton was of the devil's party, possibly without knowing it, and Shelley was right to describe Satan in *Paradise Lost* as 'a moral being . . . far superior to his God'. Empson sometimes hints at his own credo: man should not seek transcendence but 'conciliation with a secular universe'. From his Chinese days he retained the interest in Buddhism which had prompted his book on the faces of the Buddha, a work long said to be lost, but happily now recovered. No doubt the indefatigable Haffenden will soon be editing it.

Milton's God is a wonderful book, almost the best display of Empson's passionate and polemical mind. I have always admired this great swipe at Pascal and his Wager:

He argued, while more or less inventing the mathematics of Probability, that, since the penalties for disbelief in Christianity are infinitely horrible and enduring, therefore, if there is any probability however tiny (but finite) that the assertions of the religion are true, a reasonable man will endure any degree of pain and shame on earth (since this is known beforehand to be finite) on the mere chance that the assertions are true. The answer is political, not mathematical; this argument makes Pascal the slave of any person, professing any doctrine, who has the impudence to tell him a sufficiently extravagant lie. A man ought therefore to be prepared to reject such a calculation; and I feel there has been a strange and unpleasant moral collapse during my own lifetime, because so many of our present literary mentors not only accept it but talk as if that was a moral thing to do. Clearly, if you have reduced your morality to keeping the taboos imposed by an infinite malignity, you can have no sense either of personal honour or of the public good.

Whatever one thinks, whatever Pascal might have said about this, it is rather thrilling to have Christian doctrine lined up against 'personal honour' and 'the public good', and in such strong Johnsonian prose. But the voice is the true voice of Empson. He even calls Pascal 'neo-Christian', thus grouping him with his own craven and shameless contemporaries who don't even pretend to believe in their religion; 'they regard it simply as a general moral truth that one ought to tell lies in favour of the side which is sure to win.'

In his final years he continued his campaigns to protect literature from the corrupting influence of the neo-Christians and other academics who, as it seemed to him, had sold out to the religion of the Torturer God, or simply decided that common sense and human decency were not part of their remit. He worked with minute care on 'The Ancient Mariner', on *Dr Faustus*, on the question whether Mary Palmer (who published his poems after his death) was really married to Andrew Marvell. The posthumous collections, including *Using Biography* and *Argufying*, a volume of Shakespeare pieces and two on Renaissance literature, are all animated by a dislike amounting to hatred of what he took to be corrupt criticism.

In no other case were his objections more eloquent than in his defence of Donne against modern critics who seemed intent on trivialising and Christianising him. When writing his early poems Empson had tried to make them as like Donne as possible: hence all the scientific metaphors. (Some think that what he was really doing was making Donne as like Empson as possible.) He revered Donne, citing every scrap of evidence that the poet was learned in the 'new philosophy' of his day, and profoundly interested in such notions as the plurality of worlds and the thrilling possibility of inhabited planets; whether each one would require an Atonement, whether, in these Americas of the imagination, love would be more free and purer. These were real questions, and one might, for instance, believe that there could be a religion that took account of them, a religion of love. Indeed Empson believed that Donne intended his love poems to be an attack on Christianity.

The main difficulty in seeing Donne as an adept of contemporary astrophysics was that he used the new as he used the old scholastic learning, not needing to endorse either. (It is hardly possible to imagine a less Empsonian position.) When the soul arrives in heaven it won't need to bother about all the unsolved questions men labour to answer, seeking 'to know but catechisms and alphabets/Of unconcerning things, matters of fact': 'In Heaven thou straight know'st all, concerning it,/And what concerns it not, shalt straight forget.' The arguments about Donne were sometimes very detailed; disagreeing about the correct reading of a particular line in Elegy XIX, Empson took on Helen Gardner and John Carey (and me, though I was of neither party) with ferocity.

Haffenden gives a good account of this once celebrated row, not without a pardonable bias in favour of the man to whose life and work he has devoted more than twenty years. For the most part he is just in his dealings with the master's whipping-boys, and on this central issue of Donne it was proper to favour Empson though he happened, I believe, to be wrong.

Money worries in the final years required him to spend time at American universities, teaching, lecturing, and reinforcing his reputation for bizarre or clownish behaviour. A colleague at Penn State notes that 'he went back at night to a place full of rotting oranges, used tissues and odd socks', and records that 'he once, for some minutes, watched my neighbour's door lamp through my telescope, thinking it Mars.' Dining with Marshall McLuhan, 'I thought I had to explain to him that he was worshipping the devil, being a Roman Catholic. It was at his own dinner-table, but the ladies had gone for their pee, so it wasn't really rude.' On a visit to Harvard he was 'truculent and contradictory' towards Richards.

He was no longer happy in these American appointments, and began to feel isolated. Haffenden reminds the reader that Empson believed the true writer has to sustain 'the self-centred emotional life imposed by the detached intelligence', but the price of the detached intelligence is 'painful isolation'. Still, in one way or another he had a good life, enjoying the fun but capable of intense and rewarding work; not immodest but conscious of his own truly exceptional powers. Sometimes it seemed necessary to disagree with him and to take the consequences; but also to agree always that he was incomparable. John Haffenden was aware of this when he undertook, along with all the other work of retrieval he has done for Empson, this immense and magnificent biography.

16 November 2006

WHO HAS THE GALL?

....

Sir Gawain and the Green Knight translated by Bernard O'Donoghue
Sir Gawain and the Green Knight translated by Simon Armitage

The survival of poetry, especially if written before the invention of print, has often been a matter of luck or accident. Consigned to caves in the deserts of the Middle East, it might be preserved by the hot, dry climate for a couple of thousand years before somebody stumbled on it. And we are told that some hot, dry Alexandrian bureaucrat, no poetry lover, decided that seven plays by Sophocles, enough for one codex, would serve for the teaching of grammar and rhetoric. The surplus hundred-odd went for scrap. The single surviving manuscript of the Sophoclean remnant was rescued during the sack of Byzantium in 1453 and carried off to Italy. The story did not end there; the survivors were subjected to the depredations of vermin and, before the development of modern editorial skills, to the attentions of celibate, passionate scholars of the type studied by A.D. Nuttall, lately and sadly lost to us, in his brilliant book *Dead from the Waist Down*.

Of course one can look at the question from the opposite angle: how amazing it is not that so much was lost but that anything at all survived. A manuscript, now in the British Library, contains the only surviving copy of the late 14th-century romance *Sir Gawain and the Green Knight*. It lacks a title and shares the manuscript with three other poems of a devotional character, also without titles, and probably, according to the experts, by the same poet. Of this group *Pearl*, an allegory about a man's grief at the death of his two-year-old daughter, is the most brilliant and mysterious.

Written around 1400, the manuscript is usually described as physically unattractive, not in the hand of the author and hard to read. It belonged, in the early 17th century, when antiquarianism was getting started, to a Yorkshire collector, Henry Savile, and then to the antiquary Sir Robert Cotton, whose books came mostly from the dissolution of the monasteries. The Cottonian library also contained the sole extant copy of *Beowulf*, which in 1731 narrowly escaped destruction in a serious fire. After a spell in the Bodleian the collection reached its presumably final destination in the British Library.

The greatest of all Old English poems, and, after Chaucer, the finest in Middle English, might well not have survived; conceivably we would never even have heard of them. No one knows when *Beowulf* was composed, let alone when it was first recited, and there is virtually no other survivor to compare with it. And *Gawain*, a magnificent poem by any reasonable criterion, also stands alone. It has some resemblance to other examples of Arthurian romance in France as well as in England, but as Tolkien remarked, it remains 'a solemn thought' that the name of the Gawain poet is 'now forgotten, a reminder of the great gaps of ignorance over which we now weave the thin webs of our literary history'. Much arduous scholarship has gone into that weaving, but the poem remains available to the laity as a poem, a strange and delightful experience. It is a worthy contemporary of *Troilus and Criseyde*, though written in a dialect very different from Chaucer's.

It was probably the dialect of Staffordshire, Cheshire, Derbyshire and thereabouts. The author was apparently familiar with the Wirral, wild territory at the time, we're told, so he may have been an extremely gifted Merseysider. But Chaucer had the advantage of speaking the English of London, from which modern English descends. *Gawain* is linguistically a far tougher proposition, and only specialists can comfortably read it, so there already exist a good many useful translations, and now we have two more, both by established poets. One of them, Bernard O'Donoghue, is a professional medievalist as well. The other, Simon Armitage, a Northerner, claims the advantage of familiarity with dialect forms that linger in his part of the country.

The first decision the translator must take is whether or not to alliterate. We are accustomed by centuries of poetry to think the normal English verse line is the iambic pentameter, as in Chaucer. Old English preferred alliteration to rhyme, as in *Beowulf*, and much 14th-century verse also uses it, though less strictly. It is rarely used in modern poetry, though there is an extended example in Auden's *The Age of Anxiety*, but it was the norm until replaced as a structural principle by rhyme. Alliterative verse is a complicated affair, governed by quite firm rules, and *Gawain* offers a sophisticated model. Its four sections are divided into stanzas or 'fits', each ending with a device known as the bob-and-wheel: a short line, normally two words with one stress, followed by a three-stressed quatrain whose second and fourth lines rhyme with the bob. Thus:

> So in peril and pain Sir Gawain made progress,
> Criss-crossing the countryside until Christmas
> Eve. Then
> At that time of tiding,
> He prayed to highest heaven.
> Let Mother Mary guide him
> Towards some house or haven.

The effect of the bob-and-wheel is striking; it wraps up the stanza or section it is concluding with a decorative comment or summary that stresses its own difference from the routine of the alliterative verse to which it is attached. As for the rules of alliteration, O'Donoghue explains them thus: 'The rhythmic alliterative line was divided into two halves, each containing two (or in the first half-line originally three) main stresses ... The third stress (that is, the first stress of the second half-line) always alliterates with one or both of the stresses in the first half-line, but never with the fourth stress.' There is more to it, but that is enough to show the problem facing translators.

O'Donoghue argues that the formalities of alliteration cannot be imitated in modern English without introducing anachronisms of vocabulary or word order. He offers as an illustration a modern version of the third and fourth lines of the poem, rendered thus by the authoritative Tolkien:

> The traitor who the contrivance of treason there fashioned
> Was tried for his treachery, the most true upon earth –

which, self-evidently, won't do. O'Donoghue then quotes Marie Borroff's translation:

> The knight that had knotted the nets of deceit
> Was impeached for his perfidy, proven most true

This is better, making more sense of the last phrase, and also, like Tolkien, observing the rules. But O'Donoghue doesn't like it, and offers this instead:

> The man who'd betrayed it [Troy] was brought to trial,
> Most certainly guilty of terrible crimes.

This makes sense and, he claims, keeps the rhythm of the original while replacing the phonetic formalities (alliteration most importantly) with the 'normal formalities of modern English'. And so he decided to abandon the alliterative structure, and declined to allow rhymes in the bob-and-wheel passages. Armitage translates those lines thus:

> The turncoat whose tongue had tricked his own men
> was tried for his treason – the truest crime on earth.

And since he finds this satisfactory (despite the vague ending) and since he is capable of carrying on the practice with some ease and evident zeal, Armitage settles for alliteration: 'to me, alliteration is the warp and weft of the poem, without which it is just so many fine threads. In some very elemental way, the story and the sense of the poem is [*sic*] directly located within its sound. The percussive patterning of the words serves to reinforce their meaning.'

Perhaps it's a pity to make this point by reference to some of the dullest lines in the poem, but once it is made one can see how it happens that we have before us two translations that are about as far apart as they could possibly be while each retaining its own fidelity to the original. Both positions are defensible; both allow for the variety of the content and for flexibility in its delivery; above all, both are continually aware that they are handling a rather beautiful object.

One can see that the subject of *Gawain* might well appeal to Armitage. It starts with Christmas celebrations and games; the action gets going with a particularly eerie game, the rules laid down by a disguised and uninvited guest. Once he sets out on his quest Gawain has to venture through the changing seasons (there are wonderful winter landscapes) and across a wilderness, challenging boundaries and, as obliged by his oath, putting his life at the disposal of a supposedly murderous opponent. And there were other attractions; most of all the lexical challenge of the alliteration, but also the temptation to give this high romance a touch of the demotic:

> It was Christmas at Camelot – King Arthur's court,
> where the great and the good of the land had gathered,

> all the righteous lords of the ranks of the Round Table
> quite properly carousing and revelling in pleasure.

Compare O'Donoghue's:

> It was Christmas at Camelot, and there was the king
> with his leading lords and all his best soldiers,
> the famous company of the whole Round Table –
> celebrating in style: not a care in the world.

'The great and the good' is the kind of thing we get rather too much of in Armitage: he will slide in an ironic modernism when he can. O'Donoghue's 'in style: not a care in the world' is not quite so trendy, but is still fitted on like a prefabricated part. (And although he has forsworn alliteration he does have 'leading lords'.) Is either of these an improvement on Tolkien?

> This king lay at Camelot at Christmas-tide
> with many a lovely lord, lieges most noble,
> indeed of the Table Round all those tried brethren,
> amid merriment unmatched and mirth without care.

That trace of archaism is something the two new translators understandably want to avoid. Yet Tolkien still seems closest to the original; his first line makes no change in it, and he keeps 'lovely lords' as a translator today might not think proper. In the last line he has to deviate because of the changed modern sense of 'reckless' – the original has 'rechles mirthes'. He wants to keep as close as possible to the original, and would not, like these more recent translators, have supposed that archaism was a hindrance to his doing so.

When the music stops Arthur and his brilliant company at the Christmas feast are suddenly confronted by an 'aghlich mayster' ('a perilous horseman', Tolkien; 'a monstrous apparition', O'Donoghue; 'a fearful form', Armitage). The huge size of the visitor is emphasised, and the bob-and-wheel informs us further: he was green, and the next section spells out his greenness. Here Armitage scores by his rhymes:

> Amazement seized their minds,
> no soul had ever seen
> a knight of such a kind –
> entirely emerald green.

'For at the hue men gaped aghast/in his face and form that showed;/ as a fay-man fell he passed,/and green all over glowed,' Tolkien says, this time struggling a bit.

The intruder has green hair and a green beard, and wears a green gown. He leads a horse that is as green as he is, in every part down to the tail – 'to its tippety-tip!' says Armitage for some reason. The knight is 'otherworldly, yet flesh/and bone', this poet says, in the spirit though not the language of the original. Armitage enjoys taking liberties. The knight's dreadful weapon becomes 'the mother of all axes,/a cruel piece of kit I kid you not' and his courtiers had 'seen some sights', but this was 'something special'. Too much of this, as when Arthur, 'keeping his cool', says he's not 'spoiling for no scrap', and refers to his young liege-men not as 'berdles childer' ('beardless children') but as 'bum-fluffed bairns', and we may think he's enjoying himself a bit too much at the expense of the poem. O'Donoghue's 'mere adolescents' is probably too sedate.

The Green Knight, in a variant of the more usual kind of Christmas game (forfeits, for instance), offers to allow himself to be beheaded so long as his killer undertakes to meet him at a certain Green Chapel on New Year's Day a year hence, and submit himself to one stroke of the great axe. But 'who has the gall? The gumption? The guts?' Armitage's monster sneers. ('If anyone's so warlike as to give what I ask for,' says O'Donoghue – which can hardly help being more accurate.) Gawain insists on accepting the challenge and the beheading is graphically de-scribed. Armitage revels in it: 'in the standing position he prepared to be struck,/bent forward, revealing a flash of green flesh' (not in the original, but worthy of it). The head rolls away, kicked along by the no-ble company; the Green Knight picks it up and sits at the table, blood pouring from his neck, the head still talking. He reminds Gawain of his bargain, and rides off. The king assures the ladies that 'such strange-ness' was in the true spirit of Christmas.

The next year the pious and courteous Gawain, fully armed and bearing a shield with an image of the Blessed Virgin on its inside, sets forth in search of the Green Chapel to honour his knightly promise. The magnificent middle passages of the poem describe, with a profu-sion of natural detail, his journey 'through the whole of England'. At the second Christmas of the poem he is welcomed in a grand castle and made to join in the lavish celebrations. The lord of this castle proposes another Christmas game: he himself will hunt hard for three days and everything he kills will be Gawain's if Gawain, in return, hands over the benefits he may have received at the castle in the lord's absence. The hunting is spectacularly described. On each day, when the lord is absent, his wife attempts to seduce Gawain: a kiss, two kisses, three kisses. Each of these benefits Gawain faithfully confers on the lord, embracing him when he returns from the field. The blend of brutal hunt and subtle seduction is described with extraordinary power and delicacy. Gawain remembers his vow of chastity but, against his will, accepts the lady's present: a magic girdle which will protect him when the Green Knight strikes. He knew it was wrong to take it, but didn't despise the chance of survival; he thought the girdle 'could be just the job' (Armitage, of course). The account of Gawain's ordeal is masterly.

How he survived that ordeal with little more than a graze from the axe, who the Green Knight turned out to be, and why, after Gawain's return to Camelot, Arthur's knights began to wear girdles of the same design, provides the substance of what follows. We are told at the end that, since its foundation by refugees from Troy, Britain has known many such adventures and stories, but Gawain's is unique.

If I needed to choose between these new versions I should have to prefer Armitage's, despite his naughtiness. 'Stunning' is an adjective that precludes thought but Armitage uses it, along with 'No way!' and the like. Of a hunted fox it is said that he was 'convinced that his cunning had conned those canines'. When the Green Knight has to alliterate with 'the challenge at the chapel' he becomes 'the great green chap'. 'We're talking a hundred top hunters at least' is pub talk. 'Every person present performed party pieces' is a stunt. But although he kicks up his heels occasionally Armitage has done much justice to these 2530 extraordinary lines, and has paid the anonymous poet the tribute of hard poetic labour. O'Donoghue is less sparky but still a very good read. 'He grabbed the girdle and ungathered its knot/and flung it in fury at the man in front./"My downfall and undoing; let the devil take it,"' says Armitage. 'Then he snatched at the girdle and loosened its knot,/and violently flung it back to the knight./"Here, take the damned thing, and bad luck go with it!"' So O'Donoghue. Both versions will do, and the choice really hangs on the view taken of alliteration. Not to be pre-

ferred is Tolkien's 'foul be its fate,' which lacks that freshness translators ought to seek, perhaps especially in this case; for, as Armitage says
in his introduction, the anonymity of the poem makes it more attractive to the modern poet, as if he could claim it, experience its presence
and its delicate blend of chivalry and religion, of the domestic and the
uncanny, something we probably can't find anywhere else, save possibly in some paintings of the *trecento*.

8 March 2007

NOTHING FOR EVER AND EVER

....

The Letters of A.E. Housman edited by Archie Burnett

When A.E. Housman failed his final examinations at Oxford he went to London to work as a clerk in the Patent Office. After ten years of that, he was appointed, at the age of 33, to the chair of Latin at University College London. In his application for the job he very properly drew attention to his Oxford failure. Not, you might think, a glowing CV, especially as he couldn't claim any teaching experience. Yet these manifest disadvantages failed to deter the electors to the chair. They had their own criteria of eminence and saw that Housman was already one of the few. He would, before very long, be called the greatest Latinist of his age, to be named in the same breath as Bentley and Porson and Housman's famous German contemporary Wilamowitz-Moellendorff.

He was usually quite modest about his claims: 'I wish they would not compare me to Bentley ... I will not tolerate comparison with Bentley. Bentley is alone and supreme.' However, 'they may compare me with Porson if they will.' He was willing, that is, to be compared only with the runner-up for the title of greatest English classical scholar. Ordinary readers, even if they have a bit of Latin, can have little notion of what it means to know it well; those who, in their day, did know it well were ready to appoint a young man with a record of academic failure to the most influential Latin chair outside Oxford and Cambridge.

He had spent most of his London evenings in the British Museum Library working on Greek, and more intensively, Latin authors, notably Propertius, Juvenal and Ovid, and had produced some learned articles much admired by the few who were qualified to comment. Then, at University College, he began work on an edition of a long, dull and difficult first-century astronomical-astrological poem by Manilius – a text that had earlier tested the scholarship of Bentley, which was no doubt a challenge in itself. His notes on Manilius were in Latin, and the great work was published at his own expense. Its fifth and final volume appeared in 1930, 27 years after the first.

Its few readers needed to be high-calibre specialists. He made no attempt to persuade others that Manilius was worth their trouble. 'I adjure you,' he wrote to Robert Bridges, the poet laureate, 'not to waste your time on Manilius. He writes on astronomy and astrology without knowing either.' To an American correspondent he wrote: 'I do not send you a copy, as it would shock you very much; it is so dull that few professed scholars can read it, probably not one in the whole United States.' Perhaps the real experts were more interested in Housman's Latinity than in Manilius' Latin. But Manilius was his chosen life-work, and when he finished it he seems to have felt about it much as Chapman did on finishing his Homer: 'The work that I was born to do is done.' He said repeatedly that the publication of the final volume left him nothing more to do; he would now (at 71) 'do nothing for ever and ever'.

In his well-known essay on Housman, Edmund Wilson made a special point of the author's giving up work on a poet as interesting as Propertius in order to spend his life with Manilius. Wilson regarded the switch from love poems to obsolete science as evidence of an intellectual sterility all too characteristic of the English universities in Housman's day, indeed of English society more generally; and of course there was the doubtless related matter of Housman's sterile love for Moses Jackson, a friend and fellow undergraduate capable of inspiring the deep devotion of the young Housman but lacking any intention of responding in the manner desired. Moses Jackson was certainly important to the poetry, and I don't say there is nothing in Wilson's theory, but there is a more difficult and more interesting aspect of the switch to Manilius: how we should understand this life-absorbing passion for a craft that required not only a virtually unparalleled grasp of ancient languages and cultures but the possession of the exquisite divinatory intelligence required to make proper use of that knowledge? It was, he believed, a gift one has to be born with – possessed, therefore, by few, even among the very learned. And it was a resource more severely tested by Manilius than by the elegant and witty Propertius.

That he was among the few capable of the choice deplored by Edmund Wilson, indeed the first among them, made him contemptuous of rivals. His views of them could be gratuitously, though to disinterested observers amusingly insulting. As a freshman, describing his Oxford matriculation ceremony in a letter to his stepmother, he remarks of a document he was handed that it was 'written in Latin, or what passes for Latin at Oxford'. Not to be silenced by the grandeur of the institution or its famous members, he did not conceal his contempt for the scholarship of the great Benjamin Jowett, Regius Professor of Greek and master of Balliol, calling his Plato 'the best translation of a Greek philosopher which has ever been executed by a person who understood neither philosophy nor Greek'. He is said to have kept a record of choice insults for use when the need arose,[1] and he certainly preferred the harsh manner of earlier scholarly rivalries to the politer style of his contemporaries. Marginalia in his own books describe their editors and authors as idiots, asses, blunderers, thieves, egotists, ignoramuses. By way of demonstrating his amused contempt for such scholars he announced that he published his edition of Juvenal 'for the use of editors', *editorum in usum dedidit*, as if offering instruction to professionals who should not need it but all too evidently did. He had a passion for exactitude; accuracy, he said, was a duty, not a virtue. 'When,' he asked fretfully, 'will mankind begin to understand that I am more careful than they are, not less?'

He declined all academic and national honours because to accept them would be to admit comparability with other classical scholars who had received them, admiring the attitude of the 17th-century Greek scholar Thomas Gataker who refused a Cambridge doctorate because 'like Cato the censor he would rather have people ask why he had no statue than why he had one.' When he came across some self-critical words of T.E. Lawrence in *Seven Pillars of Wisdom* – 'there was a craving to be famous; and a horror of being known to like being known' – he wrote in the margin: 'This is me.' So in the course of his life he turned down everything from the OM to the poet laureateship, not to speak of many honorary doctorates. And he refused all invitations to give lectures except for the ones that he conceived to be part of his job.

There was a famous exception to this rule, the Leslie Stephen Lecture 'On the Name and Nature of Poetry', which he gave in 1933. The

---

[1] A matter carefully examined in R.P. Graves's biography, *A.E. Housman: The Scholar Poet* (1979).

lecture was a huge success, though powerfully deplored by some Cambridge dissidents, led, as some report, by Dr Leavis, or, as some less
plausibly suggest, I.A. Richards. To Leavis it seemed that it would take
years to remedy the damage the lecture must have inflicted on his students. But many others found its much softer view of poetry acceptable; and what everybody remembers best are the passages about the
emotional aspects of poetry. Housman included a number of surprisingly personal comments on this topic. Milton's 'Nymphs and shep-
herds, dance no more', he said, can 'draw tears . . . to the eyes of more
readers than one'. And tears are only one symptom. A line of poetry
can make his beard bristle as he shaves, or cause a shiver down his
spine, or 'a constriction of the throat' as well as 'a precipitation of water
to the eyes'. For so reticent a man it was a surprising performance. It
possibly upset his health, and he came to regard the date of the lecture,
May 1933, as an ominous moment in his life.

I have neglected the calm progress of his academic career. Back
in 1911 he accepted the chair of Latin at Cambridge and a fellowship
of Trinity College, where he lived for the rest of his life. His scholarly
fame was now secure, and at the same time his reputation as a vernacular poet grew to match it. The celebrity of *A Shropshire Lad* was
greatly enhanced during the war of 1914, and the two volumes of verse
that followed it were also well received. Despite his professed horror at
the idea of fame, he might have felt that at least in some ways things
were going quite well.

The life of a bachelor fellow of Trinity could hardly be described as
arduous; the company was distinguished, the wine excellent, the menus
subject to his approval and the professorial teaching load fairly light.
The days could be given to Manilius, the evenings to extensive reading
or to such avocations as research into Latin obscenities. He had a private lavatory and, declaring himself to be a philosophical hedonist, refused on principle to allow his less fortunate neighbour, Wittgenstein,
to use it. Vacations were filled with luxurious journeys.

And yet it is likely that few men, even taking into account these
amenities, would envy such an existence. Housman's own pronouncements, in prose and verse, on the meaning of life tend to be stoical;
there were things he enjoyed, but he did not seem to enjoy them very
much. And one is driven back to the position that it was the private

pleasure of his divinatory exercises that made everything else tolerable. That was the view of his colleague A.S.F. Gow, who remarked that 'a man whose mind is so perfectly adapted to the difficult and delicate tasks he has chosen out . . . cannot be wholly unhappy.'

Auden's sonnet on Housman ignores Gow's point and dwells on more furtive pleasures:

> Deliberately he chose the dry-as-dust,
> Kept tears like dirty postcards in a drawer . . .
> In savage footnotes on unjust editions
> He timidly attacked the life he led.

Even if one leaves the poems out of account, it seems that whether or not he was unhappy he was capable of describing the state of man as one of just tolerable discomfort; and of claiming that there were ways of relieving even that degree of misery. He would tour Europe in a chauffeur-driven hired car and fly to France on the fledgling air services, claiming to conquer his fears by reflecting that every crash reported reduced the probability of his being involved in one himself. He invariably celebrated the New Year with a feast of oysters and stout. On hospitable London evenings he liked to entertain his guests at the Café Royal before taking them to a music hall.

And even dons can sometimes have fun in their donnish way, as Housman did when he became a gourmet, a connoisseur of wine, and a drinker of beer at lunch because beer produced a languor conducive to poetry. A frequent visitor to Venice, he seems to have fallen in love with a gondolier. Paris offered its own pleasures. A quieter entertainment was the composition of light verse, in which long practice made him remarkably skilful. The concluding lines of 'Fragment of a Greek Tragedy', written when he was at school, are here quoted as evidence that Housman could giggle learnedly:

> *Eriphyle* (within): O, I am smitten with a hatchet's jaw:
> And that in deed and not in word alone.
> *Chorus*: I thought I heard a sound within the house
> Unlike the voice of one that jumps for joy.
> *Eri*: He splits my skull, not in a friendly way,
> Once more; he purposes to kill me dead.

Cho: I would not be reputed rash, but yet
I doubt if all be gay within the house.
Eri: O! O! Another stroke! That makes the third.
He stabs me to the heart against my wish.
Cho: If that be so, thy state of health is poor;
But thine arithmetic is quite correct.

If you like that sort of thing there are later poems that challenge you not to laugh. 'Light Verse and Juvenilia' occupy a hundred pages of Archie Burnett's Oxford edition of the poems. Being exceptionally susceptible to poetry, Housman could laugh at it. This balances his tendency, confessed in the Leslie Stephen Lecture, to cry at it. We are told by someone who was present on an occasion when he had difficulty reading the ode of Horace that begins *Diffugere nives*: "'That,' he said hurriedly, almost like a man betraying a secret, "I regard as the most beautiful poem in ancient literature.'" His audience was astonished, for he usually professed contempt for such literary judgments. However, when Thomas Hardy said his favourite Housman poem was 'Is my team ploughing', he said it was his too.

Archie Burnett, who edited the verse in almost 600 pages, has now edited Housman's correspondence in two enormous volumes, about 1200 pages. Somebody else had edited the letters as recently as 1971, but not so thoroughly. Burnett shares his hero's view on accuracy. Not many poetry lovers will want to read these volumes from beginning to end, and it must be said that they are somewhat reader-repellent. Their price and practically everything else about them suggests that they are not meant to be read except out of necessity, rather like the Manilius. The long editorial labour they required was a tribute rather to Housman's eminence in other activities than to his letter-writing. He is capable of chilly, erudite jokes, and his default style, an elegant facetiousness, can be amusing. But Burnett has collected dozens of epistolary scraps, which offer little opportunity of stylistic variation. Some are only two or three words long. A great number are addressed to Housman's publisher, Grant Richards, sometimes peremptory, sometimes indulgent – the responses varying according to the varying urgency of the business problems of the unbusinesslike Richards. The proofing and printing of successive editions of the poetry are a recurrent concern; the passion for exactitude was not limited to Manilius. What seems to be a queue of England's keenest composers sought Housman's permission to set lyrics from *A Shropshire Lad*, and they were all told, politely but coldly, that they could go ahead provided they changed no word of the poem concerned. He refused all offers of payment but insisted on the observance of the ban on omission or alteration; Vaughan Williams transgressed, and Housman seems never to have forgiven him. Repeated requests from anthologists for poems from *A Shropshire Lad* were turned down flat. A great many of these letters say 'no', very briefly, in one way or another; the shortest of them has a message of one word: 'Refuse.'

Letters to family members, especially to his brother Laurence, whom he liked to tease, can be dutifully full, but in general Housman keeps everything short. There are many brief, authoritative replies to inquiries from scholars. Here is an entire letter to A.S.F. Gow: 'The constellation is called Tr 'i gwnon for instance in Ptol.synt. VII c.5 (Heiberg vol. I ii p.82), schol. Arat.236, Vett. Val. p.13 13. I do not find *Trigonum* in Latin: in schol. Germ. ed Breys p. 109 8 sq. it is *Triangulus*.' On this, as on other such recondite allusions, the editor, perhaps wisely, remains silent. He does explain in his 'Note on Editorial Principles' that where he has found it impossible to elucidate a reference he has chosen to remain silent, rather than to multiply notes saying 'not identified' or the like; for to do that, he argues, would make the footnote number 'a false promise of enlightenment'. A sensible position, no doubt, but it would be strengthened by the omission of plainly unnecessary notes explaining that when Housman wrote 'don't' he meant 'don't'. Still, the editor is conscientious in the provision of ascertainable information about Housman's correspondents, and about his reading, which was more adventurous than one might have expected. It included *Lady Chatterley's Lover*, *Ulysses* and *Du côté de chez Swann*.

A word of mild and, as experience suggests, useless complaint about these volumes as physical objects. They are heavy and tightly bound – presumably to save space by reducing margins. You need both hands to hold them down; if you release the pressure they snap shut. Having let go to make a note one is compelled once more to force a new entrance, feeling about as welcome as Wittgenstein. Yet there was a time when Oxford editions were a pleasure to use.

If one struggles on to the end, the reward is a moving close-up of the great man in his last years. He was 74 when he gave his Leslie Stephen performance ('that infernal lecture', he now called it). He had now even less reason to rejoice in the human condition or in the Latinity of his epoch. 'I can bear my life, but I do not at all want it to go on.' He was ill, but would run up all the stairs to his room, hoping to die at the top. In May 1935, when he was 76, he told Grant Richards that 'the continuation of my life beyond May 1933 was a regrettable mistake.' He could no longer manage to walk from Trinity to Magdalene (half a mile, perhaps). Nevertheless he continued to lecture, complaining that getting to the lecture-room was more tiring than giving the lecture. A month before his death in April 1936 he described himself as an 'egoistic hedonist', adding that while George Eliot said she was a meliorist, he was a pejorist. And 'pejorist hedonist', with its English blend of Latin and Greek, fits him well enough.

5 July 2007

NOT JUST YET

....

The Long Life by Helen Small

In the opening pages of Plato's *Republic* Cephalus tells Socrates that when old men of his acquaintance get together they tend to spend their time bemoaning the lost pleasures of youth. Since sex, feasting and other laddish benefits have been curtailed or withdrawn they feel they might as well not be alive at all. But Cephalus also reports that the poet Sophocles, asked how the sex was going, made this exemplary but prim reply: 'I am very glad to have escaped all that, like a slave who has escaped from a savage and tyrannical master.' Old age, he says, brings freedom from desire; the true cause for complaint is not old age itself but the way people live. 'If they are temperate and contented, old age ... is only moderately onerous; if they aren't, both old age and youth are hard to bear.'

Youthful readers, confronted by Sophocles' anaphrodisiac calm, may dismiss this remark as just the kind of thing an old man, having reached an unimaginable stage of drooling enfeeblement, would say. There is a difficulty of communication: Cephalus and Sophocles are themselves old (Cephalus says he can't visit Socrates in Athens because he can no longer manage the walk from Piraeus) and know something of the subject at first hand; but the young know nothing directly about old age and their inquiries into the topic must be done blind. Helen Small, for instance, pronounces with impressive youthful verve and authority on a condition that must still, in a sense, be a closed book to her. Revealing her own age (42), she laments the dearth of serious philosophical reflection on the subject, and resolves to show how thinking about it 'rests on larger ... assumptions about what life is, what a person is, what a *good* life is'. This broadens the subject, for these are issues on which persons of any age are free to comment. Few of Small's witnesses are doing real old-age philosophy. Those who have had actual experience of old age are likely to be dead or very tired or just reluctant to discuss the matter with clever young interlocutors, so that much of the best thinking on this subject comes from philosophically sophisticated but honourably ignorant juniors.

In any case, Plato's belief that old age is the best age for doing philosophy (he thought 50 a good age to begin) seems to have gone the way of another ancient notion, that old persons deserve automatic respect. What, if they can think at all, do they think of old age? Closing my eyes, I ask myself with which masters, if any, my own stock notions originate. The answer for me, and I suspect for many others, is Eliot.

> What was to be the value of the long looked forward to,
> Long hoped for calm, the autumnal serenity
> And the wisdom of age? . . .
> There is, it seems to us,
> At best, only a limited value
> In the knowledge derived from experience.

And so on. 'Do not let me hear/of the wisdom of old men, but rather of their folly.' Eliot was 52 when he published these lines in 'East Coker'. Two years later the familiar compound ghost of 'Little Gidding' was even more downbeat:

> Let me disclose the gifts reserved for age
> To set a crown upon your lifetime's effort.
> First, the cold friction of expiring sense
> Without enchantment, offering no promise
> But bitter tastelessness of shadow fruit
> As body and soul begin to fly asunder.

Eliot was now 54. Certain dark consolations, admonitions rather, are offered, but the ghost's sentences echo coldly in the mind, along with 'Gerontion': 'Neither fear nor courage saves us.' These resonances tempt us to join in the complaining; but somehow they don't go deep enough to drain our reserves of cheerfulness. Small introduces Larkin's 'The Old Fools', a great poem certainly and a terrible one, here sympathetically analysed. Larkin was 51 when he wrote it, a middle-aged man already terrified by the prospect of dementia. What, then, is to be done, as the menace of senescence increases? 'Not fare well, but fare forward' is Eliot's bleak recommendation. Larkin is less stoical but no more consoling: 'Well,/We shall find out.' Both these poems are about the apprehensions of middle age and not about old age itself.

Small describes her book as 'essayistic', which it exactly is, and its being so causes her and her reader some trouble. At first the topic seems reasonably narrow: 'What philosophers and non-philosophers have had to say about old age has, in essence, changed very little since classical antiquity.' But they have had a good deal to say about life in general, and old age is a part of it. So she gives them their say, and in doing so displays admirable discursive energy and a determination to control many strands of argument.

Especially concerned with the rival claims of the aesthetic and the ethical, she includes a number of high-class fictions that refer to these claims. Among the novels about which she has most to say is *Death in Venice*. Thomas Mann was 35 when he met the original of the boy Tadzio, whose beauty prevents Aschenbach from achieving 'Platonic sublimation'. Consequently, Mann, with his aesthetic imperative, cannot offer 'a primarily moral account of what it means to live into old age, of what the value of a long life might be, and what the relation is (if any) between a long life and a good life'. Ethical considerations (always dominant in this book) are in Mann's story subordinated to the aesthetic. He wrote as an artist longing for release from the demands of form, from the need to impose form on experience. Despite his intellectual resources he was thus forced onto what Small regards as the wrong, the aesthetic track.

The question of narrative unity entails an acute problem with endings and Small gives it a chapter to itself. Fear of the end may affect the spirits of the aged, but given the choice between having an end and having it perpetually deferred, they would choose the former. Tennyson's 'Tithonus' is a great poem but it is not calculated to encourage a desire for deathlessness; and Swift's Struldbruggs would end all hesitation in the most fervent lover of existence. The story of *The Makropulos Case* is also exemplary. It counsels us not to accept such unnatural conditions. The old will not be disturbed, feeling the certainty of extinction in the very short term a topic of much more immediate interest.

The larger claim is that endings can be thought of as part of a plot, that a life resembles, or ought to resemble, a narrative with a beginning, a middle and an end, the end being thought of as the completion of a 'progress narrative'. But in fact the last years may not offer anything that could be called 'completion'. They may contain 'projects' with posthumous implications, a provision recommended by Simone de Beauvoir, or they may be spent in idleness or even wickedness, having few virtuous connections with the rest of the life in question, or with the structures of literary narrative.

Nor do readings of the past and divinations of the future of a particular life much resemble reading a poem or a story. There may be a passing resemblance to reading in the recollection and arrangement of personal disasters and pleasures now gone by, yet likely to have a foreseeable effect on the future. And musings of that sort may help to establish a personality, a self of sorts, that provides connections between past, present and future. Driven to it, we might even claim to discern a structural relationship between events in childhood, youth, middle age and old age, chronologically remote elements that pertain to one another only because of the continuing existence of a factitious self that recalls, or fails to suppress them.

In assembling such shored fragments and ghostly encounters, it might be said, but fancifully, that what we are doing bears some resemblance to the making of fiction. The old person can see himself as an autobiographical pícaro, given a self that traverses and violates, but is also changed and coloured by the landscapes of the past, yet does remain a sort of self, the kind that fiction can project – responsive to generic pressures, yet malleable. But he lacks the options open to the fiction writer. He cannot choose to end his life at a point just before death where it might best be experienced as fulfilled. Death may be, is likely to be, a little too early or a little too late.

It is on this point of choice that making a fiction and completing a life differ most sharply. To make use of one of Small's exemplary old men, it is a matter of fictive luck whether Priam ends or does not end his old age in misery, escapes or does not escape the sword of Neoptolemus, dies there and then or returns unscathed to his wife and fifty children. Should Job, his boils cured, his contest with God honourably lost, be returned to prosperity, to seven thousand sheep, five hundred she-asses, seven sons and three daughters, one of whom is named Keren-happuch, which is said to mean 'Box (or Horn) of Eye Paint'? His fate is as arbitrary as her name. As it happens, Job seems to die happy, 'being old and full of days'. To die thus at just the right moment depends, in life, not on narrative logic but on what Bernard Williams calls 'moral luck'. It is what enables a person to die when full of days, old but not in terminal misery, correctly mourned by a numerous and prosperous family. It is not an ending one can choose, it is a matter of aesthetics.

For instruction in the preferred ethical approach we must go back to Aristotle. Aristotle had high ethical standards. He believed children can't be happy, since they are still incapable of noble acts. The mature, he thought, cannot expect to escape the misfortunes of their declining years. The old will suffer biological and intellectual decline. Even if they remain prosperous into old age they may then spoil the story as a whole by being struck down, like Priam. It is permissible to call old persons 'prosperous', but not 'fortunate', or at least not until they've died in a way appropriate to the description. So Aristotle in his *Ethics*; in the *Rhetoric*, probably written when he was younger, he is even more severe on the old.

Aristotle saw the particular difficulty of judging the conduct of old people whose powers are failing by the criteria of virtuous behaviour appropriate to maturity. *King Lear* being an obvious case in point, Small gives an elaborate account of it. Is Lear mentally and morally impaired when he divides his kingdom? If he is so, and continues to be so as the action proceeds, we should perhaps take the fact into account when we judge his life. Certainly, Lear uses his age and mental frailty as an excuse for his wild behaviour, but Cordelia's answer when he offers himself for judgment is 'No cause, no cause' – she throws the case out of court. The Fool is constantly accusing and convicting Lear, but he does so with love. Indeed, for all its talk on and around the topic of justice, judgment in the play is either phantasmagorical (the mad trial of Goneril and Regan in the hovel) or corrupt, like Cornwall's interrogation of Gloucester and the venality of the justices condemned by the raving Lear; or simply a matter of faith: 'This shows you are above, you justicers.' Judging is not what is asked of us. The allusions in the final scene to the Last Days and the universal judgment that will ensue further declare the irrelevance of temporal judgment. Here it doesn't make any sense to judge. Pity is permitted; so ethics gives way to tragedy, something of which Small disapproves. She has an Aristotelian partiality to judgment.

This does not prevent her from making interesting variations on the theme of what nearly everybody feels about this play, but, surprisingly, she fails to consider Samuel Johnson's moment of revulsion as a valid response. He obviously saw the play, or at any rate its treatment of Cordelia, as cruel, immoral and 'contrary to the idea of natural justice', and he might have added that the play is cruel even to its audience. Anyway, Johnson's strongly ethical judgment takes precedence over the aesthetic, which is on the whole what Small prefers.

More generally, some of the proponents of narrative unity here considered believe that our lives make sense to us only in so far as they are seen to possess 'the temporal logic of a narrative'. A life acquires such meaning as it has over time. Some say that a sense of the unity of a human life cannot be had without both a childhood and an old age. This condition satisfied, one may acquire a sense of selfhood; otherwise, without a beginning, a middle and an end 'there would not be subjects of whom stories could be told.' So Alasdair MacIntyre; but Small does not agree. As she remarks, few lives have the aesthetic dimensions of literary narratives. Nevertheless she asks whether stories can make some contribution to the debate, and analyses Saul Bellow's *Ravelstein* to find out. This is a creative work of old age, written in the shadow of death, for which she has strong affection and respect. Her approval is of course anti-aesthetic: 'In this novel, declining to describe our lives as unified stories until we absolutely have to (until, that is, we are on the point of dying) is the only way we can hope to live out our time other than as tragedy.' She deals briefly with the ironies of Bellow's actual old age: the writing of *Ravelstein*, the begetting of a daughter, the onset of Alzheimer's. Estimating the value of those last five years – 'their contribution to a good whole life' – she merely echoes Michael Slote: 'Less exacting criteria should apply.'

Again judgment, albeit merciful. Relevant to this clemency is Small's honourable desire to claim for the old a fair share of social resources. In the course of her examination of the problem she studies Derek Parfit's *Reasons and Persons* along with *Le Père Goriot*, and Adorno's late lectures on metaphysics with *The Old Curiosity Shop* and Beckett's *Endgame*. Adorno learned from *Endgame* that it 'prepares us for a state of affairs in which everyone who lifts the lid of the nearest trashcan can expect to find his own parents in it'. This, he suggests, is the gerontology of late capitalism. Beckett himself condemned this 'over-reading', and told the actor Patrick Magee that Hamm was 'the kind of man who likes things coming to an end but doesn't want them to end just yet' – a deeper insight than may at first appear. Small, as we might expect, thinks the most important words in Beckett's play are: 'Please, no pathos.' That would allow tragedy, another surrender to the aesthetic.

In a final chapter she studies Michael Ignatieff's novel *Scar Tissue* along with developments in evolutionary theory that affect old age. Peter Medawar argued that the effect of natural selection grows weaker with time, and that old age is 'in effect a biological dumping ground' – a 'genetic dustbin'. But this will no longer do; interest has now settled on the phenomenon of the senescent 'plateau'. There is evidence that in late life senescence can come to a halt: 'Mortality rates become stable rather than (as one might expect) increasing incrementally.' This decline in the mortality of the old seems to start at about 75. Normal actuarial tables are 'not valid above that age'. Small thinks this plateau may help us to see old age as a phase of life and not as 'an ever more precipitous slope of decline'. On the other hand, we may just have to look forward to becoming Struldbruggs rather than Old Fools. One wonders in what spirit the old will receive news of the plateau. It would probably have depressed Eliot and terrified Larkin. Small is more optimistic. She deserves to feel good, for she has argued tirelessly, written an impressively researched book, and commanded the interest of sceptics more than twice her age.

13 December 2007